Over To You, Mr Brown

To Indie
For a better future

Over To You, Mr Brown

How Labour Can Win Again

ANTHONY GIDDENS

polity

Policy Network

First published in 2007 by Polity Press

Reprinted 2007

Polity Press
65 Bridge Street
Cambridge CB2 1UR, UK

Polity Press
350 Main Street
Malden, MA 02148, USA

ISBN-13: 978-07456-4222-2
ISBN-13: 978-07456-4223-9 (pb)

A catalogue record for this book is available from the British Library.

Typeset in 11 on 13pt Sabon by Peter Ducker MISTD
Printed and bound in Great Britain by MPG Books, Ltd, Bodmin, Cornwall

The publisher has used its best endeavours to ensure that the URLs for external websites referred to in this book are correct and active at the time of going to press. However, the publisher has no responsibility for the websites and can make no guarantee that a site will remain live or that the content is or will remain appropriate.

Every effort has been made to trace all copyright holders, but if any have been inadvertently overlooked the publishers will be pleased to include any necessary credits in any subsequent reprint or edition.

For further information on Polity, visit our website: www.polity.co.uk

Contents

About Policy Network

Policy Network is an international think-tank dedicated to promoting progressive policies and the renewal of social democracy. Launched in December 2000, Policy Network facilitates the sharing of ideas and experiences among politicians, policy-makers and experts on the centre-left.

Our Common Challenge

Progressive governments and parties in Europe are facing similar challenges. Perceived threats to economic, political and social security linked to globalisation, and the limitations of traditional policy prescriptions in the light of rapid social and technological change, increasingly demand that progressives work across national boundaries to find solutions. Insecurities associated with increased immigration flows, terrorism, shifts in economic power and environmental change are increasingly driving the political agenda. Responses to these challenges must be located within an international framework of progressive thinking, rooted in social democratic values.

Our Mission

Policy Network's objective is to develop and promote a progressive agenda based upon the ideas and experiences of social democratic modernisers. By working with politicians and thinkers across Europe and the world, Policy Network seeks to share the experiences of policy-makers and experts in different national contexts, find innovative solutions to common problems and provide quality research on a wider range of policy areas.

History

Policy Network was launched in December 2000 with the support of Tony Blair, Gerhard Schröder, Giuliano Amato and Göran Persson following the Progressive Governance Summits in New York, Florence and Berlin. In July 2003, Policy Network organised the London Progressive Governance Conference, bringing together 12 world leaders, and over 600 progressive politicians, thinkers and strategists. Since 2003, Policy Network has organised Progressive Governance Conferences in Budapest and Johannesburg, as well as a series of events and summits across Europe.

Activities

Through a programme of regular events, including Progressive Governance Conferences, symposia, working groups and one-day conferences Policy Network's focus is injecting new ideas into progressive politics. Meetings are held throughout the year, often in cooperation with partner organisations such as Fondazione Italianieuropei, the Wiardi Beckman Stichting, Fundación Alternativas, A Gauche en Europe, the Friedrich-Ebert-Stiftung, the European Policy Centre, the Progressive Policy Institute, and the Centre for American Progress. The outcome and results of the discussions are published in individual pamphlets that are distributed throughout the network, placed on our website and used as the basis for discussions at Policy Network events.

During 2005 and 2006, we have concentrated our energies on the renewal of the European Social Model. Our programme on the ESM was launched during the UK Presidency of the European Union and has investigated the principal means through which the various models for welfare states in Europe can be adapted to meet the challenges of the 21st century. Eighteen working papers were commissioned for the project, and six of them presented for discussion at a private seminar for the UK Prime Minister at 10 Downing Street one week prior to the European Summit at Hampton Court. Since then the debate has widened in a series of discussions across Europe in collaboration with other European centre-left think tanks in Italy, the Netherlands, France, Hungary, Germany, Spain, Romania and Finland. Similar discussions also took place around the UK.

About Policy Network

The first results have been published in a policy pamphlet, *Hampton Court Agenda: a Social Model for Europe*, published by Policy Network in March 2006. Two further books, *Global Europe – Social Europe*, edited by Anthony Giddens, Patrick Diamond and Roger Liddle, and *Europe in the Global Age*, written by Anthony Giddens, were published in October 2006. Prior to a major symposium in Brussels with EU Commission President José Manuel Barroso in December 2006, Policy Network produced a statement entitled 'Global Europe, Social Europe'. It synthesises the major points of Policy Network's debate on the future of the European Social Model and outlines a template for reform.

In 2007, Policy Network's work programme will broaden to include research on immigration and social integration, public service reform and social justice in a globalised world. More information on Policy Network's activities and research can be found on our website: www.policy-network.net.

Policy Network Team

Honorary Chair	Peter Mandelson
Director	Patrick Diamond
Executive Assistant	Suzanne Verberne-Brennan
Head of Research	Olaf Cramme
Accounts/Office Manager	Anna Bullegas
Events Manager	Joanne Burton
Web-site Manager	Matthew Carter
Policy Researcher	Constance Motte, Chelsey Wickmark
Events Assistant	Fatima Hassan
Publications Officer	Lucy Greig
Media Officer	Annie Bruzzone

Policy Network
Third Floor
11 Tufton Street
London SW1P 3QB
United Kingdom

Tel: +44 (0) 20 7340 2200
Fax: +44 (0) 20 7340 2211

www.policy-network.net

Acknowledgements

There are always many people to thank when writing a book. This particular one placed an enormous burden on everyone working at Polity Press, since the publishing process had to proceed very quickly. Special thanks are due to Emma Hutchinson, Neil de Cort, John Thompson, Gill Motley and Breffni O'Connor. My thanks also go to everyone at Policy Network, especially Olaf Cramme. Sarah Dancy copy-edited the volume with her usual mixture of flair and diligence.

Several people looked at the manuscript in an early form. Thanks in particular to Annie Bruzzone, Charles Clarke, Victor Phillip Dadaleh, Patrick Diamond, Roger Liddle, John Lloyd, Peter Riddell, James Strachan and Tony Young. They all gave extensive comments and I'm very grateful. David Held read the manuscript and helped in many other ways and I'm grateful to him as always. Anne de Sayrah, Jean-Francois Drolet, Johanna Juselius and Sharon Shochat provided invaluable help in preparing the volume. Vkay Khanna provided stimulus in our many encounters.

Above all thanks to Alena, who was a massive help, not least by uncomplainingly allowing me to work on the project most hours of the day. I even wrote some of the manuscript sitting with my laptop on the beach on holiday in Tobago. Maria helped sort out my computer tangles, while Sasha and Oscar kept me company while I was working at home.

Finally I should like to thank Tim Berners-Lee. I only met him once, when we were both awarded the Asturias Prize in Spain. As the inventor of the world-wide web, he has helped transform all our lives. Without the resources provided by the internet, the book could not have been as wide-ranging as it is. Nor could it have been published so quickly.

The subject-matter of the book overlaps to some extent with my last one, *Europe in the Global Age* (Polity, 2006). I haven't hesitated to draw upon that work where necessary, including even filching one or two figures from it.

The figures that appear on pages 25, 26, 53 and 142 are reprinted with permission from the government Strategy Unit publication, *Strategic Audit: Progress and Challenges for the UK*, 2005

London, 7 February 2007

Preface

It is February 1998. I am on my way to Washington DC. On board also are Tony Blair, Cherie Booth and a gaggle of cabinet ministers, political advisers and journalists. We are off to the White House to meet Bill and Hillary Clinton, Al Gore and a group from the US cabinet. We are flying in Concorde, the first and only time I have ever done so. Concorde – the plane that gives you three and a half hours extra to find your luggage. The plane makes its descent into Washington through a storm. As we are getting off after the landing, the pilot tells me that only Concorde, which is especially aerodynamic, could have negotiated the squalls without undue danger. It still felt very bumpy to me.

Lined up on the tarmac in the driving wind and rain is a bevy of large black limousines, straight out of some Hollywood movie. We pile in, if only to get shelter from the weather. The group in our car – three or four junior ministers and advisers – immediately gets a fit of the giggles. Labour has not been back in power for long, and all this is very new. We drive at high speed into the city, with several motor-cycle outriders in front of us, sirens blaring. The freeways have been blocked off to let us through.

The meetings in the White House last two days. On one of the evenings, we go to a dinner there. Standing in line to shake hands with the President, I am next to Harrison Ford on the one side and Barbara Streisand on the other, who both chat to me amiably. Later we are entertained by Stevie Wonder and Elton John at twin pianos.

It was a bit different from teaching sociology in Cambridge, which previously I had spent a large chunk of my life doing. My involvement with Labour politics began only at the outset of the 1990s. I had been a Labour supporter for a long while before that, but not a particularly diligent one. It was in fact Gordon Brown who got me more interested. Geoff Mulgan was his adviser at the time, and asked me to come to meet his boss to talk about my work in social theory. We had a couple of good discussions about the changing nature of modern societies, new forms of individualism and globalization (still a relatively new term then).

My more active involvement with Labour began through the agency of John Eatwell, who was economic adviser to Neil Kinnock, and taught in the Cambridge Economics and Politics Faculty, of which I was also a member. I asked John how I might get involved in the practical side of politics.

He suggested I should come to some of the lectures and seminars put on by the Institute of Public Policy Research, a think-tank in London which he had recently helped to set up. Among others at the IPPR in its early days were Patricia Hewitt and David Miliband, working upon what became the report of the Social Justice Commission. David subsequently became the head of the Prime Minister's Policy Unit (in which role he was later followed by Geoff Mulgan); he invited me to an informal weekend seminar at Chequers featuring Tony Blair, Gordon Brown, Hillary Clinton, their policy advisers and several members of the British and American cabinets.

That meeting was the first of many that I went to of a similar type. (The one in Washington was the second.) The aim of the gatherings, given the similar background of the Democrats and New Labour, was to swap experiences and debate policy dilemmas. Both parties had been returned to power after a long time in the electoral doldrums.

Offshoots of these original encounters were the Progressive Governance meetings, to which an increasing range of left-of-centre leaders came, and which have been held every year from 1998 onwards. They began in New York and Florence, followed by Berlin and Stockholm; more recently they have gone much further afield, to Brazil and South Africa, with the next one planned in Chile. Critics say they accomplish nothing, since the leaders grandstand to their audiences at home. They forget that several hundred policy specialists attend each one, and it is here that many political ideas get shaped.

I wrote my book *The Third Way* as a result of taking part in the early Blair–Clinton dialogues.[1] I saw myself then, and regard myself now, as a social democrat – a person of the reformist or centre-left. In Britain this means standing in the Tony Crosland tradition, but social democracy is of course also a worldwide movement. The title I first planned for the work was *The Renewal of Social Democracy*, which for me is what the third way was and is all about. If I had stuck with it, I imagine the book would have been much less controversial than it turned out to be. It probably wouldn't have attracted any attention outside the academic community.

Under the title *The Third Way*, it certainly did. I was amazed at the interest in it across the world. As a result, I visited political leaders and their advisers in many European countries, but also travelled widely in Asia and Latin America. One of the effects of globalization is that much the same debates are going on in most countries. Many of the most interesting discussions I had were outside the developed world.

From 1997 to 2003 I was Director of the London School of Economics. The LSE has had, and continues to have, a massive impact upon public policy, in this country and in many others besides. It formed a marvellous environment for me, and I owe a great deal to my colleagues there. The job was more than a full-time one, but I was able to continue writing (short books only).

This book began life as a pamphlet, but somehow turned into a rather longer essay. I wanted to avoid the tendency of the pamphleteer to say what should be done without giving any idea of how to actually do it. I don't agree with all the policies that New Labour's leaders have followed, or the ways in which they have chosen to put them into practice. But I do think that through two and a half periods of government so far, the country has been changed for the better. There is plenty to build on, and plenty of further innovations to make too.

I've interspersed the text with a few political jokes and quotations, all picked up more or less at random from the internet, where they appear in many different versions. I hope they lighten up the whole thing a bit. All jokes have a serious side to them – which doesn't mean that one has to agree with the point they are making. I use some of the jokes and quotes precisely to disagree with the popular wisdom they express.

Here's one for tasters. Tony Blair and Gordon Brown decide to take a stroll through the park together. 'Look,' says Tony, 'let's be honest with one another.' 'Sure', says Gordon; 'you go first.' And that was the end of the conversation.

Is, or was, the relationship between Blair and Brown really as bad as that? Well, only sometimes. It's often been said, but Blair and Brown are truly the Lennon and McCartney of modern politics. Paul had the Scottish-sounding name, but Brown is clearly the Lennon of the partnership. Like Lennon and McCartney, their relationship has been antagonistic and symbiotic.

Lennon wasn't as good without McCartney, and vice versa. Does that mean that, if and when he becomes leader of the party and Prime Minister, Brown won't be able to manage? No – Lennon recorded that sublime song 'Imagine' after he struck out on his own. I don't think being Chancellor of the Exchequer for ten years is necessarily the best preparation to be Prime Minister. The PM has to range over an enormously wide range of subjects, and face more or less unending media scrutiny. He must reach out to the nation beyond his own party. Yet by any reckoning Brown is a talented politician of unusual capacity and intellect. He could do an outstanding job. People might want something different from the Blair style of leadership – and the Tory leader David Cameron has modelled himself on Blair, hasn't he?

Introduction

The title of this book might at first blush seem doubly misleading. There is a possibility Gordon Brown might not become the next leader of the Labour Party. So I'm taking something of a risk in publishing the work at all. At the time of writing, however, he is the overwhelming favourite and in my view quite rightly so. Should Brown somehow fail to make it, the book – I believe – would not become wholly redundant. Most of the arguments I deploy below would apply whoever becomes the next leader.

A second reason why *Over To You, Mr Brown* could be seen as questionable is that Brown has been a central influence over New Labour from its very inception. Some of its most successful policies are due mainly to him. Since these policies are primarily economic, they are the underpinning of much else that the party has achieved in its ten years of government. However, there is no doubt that a Brown-led government will differ substantially – has to differ substantially – from those headed by Tony Blair.

I can't see any scenario in which Labour could win big at the next election. The party might not win at all. Labour supporters must face up to the fact that people could be irremediably fed up with New Labour, even with a (relatively) fresh face at the helm. Yet all is very far from settled. The advent of a new leader gives Labour the chance of revival – not as a party out of power, but one with ten years of real achievement to build on. At the moment, the Conservatives have no policy programme to speak of, and it will not be easy to develop a consistent one. Fresh policies adaptable to a Tory viewpoint are not waiting somewhere in the ether, ready to be appropriated by the policy discussion groups the leadership has set up. There could be major divisions looming within the Conservative Party over taxation, the EU, crime and punishment, the environment and other issues once specific policies are introduced.

I argue in the book as a whole that there are three battles that Labour has to win if it is to stay in power at the next election, and be able to enact policies that will further transform the country for the better. These are the *battle of ideas*, the *battle of strategy* and the *battle of tactics*. New ideas are essential if Labour is effectively to counter the Conservative challenge and, even more important, rekindle enthusiasm amongst the electorate. Such ideas should be based, as they were in the early 1990s, upon an analysis of the major changes affecting our society today. Winning the battle of strategy means introducing a policy framework that allows values and ideas to be put into practice. It is in turn directly related to the battle of tactics, which concerns the nitty-gritty business of actually coming out ahead of the other parties in an election.

It is probably two years before the next general election. How will Labour fare under new leadership? What policies should be kept, and what policy innovations should be made? In the discussion which follows I try to answer these questions and suggest how Labour can use the transition to its own profit.

Over the past ten years in an electoral sense the party has had the most successful period in its history. It had never before been in government for two full terms, let alone three. In spite of its long-standing hold over power, New Labour has been dismissed by many as all sound-bites and no coherent policies. Others have said that whatever policies it does possess have been mostly appropriated from Thatcherite conservatism. New Labour has simply taken the party to the right and has given up most of the progressive causes for which it once used to stand.

These views are naive and inaccurate, as I seek to show in the text. The party reversed its fortunes by adopting a new political outlook and one rich in policy content – a third way programme. Policy innovation was essential to respond to a rapidly changing world. It is only through such innovation that we can defend the values of the left. A large part of the government's task over the past decade has been to pick up the debris left by years of Thatcherite rule and prepare the country for a new era.

Since coming to power, New Labour has managed to shift the framework within which politics in Britain is carried on. As a result, the Tories have had to change ideological ground quite fundamentally in order to be taken seriously again. Tony Blair saw off a succession of Conservative leaders who clung to the old Thatcherite ways.

The UK has enjoyed a stable period of economic growth since 1997, the result of effective macroeconomic policy. Labour's emphasis upon getting as many people into work as possible was extensively criticized when first introduced, but has proven its effectiveness. Britain has something close to full employment.

These achievements have allowed large-scale investment in public services, and in anti-poverty measures. Such investment has been made without significant increases in tax rates; tax revenue has gone up mainly as a result of sustained growth. Labour's successes in tackling poverty and under-privilege more generally have been considerable. There are very few long-term unemployed in the UK, and low overall rates of youth unemployment. Compare that situation with France, where about a third of people under the age of 30 have never been in full-time work. Well over two million people have been lifted out of poverty in Britain since 1997. In France, Germany or Italy, by contrast, the proportion of people in poverty has been rising.

Overall, Labour has done a good job for the country, often in trying circumstances. Ten years on, however, a thoroughgoing overhaul of the party's ideas and policy outlook is needed. I propose in this book that Labour does so in terms of what I call a 'Contract with the Future'. What I mean by the phrase is that Labour should offer a contract to citizens to initiate a future for the country that is socially just, as well as economically and ecologically sustainable. It is the guiding thread of this whole book and to me it should be Labour's Big Idea.

I would like New Labour at this point more explicitly to rejoin the social democratic family of parties. The party in the 1990s was highly influenced by the New Democrats in the US, and in many ways fruitfully so. But the US is a different form of society from those in Europe, more tolerant of inequality, and able to draw upon immense resources compared to Britain. Its influence in the world is incomparably greater, even if in the recent period it has been undermined by the unfortunate policies of the Bush Administration. Britain is a European country, and should aspire to a similar mix of prosperity and equality to that found in the best-practice Continental states.

Themes that have been latent in Labour's thinking should be brought more into the open. For instance, a great deal of attention has been given to improving public services. Yet Labour has failed to supply a clear ideological statement of what is the governing logic of such changes. We should seek to create a society with a robust sense of public purpose, with a developed and responsive public sphere. This goal is different from that of the Old Left, which identified the public sphere with the state. The state can sometimes be the enemy of the public sphere – when it is too bureaucratic, inefficient, unresponsive to citizens' needs, or controlled by producer interests – just as commerce and markets can.

How a given service should be provided is not just a pragmatic matter – as New Labour leaders have tended to say. Efficiency, in other words, should not be the only criterion. If a service is privatized, for instance, how much control will citizens have over decisions that affect them? Will competition give people more influence or less? Will the identity of a community or area be affected? As I argue below, to answer these questions we need a clearer definition both of the role of the state and of the nature of public services than Labour has so far managed to come up with.

Social democrats these days have to be market-friendly, and accept that capitalism has proved vastly more effective in raising living standards than any version of socialism or communism were. Communism failed as an economic system because the state was quite unable to replace the enormous complexity of pricing signals that markets are able to handle every moment of the day. Sometimes the centre-left should aim at extending the range of markets rather than trying to limit them. For instance, the completion of the Single Market in Europe should bring benefits to everyone in the UK.

However, we want markets to work for the general good.

Making sure that this aim is met should be as important a part of policy as a concern with public services. New Labour has tended to treat capitalism as a 'black box'. Its preoccupation with public services contrasts oddly with lack of discussion about the nature of capitalism, which tends to be taken as a given, and which we must respond to rather than try to shape.

When New Labour came to power, the status of business leaders was very high. Corporate leaders seemed to some to have special insight into trends going on in the world. I don't believe many people think this way any longer. Some such leaders have survived and prospered. Others, however, made calamitous decisions and their businesses have been emasculated or ruined. A few became mired in corruption, and even found themselves in prison.

No business executive affects to like regulation, but it may be necessary in order to save capitalism from itself. The government has an obligation to promote corporate responsibility, nationally and internationally. It should redouble efforts to regulate tax havens, reduce money laundering, and limit tax avoidance by individuals and by corporations. The theme of responsibility has to be fundamental to Labour's political outlook. Responsibility applies to everyone – to the rich just as much as the poor. We should contest the culture of irresponsibility, or me-first individualism, that pervades some of the higher financial circles in particular.

I don't think this view means reverting to the ideas of the Old Left. The City, for example, contributes a rising proportion to GDP. It is one of the great success stories of the British economy, and should be recognized as such. But where are our versions of Bill Gates or George Soros – people who have made fortunes, but spent them for social and humanitarian purposes? Those we do have, such as the Sainsbury family, tend to come from backgrounds with established philanthropic traditions, not from the high-tech or finance sectors. Peter Lampl, who has donated extensively in the education field, was for years a businessman in the US.

Should Labour under Brown put up taxes? No – we should be thinking rather of possible tax reductions for poorer groups, perhaps as part of a trade-off with the introduction of more green taxes. There is one possible exception, though. Labour should consider a tax on the top wealth-holders. The money would not go to the Treasury, but into a trust used to help children from poorer backgrounds succeed in the educational system. Those who do extremely well should give back to the society that has provided them with opportunities, and should help the less fortunate.

I would like to see Labour now become more explicitly egalitarian. However, equality has to be pursued in tandem with economic dynamism and job creation. When I talk about Labour rejoining the social democratic family, I mean the family of avant-garde centre-left parties. The social democrats in the Scandinavian countries have suffered mixed fortunes of late as far as elections go, but they have consistently been in the vanguard of reform and modernization (not without plenty of domestic struggles). They have pioneered decentralization in public services, incentives and competition, foundation hospitals, increased voice and choice and other innovations. The Scandinavian nations are open societies, which have reconciled economic success with high levels of social protection.

Their success is not primarily the result of high tax rates, but comes mainly from policy. They have done what Labour has to do here: spend less on older people and more on the young – not by depriving the over 60s, but, on the contrary, by improving their status and rights, including the right to work; invest in women, especially in terms of job opportunities; invest in IT, science and technology; elevate educational standards and skill levels; and develop further 'flexicurity' in labour markets (the New Deal) – flexibility plus security, provided by retraining and effective career advice. The Scandinavians are not anti-business. On the contrary: Finland is ranked by the World Economic Forum as the best country to do business of any across the globe. Yet Finland and the other Scandinavian states are also the most egalitarian. The social democrats in these countries are third way political parties, prepared to embrace change – as are similar successful parties in Spain, New Zealand and Chile.

Aspiration, ambition and social mobility should be keynote ideas for Labour. This is a country in which it has been difficult for people from deprived backgrounds to do well. A lot of progress has been made since 1997, which can be further built upon. The Tories have mounted an attack on Labour on this score, saying that the level of mobility in the UK now is less than it was two or three decades ago. Don't they realize that if chances of mobility are low today, this is because of what happened at that time – in other words, when the Conservatives themselves were in power? Studies of social mobility by definition refer to people born 20 years ago or more. Labour's policies, such as Sure Start and baby bonds, should ensure that future generations do better, especially if those policies are further radicalized.

Like the Scandinavian social democrats, Labour should become serious about decentralization and devolution. Quite apart from the contribution such processes can make to the strengthening of democracy, they are important in responding effectively to globalization. Cities and regions, for example, today interact directly with the global economy – they need local leadership to help give such responses drive and direction.

Devolution is not real if it doesn't involve power, and if it doesn't involve money. It won't be easy to revive the regional agenda, since it is one of the fields where Labour policy has gone distinctly awry. The proposed regional bodies would have had very little real power. Voters were not prepared to endorse essentially toothless organizations. Yet in principle such an agenda could help the country a lot. Regions are becoming more and more important as globalization intensifies, as the experience of other countries shows. I would like to see it reactivated and strengthened, and more progress made towards simplifying the clutter of local government.

Decentralization in health care and education means further radicalizing Blairite policies, not retreating from them. Gordon Brown seems to have insisted upon watering down the Alan Milburn proposals for foundation hospitals. He did so at least in some part for good reasons. It is a policy that has to be closely monitored, in terms of both quality of care and implications for inequality. Yet if these issues can be coped with, as I think they can be, we should aim for a system giving foundation trusts more local power than they have under the watered-down scheme that Labour eventually adopted.

Herein lies one of the main tests for Brown. The Treasury, where he has spent the past ten years, could be seen as the epitome of centralizing government. One of the lines of the Tory critique as soon as Brown comes to power will be – already is – that enormous sums of money have been spent to little effect, because the state is not the vehicle to deliver true reform. So when Brown talks of the state becoming the servant of the people, he has not only to mean it, but also to show how it can happen.

'No to a two-tier system', the defenders of the centralized state will say. Yet a two-tier approach is exactly what we've had in health care and education for many years – those who can afford to, opt out. It is not a system that has worked for the poor: health and educational inequalities in the UK are worse than in most other EU nations. 'Phoney universalism' (pretending that everyone is the same) has served to exacerbate inequalities, not overcome them. Choice and voice are not intrinsically the enemies of greater equality, nor is competition. The opposite is true. At the moment these are the privileges of the more affluent – they are a core part of the 'middle-class capture' of the welfare state.

The public (state-based) and private (not for profit or commercial) sectors need to be integrated more, not less. This theorem applies both to health care and education. France, for instance, has one of the best health care systems in the world. The country has a much higher proportion of privately run hospitals and health care centres than the UK, integrated within the overall health system. In education, Labour has largely left the private – i.e. 'public' – schools alone, working with the intention of bring the best of the state system up to their level. The private schools, however, still dominate access to elite positions. They cannot be abolished, nor should they be, since many of them provide top-class education. What we could do, however, is increasingly make them open to all children, regardless of ability to pay.

Green and Brown when mixed together don't make a particularly attractive colour – a downright unpleasant one, in fact. Yet today there must be a thoroughgoing greening of the Labour Party. Along with the possible proliferation of nuclear weapons, climate change is the most urgent threat the world faces. Brown's name is going to give him quite a lot of trouble with comedians, but Brown must learn to think and act green.

Those who demand that others change their lifestyles should accept it for themselves. I would like to see every member of the cabinet driving or being driven in a hybrid or electric car – or walk if they can. Gordon Brown should make visible changes to his lifestyle. I don't think it's enough to mention, as he recently did, that he doesn't take many holidays abroad. The Parliament buildings at the moment are something of an environmental disaster area, with energy inefficiency on a large scale. Why not try to make improvements, and get parliamentarians to follow strict rules of energy conservation?

There is a new agenda here, which Labour must seize. Some of our main problems today come not from scarcity, but from abundance. This is true of climate change – think of the number of cars on the roads, the tremendous expansion of air travel and so on – but it is also true of other areas of concern, such as health. We live in the first society in which far more food is produced than we can consume. In the developed countries, starving from lack of food is unknown. Obesity, however, is a major problem; in its wake come chronic illnesses, such as heart disease and diabetes. Lifestyle change, and how to bring it about, without intruding upon individual freedoms, has moved to near the top of our most pressing concerns.

This observation applies to the 'ageing society', among other areas. Ageism is the sexism of our time. It is resonant with consequences for the economy and the wider society. Old age is no longer something that just 'happens' to people. How we age now depends a great deal upon lifestyle factors. Labour should drop the term 'pensioner' altogether. It suggests that when people reach a certain age they become dependent, unable to live an independent and flourishing life.

Among social scientists, there is an upsurge of interest in happiness, and how to maximize it. Mental illness seems to be on the increase, as does a range of forms of addictive behaviour. I don't think happiness is the sole or even dominant value leading to the good life. So rather than happiness, I speak more dryly of *positive welfare*. The welfare state in the past was based upon 'negatives' – the avoidance of risk. We need more positive goals today, for a system that has to be more interventionist – not only a safety net. Later in the book I detail what these goals should be.

I think we are approaching the end of the welfare state in the way it was originally designed. I don't mean this in the way right-wing authors do – the idea that the welfare state should be run down because it isn't needed in today's world. Rather, it has to be redesigned to be more proactive; concerned with investment and with tackling social problems at source; focused upon economic dynamism and productivity, not an organization that steps in when the job of the market is done; and more pluralistic – a regulatory agency in a welfare society, in which a variety of groups and organizations are involved in welfare protection.

The object of social policy should be the fostering of active, responsible citizenship. Lifestyle change cannot be achieved by governments acting on their own. All of the four main forces in our society will have to work together to promote it. These are the state, business, voluntary or third sector groups – and citizens. The responsible and responsive state (which I later call the ensuring state); socially and environmentally responsible firms and corporations; the responsibilities of the third sector; and the civic responsibility of citizens – these should be the energizing forces of the Contract with the Future.

As is obvious to anyone walking down the street in one of our major cities, Britain is a far more diverse society than it used to be. Immigration and cultural diversity are foremost among people's concerns today. Multiculturalism, many assert – including, most recently, David Cameron – is dead. We must abandon it in order to emphasize our common cultural heritage. I say, by contrast, long live multiculturalism! Its band of critics doesn't seem to take the trouble to understand what it actually means.

They see multiculturalism as the coexistence of closed and separate cultures, not as a means of actually integrating minorities into a dominant culture. Multiculturalism doesn't imply treating every cultural belief as equivalent to any other; it doesn't condone communities separating themselves off from the wider society; and it doesn't mean denying that a society needs a core set of values, and a generally agreed identity, to keep it going. On the contrary, it means bringing cultures and communities together, fostering dialogue between them and insisting upon common acceptance of values and laws.

Islamic radicalism, and the more diffuse feelings of alienation found in some Muslim communities, have to be understood against the backdrop of globalization.[1] The French scholar, Olivier Roy, has argued persuasively that radical Islam is not a product of religion per se, but the result of the 'deterritorializing' of Islam. The question, 'Who am I?' never came up in traditional Muslim culture – and nor did issues such as 'Should I wear the veil?' Only when Muslims are in everyday contact with other cultures do such questions become urgent and difficult.[2] In other words, we are talking here about identity politics. Much more on all this in what follows.

Whether Gordon Brown would agree with the ideas and prescriptions I have set out in this book, I do not know. I have not consulted him about them. He has certainly started to put flesh on his own views in a variety of speeches over the past few months. Brown argues for a new constitutional settlement, and has given a general outline of what form it should take. He promises a different style of leadership from that of Blair. He follows Blair, however, in regarding education as his overriding priority. Brown has spoken up strongly in favour of a British identity in the face of growing nationalist separatisms; and he has declared the need to renew a sense of national purpose. I discuss his speeches and writings in some detail below.

What he hasn't said much about so far is foreign policy. His views in this field will be of great importance – to the country at large, and to his own political future. In my view, he must seek an opportunity to show independence of mind from the current US regime. He should look for a negotiated withdrawal of British troops from Iraq, on the basis of a handover to the Iraqis in the Basra area and a difficult job well done. He should contribute to moving the international community back towards a greater emphasis upon the rule of law and the importance of international cooperation.

With the whole spectrum of international relations changing, and formidable new geopolitical players emerging, Britain hasn't a hope of influencing the course of world events if it doesn't act in conjunction with the rest of the European Union. The special relationship with America has some meaning, but it is bound to become weakened eventually, as the US increasingly turns its attention to the rising powers in the East. The worst situation for Britain would be if the country found itself stranded between the US and the rest of Europe, with little or no influence upon either.

Brown thus far has displayed little enthusiasm for the EU; but a new generation of European leaders is emerging and he could and should be prominent among them. Some of the major problems that concern us today – climate change, energy security, migration, international crime, drug-running and people-trafficking – can't be resolved by individual nations. The EU is our best hope of dealing with them in our region of the world.

Very little of all of this will be plain sailing. One can see several points of tension and difficulty for a Brown-led government.

Although there may be a nominal contest inside the party, Brown will come in as an unelected prime minister. More than 70 per cent of voters in the UK think that he should speedily call a general election. There is virtually no chance that he will do so, but such a situation could drain his legitimacy.

Much of Brown's reputation has been built on his management of the economy, where he has repeatedly won out over the many critics who have announced across the years that it is all going wrong. However, at this point there seem to be some cracks appearing in the edifice, such as the recent unexpected rise in inflation, an overvalued housing market and a continuing rise in levels of personal debt.[3] A cash crunch is looming in the public services, just at a time when progress needs to be renewed to convince the electorate that Labour has handled reform in a competent way. Funding cannot continue at the levels of the past few years.

There could be problems maintaining order within the party. Brown will have to face down the Old Left, and deal with potentially fractious trade unions, just as Blair did. If Brown concedes too much to the traditionalists, he could perhaps keep the party happy, but his tenure as Prime Minister will be short. The police inquiry into the loans for peerages might present problems that will run on into the Brown era. At the time of writing, the outcome of the investigation is unknown, but even if no prosecutions are brought, and even though Brown himself is not directly involved, mud has a way of distributing itself widely and sticking.

A further and quite fundamental worry is the status of the UK itself. How strong will Scottish, Welsh and English nationalism turn out to be? Currently, they are all on the rise. Brown has set out his stall for a reinvigorated British identity, and this is the right thing to do. But will the three mainland nations nevertheless start to pull apart?

A Brown-led government will have these and other problems to overcome if Labour is to get a fourth term in office. It is likely to be an uphill struggle all the way. The biggest obstacle of all is not the Tories, but public disenchantment – not only with the Labour Party, but with politicians more generally. Brown must show real leadership quality. Otherwise a jaded electorate will vote to 'give the others a chance', as happened in Labour's favour in 1997.

In the chapter 1, I analyse the origins of New Labour, which were deeply bound up with the thinking of the Democrats in the US in the run-up to the Clinton presidency. Labour took many worthwhile ideas and policies from the New Democrats, but this connection also explains where the government could do better. I look at Labour's main successes over the past ten years, as well as where it has fallen short.

Tony Blair listens to a reporter's question with Gordon Brown, at a news conference at Labour Party headquarters in London, Tuesday, 29 April 1997. Two days remain before the general election.

1

After Ten Years: Labour's Successes and Failures

The Internationale – New Labour Version:

> *The people's flag is rosy pink,*
> *It's not as red as you might think.*
> *Even if you're a millionaire*
> *You can happily vote for Tony Blair.*
>
> *You're free to wear your pin-striped suit*
> *We really do not give a hoot.*
> *So people think we're still sincere,*
> *We'll sing the red flag once a year.*

Great poetry it is not, but its meaning is clear enough. The Red Flag has actually now been dropped from the Labour Annual Conference, although it is sometimes sung in other settings. Is New Labour now a wholly middle-class party, which has deserted its traditional values and its mission to speak for the interests of the underprivileged? No: but the class structure of our society has changed dramatically. By far the greater majority of the population today works in service or knowledge-based jobs, not in manufacturing. All centre-left parties have to appeal to a wider coalition than in the past.

The third way is not an especially luminous term. And it lends itself to easy humour, some of it much too easy: no way, Milky Way, Frank Sinatra's *My Way*, and so on and so on. I've lost track of how many times people have suggested to me that we should now be looking for a fourth way. Also, the term 'third way' is not new – I traced the first use of it to the late nineteenth century.

Perhaps for these reasons, since New Labour adopted it, the idea has been widely misunderstood, wilfully so in many cases. I see it as a label for upgrading left-of-centre thinking in the face of the profound changes affecting social and economic life today. It doesn't matter whether one uses the term itself or not. Social democrats across the world have had to rethink their approach and policy programmes in similar fashion.

The 'first way' was traditional social democracy – in the context of this country, Old Labour – based upon an unswerving faith in the state, Keynesian demand management and reliance upon the working class as the main basis of voter support. In left-of-centre circles, it held sway for some four decades after the end of the Second World War. It was a defining political standpoint for other parties too, because it set the terms of political debate. The 'one-nation Tories' accepted the importance of the welfare state and much about the mixed economy.

The 'second way' was Thatcherism, or free market fundamentalism. Thatcherism was founded upon a belief in the primacy of markets, the need to reduce the scope of the state and minimize taxes, and upon a relative indifference towards social justice. Friedrich von Hayek, one of Mrs Thatcher's (or, more accurately, Keith Joseph's) main intellectual influences, in fact described social justice as an incoherent notion. Mrs Thatcher set about demolishing one-nation Toryism, and she was successful. But in a wider way she undermined conservatism *tout court*. If allowed to run rampant, markets undermine social cohesion and also act to dissolve tradition. Yet conservatism without respect for the past, without a sense of the importance of traditions – and where 'there is no such thing as society' – is arguably not conservatism at all.

Neither of these political philosophies proved able to cope with the demands of a social world that has changed so dramatically and which continues to do so. A third alternative is required. Thatcherism today is as dead a philosophy as traditional leftism, although of course there are those who are reluctant to abandon either. Belatedly, the Conservatives have recognized this point too, under David Cameron's leadership. Compassionate conservatism is the response of the moderate right, not just here but in other countries too.

The New Democrats

From the early 1990s onwards, or perhaps even earlier, Labour was strongly influenced by the New Democrats in the US – an influence, of course, that extended to the very renaming of the party. It was the New Democrats who repopularized the term 'third way', although it has sometimes been used by other left-of-centre parties too, such as the Swedish Social Democrats. Like New Labour, the Clintonite Democrats were often seen as bereft of guiding ideas, a party driven mainly by pragmatism. In fact, the policy analysts who guided Clinton's path to the presidency developed both a cogent analysis of social and economic change and some powerful policy responses to it.

The traditional outlook of the Democratic Party, they argued, must be reshaped in the light of the development of a more global economy, the shrinking of blue-collar work and therefore the working class, the increasing role of IT and of service industries and, internationally, the ending of the Cold War. The customary suspicion of markets and of entrepreneurialism must be dropped, since a healthy economy is the basis of effective social policy. The state and government still have important roles to play, but they themselves must be reformed to make them more efficient and responsive to the needs of citizens.

David Osborne and Ted Gaebler's *Reinventing Government* became a sourcebook for the New Democrats.[1] The authors pointed out the extent to which businesses changed in response to the new global environment – decentralizing hierarchies, empowering their employees and getting close to their customers. The voluntary sector has also launched innumerable new initiatives. By contrast, argued Osborne and Gaebler, the state often remains slow-moving, inefficient and centralized. It needs reform to cope with 'the rapidly changing, highly competitive, information-rich society and economy in which we live'.[2]

Introducing choice, competition and market incentives into the state sector – and reacting against the 'big state' – became driving motivations of Clinton's New Covenant of citizenship, and certainly survived as a core part of the ethos of New Labour. So too have other major emphases. They included some very important reorientations for the centre-left.

The mantra of the New Democrats, often repeated in their literature, was *opportunity*, *responsibility* and *community*. In our discussions with Clinton and his advisers, these terms were the ones he usually came back to. 'Opportunity' meant putting life-chances, rather than traditional redistribution, at the forefront. As far as possible, the object of social policy should be to clear away the barriers that prevent those at the bottom from being able to realize their aspirations. Intervention to pursue such a goal, however, has to be mainly at the community rather than the individual level. Community breakdown is at the origin of many of the problems that confront the poorest groups in society. 'Community action zones' were one of the New Democrats' innovations.

Welfare reform is essential, based upon the idea of citizen empowerment. Welfare should provide, in a celebrated New Democrat phrase, a 'hand-up rather than a hand-out'. Instead of unemployment benefits being paid whether someone actively looks for work or not, welfare to work should be the guiding principle. The unemployed have a responsibility to look for work, and it should be the aim of policy to promote this endeavour. Tax credits were a favourite policy mechanism of the New Democrats. As applied to poverty, they offer several advantages. They are not felt to be demeaning, as orthodox benefits often are. They form an incentive to get into work for those outside the labour market. Since getting a job is the best way out of poverty, tax credits enhance both economic dynamism and social justice.

The citizenship contract, the New Democrats argued, has to be rewritten to emphasize responsibility, not only rights. The Old Left focused on citizenship rights to the detriment of citizenship duties, which are just as important. This emphasis connects to welfare reform: those who can work should be expected to do so, rather than remain a burden on other citizens. A vital source of New Democrat thinking was the need to guarantee personal security, especially in relation to crime. Crime is a worry for almost everyone, but in poor neighbourhoods it tends to converge with other social problems, such as drug-taking and drug-trading, high drop-out rates from school and gang violence. The rightist policies of 'getting tough on crime' have failed. The answer is not to abandon them, however (a big break with previous Democratic thinking), but to combine them with an attack on the conditions that breed crime. Tony Blair (some say Gordon Brown) may have coined the phrase 'tough on crime, tough on the causes of crime'. But this comes straight from the New Democrat rulebook.[3]

Finally, at the international level, the New Democrats stressed the importance of free trade for the economic development of rich and poor nations alike, and the need to support the spread of democratization. Democracy tends to become diffused around the world because of the impact of the information revolution, since that revolution undermines the ability of states to monopolize ideas and information.[4] In the global era, the distinction between foreign and domestic policy is disappearing. Post-1989, some of the main threats to the US come not from other states but from non-state actors – an analysis fully borne out on 9:11, although few if any anticipated an attack of such magnitude.

Many of these ideas were taken over by New Labour and adapted to a British context. One can't simply say that New Labour owed its programme to the American Democrats. Labour's up-and-coming politicians and advisers were often in the US in the late 1980s and early 1990s and contributed to the evolution of the Democrats' ideas. Those in and around the Labour Party also looked elsewhere for relevant themes and policies – such as to Australia. In spite of its American terminology, the New Deal, for example, differed from the welfare-to-work programmes set up in America. The economist Richard Layard, one of its initiators, had Sweden in mind as much as the US in drawing up his ideas.[5] And there was important indigenous work too, such as the report of the Commission for Social Justice I referred to the Preface, which was published in 1994 and had a strong influence upon New Labour's outlook.

New Labour's Policy Programme

The programme New Labour built from these various sources was a powerful one, and has served the party well both in the lead-up to the election of 1997 and the period of government since then. Eight major themes form the basis of that programme, as I see it anyway, and as I tried to help shape it. It was, from the beginning, far more systematic than the critics have acknowledged:

Put the economy first. A robust economy is the precondition of effective social policy. Increasing the rate of employment – getting a high proportion of people in work above a decent minimum wage – is at least as important as reducing unemployment. Flexibility in labour markets is a must, but has to be coupled to ways of ensuring that workers can move on easily between jobs. Both these ideas were highly controversial in the beginning, but now have become much more widely accepted. Protect the worker rather than the job is the guiding theme. Macroeconomic policy should concentrate upon creating stable economic growth. Tax revenue for the state should be generated primarily through job creation and economic success. 'Prudence' was Gordon Brown's name for the balanced budgets that the New Democrats emphasized so strongly. In the past, left-of-centre parties were wedded to 'tax and spend' – in other words, borrowing way beyond what a country could afford.

Hold the political centre. We no longer live in a society where support from a single class group can deliver the foundation of political success. Labour was originally the party of the working class, but the working class is shrinking away. In the UK, by the latest calculation, only 12 per cent of the labour force now works in manufacture. The knowledge-based economy – more properly called a knowledge-based and service economy – is a reality. New occupational groups are appearing, such as 'wired workers'. Wired workers are not working class, but they are not traditional white-collar workers either. Their attitudes and outlook are different from those of these earlier classes. Labour must appeal to such groups while still keeping its traditional constituency – not an easy task for any left-of-centre party today. Keeping a grip on the centre is not the same as relapsing into conservatism: the point is to shift the centre to the left – to gain widespread support for social democratic policies.

Create a new citizenship contract, based upon obligations as well as rights. If the point of policy, in many circumstances, is to empower citizens, then it is vital that empowerment be balanced by responsibility. People should be free to live their lives as they choose, but freedom carries personal and social responsibilities with it. 'A hand-up, not a hand-out' means accepting obligations, in this case the obligation to work if one can – albeit perhaps with the help of the state. Exactly the same principle applies to the family. The obligations of parents to provide for their children, for instance, still stand even if a marriage or relationship breaks down. The traditional left tended to focus much more on rights rather than obligations; but a society based only on rights would lose all sense of community. The right has long placed more stress upon the duties of citizens. Yet without freedoms a society risks succumbing to authoritarianism.

In pursuing social justice, *concentrate upon the poor* rather than the rich. Focus especially on reducing child poverty. Reducing child poverty means having far-reaching policies, because the proportion of deprived children in Britain is higher compared to other countries. Having a decent job is the best route out of poverty for all those capable of work. Women's wages still trail those of men. Even though many women now work, they still bear a disproportionate share of the household chores and child care – these issues need close attention. Strengthening the family is a major object of policy, but we have to recognize the complex nature of family life today. Those in gay relationships should have similar rights and obligations to heterosexual partners. To reduce poverty, we should concentrate upon a redistribution of life-chances. Equality of opportunity should be the keynote, since economic dynamism depends upon creating an aspirational society.

Invest in public services, above all education and health care, but only on condition that they are reformed, and reformed quite radically. 'Education, education, education', for three reasons: an educated citizenry is more easily able to cope with change and diversity; jobs for those without skills are becoming more and more scarce; and early years' education is an essential tool in helping children from deprived backgrounds escape from poverty. Investing in children should be a priority, as should providing adequate child care now that so many women are in the labour force.

Efficiency, but also increased choice and voice, are of crucial importance in the public services. Centralized delivery by the state is by no means always the best way of delivering these objectives. Third sector groups or commercial organizations, if properly regulated, can sometimes be more effective than direct control by the state. We have to decide in all instances which combination most effectively creates public goods. It is gratuitous and wrong to counterpose, as so many critics do, 'public' (state-based) services and 'private' (not-for-profit or commercial) ones. The real test is which serves the public interest best in any specific context – I expand on this point in what follows.

Do not cede any issues to the right; instead, seek to provide left-of-centre solutions to them. The left in the past has typically tried to explain away, rather than directly confront, questions to do with crime, social disorder, migration and cultural identity, as if the concerns ordinary citizens feel about them were misplaced or irrelevant. Hence crime was assumed to be largely an outcome of inequality: when inequality is reduced, levels of crime will fall too. Whether this view is correct or not, crime and anti-social behaviour are problems for citizens in the here and now, and have to be dealt with as such. 'Tough on crime, tough on the causes of crime' is not just a sound-bite, but, if elaborated properly, a policy principle.

Immigration is largely beneficial for the host society, *but it has to be regulated*. A large influx of unskilled immigrants cannot be readily absorbed. However there are many areas where more skilled migrants are needed and there should be positive incentives to help attract them. (Much more about all this in what follows.)

Pursue an activist foreign policy. Foreign and domestic policy overlap far more than in earlier times. The yawning division between rich and poor in world society, for example, is not only unjust, but impinges directly upon our society – in the shape, amongst other things, of increasing migratory pressures.

The UK faces no visible threats of invasion from other nations, but must be prepared to assume an active role in the wider world. This task means reshaping the military to be able to respond rapidly to situations where armed intervention may be called for, either acting alone or in conjunction with the armed forces of other countries. Interventionism is a necessary doctrine in a world where national sovereignty has lost much of its meaning, and where there are universal humanitarian concerns that override local interests. (For further discussion, see chapter 8.)

What Went Right, What Went Wrong?

The universal experience of left-of-centre parties is that, almost as soon as they get into power, many of their erstwhile supporters declare them a disappointment. This process normally starts very rapidly after an election is won. The usual complaints are either that they have abandoned their ideals, or that their progress in achieving change is too slow – usually both. Of course, they also get lambasted from the right too. In most countries, and certainly in the UK, the political right has long assumed that it is the natural heir to power. Labour has from the beginning been subject to a constant barrage of attacks from the left as well as the right.

Blair has variously been accused of: rule by focus groups – and precisely the opposite, not listening enough to what the public wants; control freakery – and its contrary too, presiding over a divided party, especially being unable to handle his Chancellor; lacking an overall agenda or vision for the country; favouring markets at the expense of the public sphere, or otherwise acting as a Thatcherite; failing to produce economic redistribution and to reduce inequality; cosying up to the rich; dissimulation or outright lying in the lead-up to the Iraq war; sticking by colleagues he should have fired – but also dismissing others he should have stood by; privatizing education and the health service; failing to promote the cause of the EU; undermining liberty by favouring the introduction of ID cards and by his policies on crime and terrorism; and probably numerous other failings or betrayals too.

Most of these accusations seem to me either misleading or false. When Blair first came to power, he said 'We were elected as New Labour and we shall govern as New Labour.' He made a similar assertion in each of the three elections he has fought as leader. He was right to do so. It will have to be Gordon Brown's theme tune too, although he will want to couch it in a different language.

Labour has currently been in power for almost ten years. What are its chief successes and what are its major shortcomings? In other words, what array of problems and opportunities will Gordon Brown inherit as Prime Minister? I deal with these questions only in outline here. A decade is a long time for a party to be in government, and policies have been initiated in a diversity of different areas. All success is relative! Most of the areas I describe as successful continue to have their problems; and there is almost always more work to do. Failures can sometimes be more unequivocal, but most are relative too.

First of all, Labour has won three elections on the trot. Nothing much can be accomplished by a party out of power and Labour has actually been out of government for most of its history. Tony Blair has memorably described its past history as essentially 'a pause in somebody else's narrative'. The party had never been in government even for two full terms before. Most commentators seem to have grown quite blasé about Labour's electoral victories, speaking dismissively of the low turnout in the last election, and so forth. Yet if one looks to the US and Europe, Blair is the only left-of-centre leader to have stayed in government over the past decade. Bill Clinton and the New Democrats are long gone, and so are Lionel Jospin and the left coalition in France, as well as the SPD–Green coalition in Germany. The same is true of the social democrats in The Netherlands, Denmark and, most recently, Sweden.

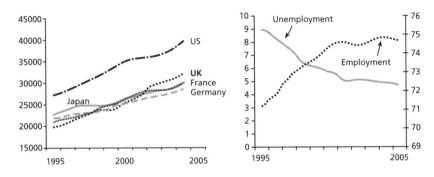

The UK has enjoyed strong and stable growth in living standards
US dollars, GDP per capita, current prices and PPP, 2004

Employment is high and stable, unemployment low
per cent aged 16 +

Figure 1.1: Over the past decade, considerable progress has been made towards the UK's economic goals

Putting the economy first is a policy that has worked, as has that of concentrating upon work- and job-generation. Ceding control of interest rates to the Bank of England was a bold decision, but one that has also paid off. The economy has been largely stable over the past ten years, with good growth rates, and has out-performed those of most of the other developed countries. About 75 per cent of the labour force is in work, as compared, for exam-ple, to only 63–4 per cent in France and Germany, while in Italy the figure is only 51 per cent. Having a high proportion of people in work has generated most of the tax revenue made available to spend on public services and new welfare measures. The minimum wage has been set at a substantial level and has not cost jobs as so many critics predicted. There are worries about the economy, as noted earlier, but it looks stronger than most of its competitors among the industrial countries.

The New Deal, tax credit policies, Sure Start and other initia-tives have all had their difficulties, but have mostly proved their worth. There is still some way to go with other policies, such as those designed to help disabled people get back into work, but there is no reason why they should not meet with a reasonable level of success. New Labour quite rightly kept some of the

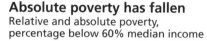

Absolute poverty has fallen
Relative and absolute poverty,
percentage below 60% median income

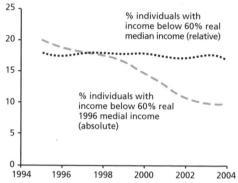

Figure 1.2: The decline in poverty from a 1996 baseline is very large

reforms Mrs Thatcher made to labour markets, for instance the law obliging unions to ballot their members before going out on strike. However, it is a mistake to see labour markets in the UK as unregulated. Provisions like the minimum wage and the New Deal mean that there is a balance between the rights of workers and the need for flexibility, although there is plenty of room left for debate about whether it is the right balance, since the interests of employers and workers may differ, sometimes quite sharply.

The Thatcherite period was one of steeply rising inequalities and expanding numbers of people living in poverty. It has been a very difficult legacy for New Labour to confront. Some say that economic inequality has continued to rise since 1997, but this is an error, based upon looking at data for individuals rather than households, which is much more important. Overall, inequality by this measure has declined – and at a minimum the seemingly implacable rise noted over the previous twenty years has been halted. The proportion of people living in poverty has been brought down by more than 2.5 million since 1997 – far more if one calculates against an absolute baseline rather than a relative one (see figure 1.2). Previous Labour governments produced a great deal of rhetoric about lowering inequality, but mostly weren't in power long enough to make any real changes.

Large amounts of tax revenue have been put into the public services, including especially education and health care. Has the money been well spent? The government has come in for a great deal of criticism on this score, but, by and large, objective indicators show that the answer is 'yes'. Most controversial has been the introduction of commercial providers into certain areas, in education and health, as well as in transport and other areas; and the use of mixed funding streams for building projects, in the shape of public–private partnerships. Among the most contentious of all was the decision (taken by Gordon Brown) to support a public–private scheme for the renovation of the London Underground, pushed through in the teeth of fierce opposition from the mayor, Ken Livingstone. I come back to these questions later.

Many would put crime and migration into the category of Labour's failures, and it is true that there have been major problems. However, crime rates have come down substantially and the UK has made a more successful adaptation to increasing cultural diversity than most other European countries. Such policies have also been crucial to Labour's electoral achievements. In several other countries, left-of-centre parties largely ignored these problems and, as a direct result, fell from power. These things having been said, Labour does need to rethink its policy on crime at this juncture. It has depended too much on the criminal justice system rather than taking a wider view of crime prevention. (See chapter 3.)

As a result of the above policies as a whole, the UK has shifted in a more social democratic direction. A key indication of this transformation is provided by the changes in the doctrines of the Tories since the arrival of David Cameron. Under Tony Blair's leadership, Conservative leaders from John Major through to Michael Howard have been successfully challenged. All of them tried to stick to an essentially Thatcherite agenda. Cameron, by contrast, has sought to move quite explicitly onto New Labour's ground. He rejects tax-cutting as an overriding objective; he has expressed his commitment to the NHS and other public institutions; and he emphasizes the need to reduce poverty.

On balance, therefore, Labour has been a successful government on the domestic front, so long as one doesn't measure it against unrealistic expectations. Of course, all is not rosy in the garden. Where has New Labour fallen short? Where are its main continuing problems? I believe they are also considerable.

There has been something of a failure of ideology. In 1997, two of the great difficulties facing the country were the run-down nature of the public services and the growth of inequality and poverty. Tackling these problems quite rightly became a basic part of Labour's programme. Yet no clear political vocabulary was developed in which to express these concerns – one of the main reasons why New Labour has been so widely accused of staying too close to Thatcherism.

Reform of the state is a fundamental part of the New Labour agenda – a different orientation from the traditional left, which had more of an unquestioning reliance on it. However, it must be made clear that state reform, including the introduction of non-profit and commercial organizations, is not an abandonment of Labour's public purpose. A clear distinction must be made between the state and the public sphere.

New Labour is a party concerned in an essential way with social justice, but one could be forgiven for doubting the strength of this commitment. The chief reason is that Labour has been coy about its egalitarian aspirations, couching them in the vague language of social exclusion; and that it has in fact set up such a diversity of programmes that it is difficult to extract the main thread from them. It is right to put a stress upon opportunity rather than traditional redistribution, but a more powerful vocabulary for expressing this concern to citizens is needed.

Constitutional reform and devolution remain to a large extent in limbo. Labour's reforms, most notably the creation of the Scottish Parliament, the Welsh Assembly and the Northern Ireland Assembly, have been substantial and have changed the country significantly. The largely successful promotion of peace in Northern Ireland has been a major plus factor, driven in substantial part by Tony Blair's personal involvement.

Yet Labour even now seems to have no developed view of what devolution should mean for the country as a whole – should Britain become a more federal country or not? The Regional Development Agencies are effectively agencies of central government with some responsibilities for the regions. Labour has also struggled with the problem of how to reorganize local government, with its patchwork of different councils. Elected mayors have only been endorsed in thirteen cities. In one of these, London, the government actively sought to block the leading candidate, Ken Livingstone, who at that time was regarded with great suspicion in Labour Party circles.

Labour more or less completely left to one side any attempt to influence corporate capitalism. One can see why. The party wanted to get support from quarters that had previously harboured great suspicion of it. Hence the 'prawn cocktail initiative' to woo the City by the Labour leadership in the mid-1990s. There was a brief flirtation with 'stakeholder capitalism' in the early period of Tony Blair's leadership, but that quickly fizzled out. Labour's inaction with regard to capitalism contrasts with the fervour of its reforms of public services. I don't mean to say that we should go back to Old Labour's hostility to markets and to entrepreneurs; but we should work out more explicitly what sort of capitalism we want.

The 1997 manifesto stated that 'we will put concern for the environment at the heart of policy-making, so that it is not an add-on extra, but informs the whole of government'.[6] Major initiatives were in fact made, such as the introduction of an energy tax and signing up to the Kyoto agreements. Yet in a speech made in 2001, Tony Blair admitted that, with other questions to concentrate on in the first few years, 'environmental issues slid back down the political agenda'.[7] Full recognition of the implications of climate change has only come late on and without, so far, adequate policy innovation. Much the same could be said of transport, an overlapping issue. It was left to Ken Livingstone to pioneer road-charging, while the railways are only now recovering from several years of vacillation and indecision in the way they were managed.

Blair has long stated himself to be a strong pro-European, and I believe genuinely so, but he has been unable either to reverse British euro-scepticism or put Britain more at the centre of Europe. He has said that New Labour is 'at its best when it is at its boldest', but he has not applied that principle to UK membership of the EU. He was not willing to take the gamble of pushing for the UK's entry to the euro early on when he might have been successful. Britain appears almost as much the 'reluctant European' today as it did in 1997. The main areas where Britain has had an impact is in supporting enlargement and pushing to upgrade the EU's rapid military deployment capacity. In Europe, for a left-of-centre politician, Blair's closest allies have been strange ones – the right-wing leaders, Mr Aznar in Spain and Mr Berlusconi in Italy. The alliances preceded the war in Iraq, although they were further strengthened by it.

These problems relate to difficulties of foreign policy, which in the end have done more than anything else to reduce Blair's personal popularity and damage the standing of New Labour. One cannot say that New Labour's foreign policy has been an unequivocal failure; quite a range of successes have been notched up. The speech Blair gave in Chicago in 1998, making the case for an interventionist foreign policy in pursuit of humanitarian goals, remains an outstanding one. That policy was pursued with some degree of success in Bosnia, Kosovo, Sierra Leone and Afghanistan. Iraq, however, proved a step too far, as did Blair's seemingly obsessive closeness to George W. Bush.

If Iraq had possessed weapons of mass destruction, especially if he had been close to acquiring nuclear weapons, I think the invasion would have been justified. Saddam Hussein had already initiated two major wars, involving the loss of a million lives; he had deployed chemical weapons in an utterly ruthless way to quell an uprising of the Kurds; UN sanctions were not only failing, but Saddam had been prepared to divert revenue allowed for humanitarian purposes to his own ends, even though children were starving.

As a result of the Iraq adventure, Blair has been accused of lying and even losing his mind. The *New Statesman*, never friendly to Blair at the best of times, in July 2003 published an article entitled: 'Blair, plausible psychopath, "set to implode"'. 'The question of Tony Blair's sanity', it proclaimed, 'is one that can no longer be avoided.'[8] The article seemed to have been written in all seriousness and quoted reputable psychotherapists who described him as a psychopathic personality. Far more people just think he lied in justifying the case for war.

Blair – Bliar? I don't think so. The Hutton Report was very thorough, and found no evidence of intent to deceive the public. Sections of the press had earlier built up Lord Hutton as someone who would uncover the truth, but what they had in mind was information that could bring the government down or at least seriously embarrass it. When nothing of the kind was forthcoming, they turned on its author. I don't have any doubt that Blair acted in good faith, given that all the intelligence communities believed that Saddam possessed chemical and biological weapons. Saddam's behaviour seemed incomprehensible otherwise, since he went to every length to block the weapons inspectors and resist UN sanctions.

What was shocking to me was the fact that the evidence that Saddam possessed WMD turned out to be so thin. I had assumed that what was revealed to the public in the run-up to the war (not much, since it included the dodgy dossier) just scratched at the surface. I had thought that there must be much more detailed evidence that could not be disclosed before the war, because it would compromise sources within the country, but there was nothing. Colin Powell's presentation to the UN of the photographic evidence of Iraq's WMD turned out after the event to be an embarrassing pretence – embarrassing for him personally, but also for the whole Western defence community. (For further discussion, see chapter 8.)

A cardboard effigy of Gordon Brown holding scissors, depicting cuts in the health sector, decorates a room at the Conservative conference in Bournemouth, Sunday, 1 October 2006.

2

The Contenders: Brown versus Cameron

Question: What's the difference between Tony Blair and God?
Answer: God doesn't think he's Tony Blair.

Question (asked in relation to Blair's propensity to travel the world): What's the difference between Tony Blair and God?
Answer: God is everywhere in the world. Tony Blair is every-where in the world except for the UK.

Like him or not, Tony Blair is a global figure. In the post-war period Winston Churchill and Mrs Thatcher are the only other British prime ministers to have been known across the world. The Labour Party probably would have won under John Smith in 1997, and I have no doubt Smith would have proved an outstanding leader. Yet without the ideological changes pioneered by Blair, it is highly unlikely that there would have been the landslide that actually occurred. He has provided the leadership that has guided Labour to three suc-cessive electoral victories. No previous Labour leader has even come close to matching that level of accomplishment. It would be hard to deny, however, that he has over-reached himself in foreign affairs. Brown as yet is quite unknown on the international stage and will have to make his presence felt quickly and forcefully.

Over the past four or five years, as one would expect, there has been a decline in the proportion of the electorate agreeing that Tony Blair has been doing a good job, and support for Labour more generally has fallen. After one year in government, in May 1998, according to Mori polling, 67 per cent of the population expressed approval of the way Blair was running the country. By May 2002 that percentage had declined to 39 per cent, although with some fluctuations in between. In July 2006 Blair's approval ratings reached their nadir, at 23 per cent. By December they had recovered to 30 per cent.[1]

A poll reported on 9 January 2007 showed that Labour still had 32 per cent overall support, but at that date the Tories had climbed to their highest point for fourteen years, standing at 39 per cent.[2] Those satisfied with the government numbered 22 per cent, with 72 per cent saying they were dissatisfied. If one looks across a whole range of polls, there has been considerable variation over 2006 and into 2007 – both over time and between the different polling organizations. The overall position, however, seems clear. The Tories have taken a lead over Labour as of early 2007 of some 6–7 per cent, perhaps more.

David Cameron's approval ratings have improved during the Blair–Brown interregnum. In some polls, he has reached as high as 40 per cent support when people are asked who they would favour as the best leader for the country. However, most voters are reserving judgement about the 'New Tories', recognizing that they have not fleshed out their policies. Over a third of respondents say they don't know enough about what Cameron stands for to make up their minds about him. Cameron is rated as more dynamic and personable than Gordon Brown; however, when asked about who would be the stronger leader, Brown comes out ahead.

Twenty years ago, the economy, unemployment and inflation headed the list of people's main worries. Now, when asked what they see as the most significant issues facing Britain today, these concerns rank low down. Only 8 per cent of citizens see the state of the economy as among the key problems the UK has to face, 6 per cent list unemployment and 2 per cent inflation. Immigration is at the top of voters' worries, cited by 40 per cent of respondents. It is followed by the NHS at 38 per cent, defence and international terrorism at 37 per cent and law and order at 30 per cent.[3] Worryingly for Labour, in spite of their lack of concrete policies, the Tories are currently ahead in several of these fields. They have a seven-point lead over Labour on law and order; and a six-point lead on immigration in one recent poll. In some surveys, Labour now trails the Tories on the NHS, as well as on education and the environment.

How should one interpret these various findings? At the time of writing I would say it is all to play for in British politics. Six to seven points behind is not a lot at this stage in the electoral cycle. A certain amount will depend upon personalities. How will Gordon Brown perform if and when he becomes Prime Minister? Will he be collegial? Can he compete with Cameron's youthful verve? In turn, will Cameron be able to develop gravitas? Will he be able to hold together a party that mistrusts some of the innovations he is trying to make?

In spite of what is often written, I don't think politics is mostly about personal qualities and even less is it about personal presentation and spin. The battle will be won more on the ground of ideas and policy. Voters do not follow policy debates in any detail, but they do have a sense of whether what a party is offering has substance or not. The advent of a new leader – even one who is already a familiar face – gives Labour the chance to refresh its programme in the eyes of voters while building upon the substantial achievements it has to its credit. At this point, therefore, it is worth reflecting upon what the main rivals stand for, according to their own testimony. I concentrate primarily upon Brown and Cameron, with a shorter section on the Liberal Democrat leader, Menzies Campbell.

Gordon Brown's Political Outlook

Brown's political philosophy is often said to be to the left of that of Tony Blair – meaning that he leans more towards the Old Left. But his speeches and writings over the past few years reveal nothing of the kind. Brown is a believer in the need for economic dynamism and flexibility in the face of the rapidly evolving global marketplace. The left must learn to recognize the many virtues of markets rather than always turning to the state. Sometimes progressives must try to make markets function more effectively rather than trying to block or limit them, but we have to resist protectionism both on a national and international level.

However, Brown emphasizes, Mrs Thatcher was wrong in assuming markets were the solution to everything. We should not let the market invade the whole of our lives; moreover, there are clear circumstances in which markets fail. A market economy is not the same as a privatized economy. For it to function properly, we must have a judicious mix of liberalization and regulation – 'liberalize where possible and regulate where necessary'.[4]

Competition can and should have a role in health care, for example, as should choice. However, health is not and cannot be a commodity like any other. Use of health care for the individual is inherently unpredictable, and cannot be planned like the weekly food shop. For this reason it is both most efficient and most equitable to pool coverage of health care; it cannot be left to private insurance. Private insurance policies that 'by definition rely for their viability on ifs, buts and small print and can cover only some of the people some of the time should not be preferred to policies that cover all of the people all of the time'.[5]

At the centre of Brown's thinking are ambitious plans for education. In his pre-Budget report of December 2006 he announced a large new package of support for schools. Head teachers will get an increase in the amount of money they receive per pupil, and will be able to spend the cash as they see fit. Secondary schools will on average receive £200,000 more per year. More small-group teaching will be available in schools at all levels. Classrooms will have more equipment and space per child. In response to the Leitch Report, the Chancellor promised that the number of apprenticeships would be doubled. A target has been set of 90 per cent of adults holding at least five GCSEs by 2020.[6] Brown sees continuing progress in education as vital if the UK is to prosper as world economic competition intensifies.

Brown is widely regarded as a centralizer, but in fact he has regularly proclaimed the benefits of devolution and decentralization. For many years he has spoken of the importance of a partnership between national and local government. He advocates a 'new localism', where local authorities are at the heart of the delivery of welfare and public services; and where civil society groups play an important role too. Those providing public services should be empowered to take decisions that affect the locality and be accountable to that community. Active citizenship and personal responsibility are two of Brown's most frequent emphases, just as they have been for Blair. There must, however, he stresses, be a balance with the national state, since otherwise standards might vary widely, local corruption creep in and geographical inequalities become magnified.

In talking of inequality, Brown puts a strong emphasis upon equality of opportunity, the need to overcome 'unfair privilege'. Markets can generate great wealth, but in and of themselves they do not create a fair society. Government must intervene to try to equalize life-chances. His vision, often stated, is of a social order in which 'individuals [are] empowered and equipped to realize their potential, a positive view of liberty for all'. But, he says, echoing the consistent New Labour theme, freedom must be matched with responsibility.

These themes tie in with Brown's musings on British identity. Sceptics say he is just trying to legitimate his Scots background in an English context, but there is plainly much more to it than that. 'Britishness' is arguably the idea that connects the elements of his political outlook. The 'golden thread' that defines what it means to be British is 'the individual standing firm for freedom and liberty against tyranny and the arbitrary use of power'.[7] However it also stands for 'fairness' and civic duty. Britishness should not be identified with conservatism, in the sense of a clinging onto the past. On the contrary, it is distinguished by its capacity to evolve.

Many years ago Tom Nairn wrote a book called *The Break-Up of Britain*.[8] It was not imminent then, but some believe the prospect is closer now. The state of the union has become a matter of renewed debate since current polls show that the Scottish Nationalist Party is doing well in the run-up to the May elections. If the party should form a government, it has pledged a referendum on full independence, although without defining in detail what that would mean.

Brown has mounted a counter-attack against what he sees as the 'dangerous drift' to separatism. Some Tories have started speaking about 'English votes for English laws' at Westminster; support among English voters for separation is also higher than it was. Brown has gone on the offensive. In an article published in early January 2007, he spoke of a dangerous drift towards a 'balkanization of Britain'.[9] In the past, we could get by with an implicit idea of Britishness. But when 'our country is being challenged in Scotland, Wales and now England by secessionists', we have to be much more direct about it.

Brown tends to brush away the 'West Lothian question' – posed by Tom Dalyell, the Labour MP for West Lothian in November 1977, during a Commons debate about devolution to Scotland and Wales. 'For how long', Dalyell enquired, 'will English constituencies and English Honourable Members tolerate … at least 119 Honourable Members from Scotland, Wales and Northern Ireland exercising an important, and probably often decisive, effect on British politics while they themselves have no say in the same matters in Scotland, Wales and Northern Ireland?' In response, Enoch Powell said: 'We have finally grasped what the Honourable Member for West Lothian is getting at. Let us call it the West Lothian question.'

According to Brown, this imbalance has to be understood in the context of a greater one. England amounts to 85 per cent of the Union, he remarked in an interview, and can outvote anyone else in it. Hence devolution to the nations is effectively a balancing mechanism.

Britain today, Brown argues, needs a renewed sense of national mission. The Union Jack has been appropriated by the British National Party, but it should be reclaimed by progressives. The flag 'should be a symbol of unity', 'a flag for tolerance and inclusion'.[10] We should in fact develop more rituals to sustain these commitments. Where is our equivalent, he asks rhetorically, of 4 July in the US, or 14 July in France?

In Brown's thinking, this emphasis is consistent with profiting from globalization – indeed it is vital for it. Britain should develop a new sense of national economic purpose, geared to a world of rapid change. That purpose should be to sustain a competitive economy while enriching public institutions and furthering social justice, nationally and internationally too. A new settlement in this country would take the following form: constitutional reform, including further devolution; a new citizenship contract; the rebuilding of civic society; the renewal of local government; the integration of minorities into British society; and a commitment to both patriotism and internationalism.[11] In recent speeches, Brown has made clear in addition his commitment to Labour's overall approach for countering jihadist terrorism.

David Cameron and the 'New Tories'

Emblazoned along the top of the Tory website as of December 2006 there is the slogan 'Stop Brown's NHS Cuts!' It's a cheek to accuse of cuts the man who, as Chancellor, has presided over record levels of investment in the health service. That apart, in political terms what does such a headline message mean? Have the Conservatives under David Cameron really changed, or are they, as some Labour critics like to say, 'the same old Tories' underneath a veneer of new rhetoric? After all, David Cameron was a speech-writer for the Tory leader who preceded him, Michael Howard, who pursued what was nominally a very different agenda.

The jury is still out on the issue. Cameron is making a serious effort to create a Conservative philosophy distinct from that endorsed by Mrs Thatcher and her successors. Yet it is not at all clear at the moment what it will amount to.

The points of overlap with New Labour are very considerable – sometimes this fact is acknowledged by Cameron, sometimes not. The NHS is a good starting-point, in fact. Gone is the theme, 'There is no such thing as society'; gone the ideas of the minimal state, the overriding commitment to tax cuts and the indifference to public services. In a speech to the King's Fund, Cameron affirmed his commitment to the 'NHS ideal' and rejected any move towards a private insurance-based system, therefore tracking the conclusions of Gordon Brown. In his speech he used words that even Aneurin Bevan might have blanched at: 'I believe that the creation of the NHS is one of the greatest achievements of the twentieth century.'[12] There isn't exactly any detail in the Tory plans for the NHS, but he has said firmly that spending on public services will rise in real terms under a Conservative government.

The Tories will support foundation hospitals, but want to free up all hospitals from close state surveillance. The Tory critique of Labour's tax policies is now a limited one – it concentrates on the need for a more simplified tax system and less regulation.

Cameron is self-consciously trying to lead the Conservatives back to the centre-ground – the new centre-ground as defined by Labour. He once more echoes Labour in saying that economic stability is the Tories' number one priority. He emphasizes the importance of globalization and, like his opponents, rejects protectionism. His version of compassionate conservatism endorses the need for policy intervention to reduce poverty and under-privilege, putting the emphasis upon opportunity and aspiration as the key. He has accepted that reducing poverty means reducing relative poverty. In other words, he has rejected the Thatcherite idea that it doesn't matter how much inequality there is as long as absolute poverty declines.

He seems happy to lend support to the idea of Britishness, in spite of a strong trend within his party towards emphasizing English separatism. Cameron has taken over the New Labour principle of matching rights with responsibilities. The idea of fostering a sense of national identity comes in for some praise, as do citizenship ceremonies, the oath of allegiance and the requirement to learn English for immigrants wishing to become naturalized. As he quite often says of Labour's policies, he accepts them, but he 'wants to go further' – in this case making it a requirement for existing citizens to learn English where they do not speak it to a satisfactory level.[13]

The story continues with terrorism and crime. Fighting international terrorism has to be a 'consuming concern' of government today; it is much more challenging than dealing with the terrorists of the past. Counter-terrorism policy must 'balance the rights of the suspect with the rights of society as a whole'. He rejects ID cards, but argues that phone-tap evidence should be open to being used in court. The Tories supported the intervention in Iraq under previous leaders and Cameron continues that endorsement. He broadly accepts Labour's approach to international relations, including Blair's principle of liberal interventionism.

What are the differences with Labour, and is there a coherent political philosophy underlying the whole enterprise? There is a philosophy of sorts, although at the moment it doesn't look very robust. It centres upon the idea of social responsibility. 'Building a strong society', Cameron says, 'is not just a task for politicians. We are all in this together.'[14] Civic organizations, such as churches, can take over some of the functions now mainly in the hands of government; and citizens have to accept obligations too. Mrs Thatcher's governments restored a sense of economic responsibility to the country. The task today is to do the same for social responsibility. The family has a core part to play, because it is a place where commitments to others are forged and sustained. However, he is not a Tory traditionalist in this area. He makes a strong case for marriage, but supports civil partnerships, and he is anxious not to stigmatize single parents.

He also says he supports investment in child care, which is another concern where his main quarrel with New Labour is that it 'hasn't gone far enough'. Increased flexibility between work and home is one of his main emphases, along with a stress upon the importance of improving quality of life. He is critical of measuring economic progress only in terms of GDP growth and he wants to put improving 'general well-being' at the centre of Conservative policies. Well-being in turn presumes sustainability and implies giving high priority to environmental questions. It is the first time, he says, that a major British political party has given the environment equal billing with social and economic priorities.[15] Labour is only in the business of short-term responses to our problems; Tory policies will be 'built to last'.

Cameron's 'hug a hoodie' speech fits with the themes just mentioned.[16] The anxieties caused by crime, especially in poor neighbourhoods, he argues, wreck any sense of general well-being at the same time as they undermine any sense of community. People often see hoodies as aggressive, wearing 'the uniform of a rebel army of young gangsters'. But wearing a hood is more often defensive rather than aggressive. Children who have suffered years of abuse and neglect need care and understanding, not just hard-nosed policing. Emotional security matters more than anything else if children are to achieve self-respect. Where the family fails, community groups should step in to give help.

In late January 2007, Cameron gave a speech about national identity that paralleled Brown's speech a short while before – but with two or three crucial differences.[17] Instead of Brown's 'balkanization', Cameron's metaphor was of multiple Berlin walls. There are 'five Berlin walls of division that we must tear down together'. These are extremism, uncontrolled immigration, poverty, lack of access to education and multiculturalism. The extremists include the British Nationalist Party on the one side and 'those who seek a sharia state' on the other. Cameron does accept the benefits that immigrants have brought, although he does not expand on the point. It is 'uncontrolled immigration' that is the problem.

The persistence of poverty means that there is 'an emerging underclass of people being left behind'; while the 'educational apartheid' between good and inferior schools blocks the chances of social mobility. Multiculturalism is singled out for special censure. It is said to be an approach 'which focuses on what divides us rather than what brings us together'. It has led to social housing being allocated along ethnic lines, and has served to 'create resentment and suspicion'.

And What About Mr Campbell?

David Cameron's speeches might be light on policy content, but those of Menzies Campbell are even more so. Being the third party, the Liberal Democrats tend to define themselves more in terms of what they are against than what they are for. Campbell is a Scot, but his Scottish background rarely seems to be raised as an issue among critics in the way Gordon Brown's is. However, should there be a hung parliament in the next general election, and Labour and the Lib Dems get together, there would be not just one but two Scots running the British government. (Well, so what? – see below, chapter 9.)

Before he became leader, Campbell voted against foundation hospitals, university fees and ID cards – positions he seems to have stuck to. His main field of specialism was foreign policy, and he has consistently opposed the Iraq war. He says he wants the Liberal Democrats 'to be modernized, to be professional, and to be credible and united' in order to 'make a reality of three party politics'.[18]

Campbell is as firm as the other two leaders on the importance of environmental questions. As he puts it, 'we need to make a priority of the environment as an issue of conscience and necessity', which will mean 'changes in all our behaviours'. He has endorsed the findings of a Liberal Democrat policy group on taxation.[19] Its report proposed a 'green tax switch', with increased taxes on aircraft emissions, a steeply rising vehicle excise duty, the introduction of a carbon tax, and indexing fuel duty to inflation. The Liberal Democrats are against the use of nuclear power.

The income from the new green taxes would be used to fund measures to help alleviate poverty and simplify the tax system. The Lib Dems propose to abolish the 10p starting rate of income tax, which would mean that two million people would no longer pay income tax at all. The basic rate of income tax would be cut by 2p; and the starting level for those who pay the 40 per cent upper rate of taxation would be raised to £50,000 a year. In the longer term, they intend to raise the income tax threshold much further, to the equivalent of the national minimum wage.

Campbell says he is 'an instinctive liberal' and is 'a passionate advocate of civil liberties, equal opportunities and constitutional reform'. There must be a return of powers to Parliament, with the executive being held to account, and an elected Lords. Constitutional reform should go along with decentralization. The state should 'give power away' to 'people and communities'. 'I will seek to reduce the power of an over-mighty state, with community services, locally provided, democratically accountable. Locally elected people should be responsible for local schools, local hospitals, local police and local transport.'[20] National voting should be through proportional representation.

Campbell wants the troops brought back from Iraq, although not with a set timetable. He says he is a strong internationalist, and he is an advocate of the importance of the EU. The invasion of Iraq flouted international law, and Britain should declare a recommitment to the basic principles of international governance. 'Britain has a unique role to play at the heart of our international system and we must restore political confidence in international institutions and the international rule of law.'

A Brief Assessment

The Liberal Democrats seem far from having worked out a consistent position. The party was put together from two different ones, and the divisions in thinking are still apparent. The Liberals wanted freedom from state interference, in personal life as in the economy. A good example of this style of thinking was provided by the *Orange Book*, subtitled 'Reclaiming Liberalism' and published in 2004.[21] The contributors spoke of retrieving some of the traditional building-blocks of liberalism, which included 'defending against the nanny state', a sceptical view of Europe and a greater role for markets in the public services. The social democrats within the party, on the other hand, are for increasing taxes, a larger role for the state and are wary of state sector reform. Campbell has to walk an uneasy line between these two.

Gordon Brown will have quite a few problems if and when he becomes Prime Minister. He can expect a furious onslaught from the right-wing press, who scent an end to years of Labour domination, and can't wait to see the natural order of things restored. He is New Labour through and through, as I have tried to show; but the Tories will paint him as a traditional socialist with a faith in the state and a believer in regulation for regulation's sake. He does not have the personal appeal that Blair has, or did before his relationship with the electorate soured.

Cameron's Tories represent a challenge for a Brown-led government, at least given the widespread disenchantment with Labour. What are their weaknesses? There are plenty of them, and future Tory success will depend a lot upon whether these can be repaired.

There is a strong sense that Cameron remains a political lightweight. His philosophy has a certain consistency, but it is almost completely devoid of substance. He defends his approach by saying that you have to lay the foundations before building a house, and only later construct the walls and the roof. However, the analogy is a false one. There is no point in constructing foundations if there is no design for the building as a whole; architects' drawings have to come well before the actual building process. They have to be all-inclusive as well as carefully detailed and thought-through.

The Tories have set up a range of groups to report back on policy issues. But such groups might find it difficult to construct an overall policy framework, which cannot be built in a piecemeal way. Moreover, what happens if they propose approaches that don't even fit with Cameron's reorientation of the party? At the moment Cameron's vagueness allows him to duck the difficult questions. For instance, responding to climate change will involve confronting some vested interests, such as the motoring organizations: is he prepared to do this? If the tax system is to be simplified, how will this goal be achieved? What taxes will be kept and which modified or abandoned? The policy group on taxation has already reported back. Cameron distanced himself to some degree from its conclusions, which were essentially tax-cutting ones.

Since he has said little about the role of the state, he is probably hedging his bets on the issue – hoping to have his cake and eat it. It isn't possible. At some point he will have to come off the fence and say if he is still a supporter of rolling back the state. Certainly there will be much pressure on him to revert back to views he has supposedly distanced himself from.

What seems to be Cameron's basic idea, that of social responsibility, is an intrinsically vulnerable one. It is not in any sense novel, but part of the standard pack of compassionate conservatism in the US.[22] Responsibilities have to accompany rights; and third sector groups should play a part in delivery of welfare measures, especially at the community level. However, it is surely plain that such groups must be in some way regulated by the state and that the state has to continue to play the main role in welfare delivery. Voluntary groups by their very nature tend to be unstable, since they have no regular funding and depend upon a continuing moral commitment from their members. Moreover, the activities of such groups, by being clustered more in some areas than in others, might reinforce existing inequalities if government does not have a role.

The 'New Tories' at present completely lack the core element that has put Labour in a strong position over the past ten years –

an analysis of the key trends in the contemporary world and how best to respond to them. It is just such a standpoint that should really serve as the foundation for the 'house' they are trying to build, since policy plans should be constructed around it. The earlier Tory incarnation, Thatcherism, did have just such an analysis, and it was influenced by reputable social and economic thinking coming from Hayek, Friedman and others. However, it is just this world-view from which Cameron now wants to break away.

Compassionate conservatism in the hands of George W. Bush turned out to be virtually meaningless in practice. Swingeing tax cuts were introduced that heavily favoured the privileged. Levels of poverty in the US, which went down during the Clinton years, have climbed again. Bush had plans to further reduce welfare expenditure, but these were blocked. Cameron himself has a fresh agenda. But will it be implemented should the Tories form a government after the next election? One could be quite sceptical, since a hard core of Conservatives are not at all convinced.

Much of the party has precisely not discarded 'Old Conservatism', and it is just these groups and currents of thought that are likely to cause David Cameron trouble – in relation to taxation, family policy, ethnic minorities and more besides. Cameron's tirade against multiculturalism was surprisingly inept and crude – so much so, that one begins to suspect dangers lurking behind the text. Will Cameron use such attacks, coupled with an onslaught on immigration, as a way of returning to the right-wing populism of his predecessor Michael Howard?

Cameron is explicitly an Old Tory in one area: the European Union. Here he out-Thatchers Mrs Thatcher. If we look back to her Bruges speech, which at the time was widely regarded as 'putting the EU in its place', we see that she was at that point far more pro-European than any of her successors as Conservative leader have been. There is a complete inconsistency in Cameron's thinking here. On the one hand he wants to make the environment a priority for the Tories. On the other, he disparages the EU, which is vital to realistic policy-making on the issue.

In the following chapters I elaborate what Labour's policy framework for the next few years should be. I start by considering the nature of globalization, what has changed in the wider world since 1997, and how a Brown-led government should respond. Even over the space of ten years the world has moved on considerably. I will then look at the key issue of public services before moving on to consider what should be Labour's view of markets and their social role. Labour should restore its egalitarian purpose; I show how this goal might be achieved.

In the second half of the book I look at some of the core issues that have come to the fore, including climate change, cultural diversity and how to handle it, the European Union and foreign policy. Finally, I consider the ticklish issue of trust and democracy. Can Labour recover the confidence of citizens? It is a lot to range over, and I apologize if I don't cover it all in the detail it warrants.

*US Federal Reserve Chairman Alan Greenspan talks with Gordon
Brown at Lancaster House in London ahead of the continuation of the
G7 Finance Ministers and Central Bank Governors' meeting, Saturday,
5 February 2005.*

3

The World in Flux: How to Respond?

The following are queries posed by customers in a large computer store in London:

> I'd like to buy the internet. Do you know how much it costs?
> Can you copy the internet on the disk for me?
> I would like an internet, please.
> I just downloaded the internet. How do I use it?
> Will the internet be open on bank holiday tomorrow?
> I don't have a computer at home. Is the internet available in book form?
> We're going on holiday for a month. Can you suspend the internet for us, please?

The internet has revolutionized much in our lives over the past ten years, and is a major factor in the intensifying of globalization; but not everyone yet quite understands it.

Globalization: What Is It?

Globalization – it's the theme tune of our times. A word that was barely in use some twenty years ago – and then only among academics – has now become common coinage. It is unattractive and cumbersome. Rarely can any academic notion have passed so thoroughly into the language – or, rather, the world's languages, since it is now spoken of everywhere.

It is no longer just a technical idea, but has entered the arena of real social and political conflicts and it is coloured with emotions. Those who are against globalization see it as the source of many, and even sometimes most, of the ills of the world. For them, globalization is essentially a destructive force and also one linked above all to power. It is an expression of the dominance of the Western nations, and corporations based in the West, over the poorer regions of the world.

Even as late as the mid-1990s it wasn't easy to get politicians to take an interest in globalization. I tried hard enough, but without conspicuous success. The New Democrats were in effect talking about it, but without using the term very much. In a few short years all that has changed. 'Globalization' now peppers the speeches of Tony Blair, and especially Gordon Brown. It is right and proper that such should be the case, since we live in a world marked by an onrush of change going far beyond the borders of any one country. But what does the term actually mean?

The simplest definition of globalization is the increasing interdependence of world society. However, we have to put some flesh on these bare bones. Globalization is often thought of solely as an economic phenomenon, even by some of the most sophisticated commentators on the subject. Martin Wolf, for instance, defines it as 'the integration of economic activities, across borders, through markets'. And he adds: 'What we are talking about is movement in the direction of greater integration, as both natural and man-made barriers to international exchange continue to fall.'[1] Seeing globalization in any terms other than the economic, he says, makes the whole thing unmanageably broad.

The world is certainly becoming much more interdependent economically. The trends in this direction are very evident. But globalization is so obviously not only economic that it is hard to see how anyone could seriously think otherwise. Throughout this book I stress the importance of communications media as one of the dominant forces of change in our lives. The world has become interconnected electronically in ways that are far more radical and far-reaching than was ever true before. I would in fact date the beginnings of the global age to the late 1960s or early 1970s, the first time at which an effective satellite system was sent up above the earth, making instantaneous communication possible from any one point in the world to any other.

Increasing economic interdependence would not be feasible without these developments. Twenty-four-hour money markets, for instance, could not have existed previously. Or consider credit cards, which now have two billion separate transactions everyday, and which can be used in the majority of countries around the world. Another example is the significance of news media. The Iraq war was probably the first to be watched by a truly global audience. Embedded journalists filmed the struggle on the ground, while the images they produced were watched by many millions in real time.

Globalization is often treated as if it were about development issues alone. Open books on the subject and they will usually concern divisions between rich and poor in world society, the influence of the UN, the World Bank, IMF and so on. The industrial countries figure as the driving forces of change, to which the rest of the world must accommodate. Such a perspective is as common among those who favour globalization as among those who are hostile to it.

Yet globalization is affecting the developed countries just as profoundly as any others in the world. This is true on an economic level: in 1970 the developed nations produced 90 per cent of the world's manufactured goods. That proportion has now declined to 60 per cent and is set to fall much further. However, it is true in many other respects too. The fact that news is now provided on a continuous basis, and concerns a whole range of electronic as well as the more traditional print media, has deeply affected politics and government (more on all this in chapter 9).

Globalization is treated by almost everyone as 'coming from the outside'. 'How do we cope with the challenges of globalization?' must be the FAQ of the moment. But it doesn't, and can't, just come 'from the outside'; it is driven by a variety of processes in which, individuals, groups and organizations participate. Every time I switch on the TV and see pictures from the other side of the world, I not only 'encounter', but also actively contribute to, globalization. The same is true when I get some cash from a hole-in-the-wall machine. Someone harvesting a coffee crop in Guatemala is not just experiencing globalization, but also playing a part in it.

The point may seem trivial, but it is not. Globalization is not a force of nature; it is made by human beings and their endeavours. Nor is it produced only by large anonymous agencies 'out there' against which we all have to struggle. It is enmeshed in a diversity of aspects of our everyday lives, and the 'our' now includes people in all countries. Hence there is nothing ironic in pointing out that the demonstrations organized against globalization made prolific use of the very influences they oppose – the internet, mobile phones, television and so forth. The same is also true of the religious fundamentalist movements that contest modernity itself.

Globalization is not just a synonym for the global dominance of the United States, or of the West more generally, whatever critics may say to the contrary. It is obvious that the affluent countries tend to dominate world institutions. Virtually all the technologies of communication that have been so important in creating greater global interdependence emanated from the developed countries. These countries have also taken the lead in opening up world markets. Yet globalization is by definition a two-way set of processes, not just a system of imbalanced power. What happens in the US economy has a great influence over the world economy as a whole. But the US does not control that economy – no single nation, or even group of nations, does.

Although globalization is the dominant force, or set of forces, shaping our societies today, it is a serious mistake to attribute everything to it, to praise it too much or to blame it too much. There are many other sources of change that are only loosely connected with growing world interdependence. Take, for example, the decline in manufacture in the economies of the industrial countries, one of the most important economic trends of recent years. The reason is partly because of global factors, especially the increasing shift of manufacturing production to developing countries. But just as important are increasing productivity and technological change in the industry itself. For instance, because of automated assembly-line production, it takes far fewer workers to make a car than once it did.

**The cost of communicating
globally has fallen dramatically**
Index of costs

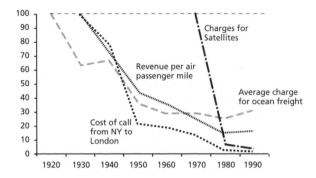

Figure 3.1: Rapid technological change in communications is likely to continue

Or look at some of the dilemmas that face European societies. Europe's welfare states are under strain. Some of the major influences involved are external, especially the problem of creating economies that are successful in an increasingly competitive world marketplace, and therefore capable of supporting large-scale welfare expenditures. Yet others are largely internal. For example, the ageing population comes from improvements in medicine and overall health, coupled to a falling birth rate. It is at most loosely connected to globalization.

Changes since 1997

Since 1997, globalization has further intensified. Information technology and electronic communication are penetrating our lives even more than before. In the Preface to this book, I thank Tim Berners-Lee, who developed the world-wide web. When I wrote *The Third Way* ten years ago, I had to spend hours going back and forth between libraries. Now I can access most of what I want to read on the computer, and only occasionally need to go and check a book in a physical way.

In 1997, the internet was in its infancy; now, nearly 70 per cent of the population in the UK is online. The knowledge/service economy is continuing to develop apace. Welfare reform remains central to the political agenda as the speed of economic transformation accelerates. Flexibility and adaptability are key attributes in many areas of life, stretching well beyond the strictly economic domain.

Labour's programme has its origins in the late 1980s or early 1990s. No matter how substantial it has been, it will not snugly fit the world of 2007. What are the main changes or issues of concern? Some are new problems, or ones that have evolved in a particular way. Others are more long-standing, but for one reason or another have come more sharply into view.

Globalization has been advanced not only by economic factors, or communication, but by political developments too. The most momentous was the ending of the bi-polar world. From that point onwards, we all clearly lived more in 'one world' than before. However, the post-1989 world has turned out to be less benign than many in the early 1990s imagined or hoped would be the case. The point that domestic and foreign policy are difficult to distinguish has even more force. Both in the international sphere and in everyday life there are new insecurities and anxieties. It was widely anticipated that there would be a peace dividend after the end of the Cold War, coupled to increasing stability in the international arena. The nature of the international system certainly has changed – we now worry less about strong states and more about weak ones, and the impact they have upon ethnic breakdown, terrorism, crime and drug-running. Yet anxiety and uncertainty are the order of the day.

The rapid economic rise of China and India and other developing countries has disposed of the idea that globalization benefits the West at the expense of the rest of the world. They owe their development to embracing the world marketplace, not hiding away from it. How far their progress represents a threat to jobs in the industrial countries remains to be seen, but is now a matter of fierce debate. China is scouring the world for energy sources to sustain its speedy economic growth. World prices for fossil fuels have risen steeply since 1997, giving rise to anxieties about energy security. But if prices stay high, such a situation might help us adapt more readily to the exigencies of climate change, which has finally become the prime political concern – as it should have been at an earlier date.

Manufacturing has staged something of a mini-recovery in the UK, but it is very unlikely that any net jobs will be created in this area in the future. There are new forms of competition to be confronted, with the advent of the international outsourcing of IT-based work. Jobs that workers had thought safe until now from competition from abroad are at risk. According to the American economist Gene Grossman and his colleagues at Princeton University, any service job can in principle be outsourced if it displays the following four characteristics: it involves the heavy use of IT, its output is IT-transmittable, it comprises tasks that can be codified and it needs little face-to-face interaction.

IT outsourcing is in its infancy, and no one knows how far it will go. Alan Blinder believes that between 30 and 40 million jobs in the US will be open to outsourcing in the future, making up 20 per cent of all non-manufacturing occupations. The same is likely to be true of the other advanced economies.[2] It doesn't mean that all those jobs will in fact be off-shored, but workers in them might be exposed to competition from people overseas who will do the same work, to the same standards, for much lower wages.

The UK must be prepared and the government will have to keep a very close eye upon immanent trends. Grossman and Blinder actually speak of what they call a 'new paradigm' of globalization that is coming into being, marking a distinct and challenging phase in the evolution of world economic interdependence. Electronic off-shoring is the basis of the new paradigm. The 'old paradigm', which has held sway for the past thirty years, affected whole economic sectors, or firms within those sectors. The US and Europe began to lose competitiveness, for example, in the iron and steel industry, shipbuilding industries and so on.

In the next phase of globalization, competition occurs at the level of the individual job, or type of job, rather than at industry or trade level. The same type of job, in other words, can be outsourced across firms and industries of widely different types. It will therefore be less useful in the future to see the winners and losers from globalization in terms of the sector to which they belong or even their skill group. The consequences are potentially very important. The winners and losers will be more difficult to predict.

The wages of many jobs are set by the fact that (at the moment) they are not affected by international competition. A cab-driver in London earns a lot more than a cab-driver in Manila not because he or she is a better driver, but because, in its very nature, cab-driving is non-tradeable. It will remain so, unless someone discovers a way of driving taxis remotely. The same does not apply at all for a host of workers in offices, hospitals or banks who previously believed they were safe from direct competition from workers overseas.

Many possibilities exist that need to be teased out, since these processes were not previously appreciated or understood. Take as an example the work of surgeons. More and more operations will almost certainly be carried out at a distance, with the doctor perhaps many thousands of miles away from his or her patient. It may be possible for the surgeon to carry out many more operations in the working day than when he or she was confined to a single hospital. Should this happen, the best surgeons will be in much greater demand than the less good ones, who will find their income dropping and perhaps their livelihood disappearing altogether. Globalization will be helping one highly qualified worker, but harming the prospects of the other – even though they are both in a sector where overall Western countries have a competitive edge.

Off-shoring has thus far only affected a small proportion of jobs in the advanced economies, so all this is at a relatively speculative stage. But there are some clear policy implications. Wherever possible, skills training should not be too specialized. What will matter most will be flexibility and adaptability, at the level of both the firm and the overall workforce.

Climate change has shot up the political agenda over the past year or two. It is worth asking why this is so, since it has been known about for at least three decades. Three reasons seem most important. First is the visibility of disasters likely to be related to climate change. Hurricane Katrina impressed itself on people's consciousness well beyond the United States itself. A city in the richest country in the world was devastated in a period of twenty-four hours. As a direct result of the heat wave in Europe in 2003, which certainly represented abnormal weather conditions, 35,000 people died.

The second reason is the accumulation of scientific evidence. The case that climate change is a reality, that it is the result of human activities and that it is already happening becomes stronger with each passing year. The third reason: defending against climate change overlaps with concerns about high oil and gas prices, and with the wider issue of energy security. These factors are important politically. If we are at the end of the era of cheap energy, non-fossil fuel energy sources become both more competitive and more relevant to our needs. Worries about depending upon potentially unreliable suppliers provide further motivation. Coping with climate change will demand binding international agreements, going well beyond Kyoto; technological innovation is bound to make an important contribution, especially if there are some clear breakthroughs in key areas.

In the sphere of international relations, 9:11 signalled a massive shift both in global and national politics. It was the first major attack on the American mainland for two centuries. Its connections with radical Islam have opened up fissures within countries with substantial Muslim majorities and more generally between the Muslim world and the rest of the international community. The shock-waves are still being absorbed, and with some difficulty. Migration and its implications for national identity and the welfare state have come even more sharply to the fore than a decade ago.

Partly as a result of these developments, one could say that 'the' social problem of our times is how to reconcile different beliefs and practices within a society that remains unified and inclusive. We like to see national character as something stable – in the case of Britain, an island of continuity among more unruly neighbours. Yet, in the words of the historian Robert Winder: 'Britain has absorbed migrants at a thousand points and times.' Its history isn't simply one of continuity, but 'the sum of countless muddled and contradictory experiences'. Or, as Daniel Defoe commented: 'A true born Englishman's a Contradiction, In Speech an Irony, in Fact a Fiction.'[3]

Nevertheless, there are major differences today from the past, with the progress of mass air travel and instantaneous electronic communication. Now migrants can and do come from all over the world, and can arrive within a few hours of setting out. The EU expanded by ten new states in 2004, with two further ones now accepted. Most of the new member states are relatively poor. Those who come to the UK from such countries aren't migrants in the proper sense of that term; they are citizens of the Union, and free to move to where the jobs are. Wild stories abound in the popular press about floods of people coming to the UK bent upon exploiting the welfare system. It isn't surprising that members of the public rate immigration, and cultural diversity more generally, as one of their major concerns.

Against the backdrop of a more fluid and diverse society, the nature of poverty and deprivation is changing quite rapidly. 'Classical' poverty is still widespread. That is to say, in spite of the improvements the government's policies have made to the lives of some, many people still have to struggle to make a decent living – their lives are dominated by scarcity. Unemployment, or failure to find regular employment, remains a problem locally and in some regions. Single-parent families and workless households are heavily over-represented among the poor – one of the main factors creating child poverty. Among younger people, rough sleeping has declined, but homelessness has been on the rise. Some half a million people, most of them young, live in temporary hostels, squats or the floors of friends.[4] There may be about the same number of illegal immigrants, failed asylum-seekers and unregistered students in the country. They work in the secondary economy, where the minimum wage is ignored and where they are not eligible for any normal benefits.

However, some problems have little to do with deprivation as such. Mental illness, for example, is worryingly prevalent, and perhaps on the increase. About 15 per cent of adults at any one time are suffering from some form of classifiable mental disorder – a serious and chronic one in the case of half of these. Quite apart from its other damaging consequences, mental illness is now arguably a more challenging economic problem for the society than unemployment as such.[5] Other lifestyle-related practices widespread in Britain include binge-drinking and drug-taking, some of which may be relatively harmless, but quite often also involve serious difficulties of addiction. If one adds in levels of personal debt, which are highest in younger age groups, together with the struggles of many single parents, these phenomena suggest that, apart from the frail elderly, it is the young rather than the old who are bearing the greatest burden of risk in today's society.

Beyond the New Democrats

What are the implications of the emergence of these diverse issues for Labour's overall political approach? The triad of opportunity, responsibility and community that was inherited from the New Democrats has certainly not lost its relevance. Defining in policy terms the relationship between them still frames many questions with which the government has to deal. However, such notions need to be complemented with other ideas and concepts.

If there are three terms that capture the main goals (and dilemmas) of left-of-centre political reform today, they would be *security*, *identity* and *diversity*.

Security, because of issues arising with the further advance of globalization. We are not talking here only of influences affecting the international arena (the old meaning of 'national security'); forces such as climate change drive right into the centre of our society and deep into our everyday lives. They create new and profound risks, on a collective as well as an individual level. Like most of the issues that confront us, they cannot be dealt with only by individual nations. Nor can they be left to government alone to cope with; all demand citizen involvement and many presume lifestyle change or at least adaptation. 'Security' can no longer mean only 'social security', and it cannot be cleanly separated from threats of a global rather than only national kind.[6]

Identity, because these self-same forces tend to challenge traditional identities, national, local and personal. Identity can no longer be taken for granted, but has to be achieved, explored and developed. National identity cannot be the same in a more globalized world; its nature and dynamics are different, even from the Cold War period. Virtually all nations are rethinking their identities, a process that can be divisive and even destructive if handled poorly. These self-same processes are driving a resurgence of local nationalisms within established nation-states, as widely scattered as Quebec in Canada, the Basque country in Spain and France, and Kashmir in India. Scottish and Welsh separatism, together with an English nationalism that is gaining strength, are not developments unique to this country.[7]

National identity remains an essential part of who one is – not having a passport leaves a person without roots and to a large degree without rights too. Social identity is even more important, because everyone needs to be part of social groups that lend meaning and motivation to life. Personal fulfilment demands a sense of continuity and integrity of self; in turn, lack of self-esteem and confidence are related to a variety of individual problems, including some of the most prominent forms of mental illness.

Multiple identities are an inherent part of cosmopolitanism, itself intrinsic to globalization. Many are comfortable with being, for instance, English, British, European and, in a vaguer sense, a global citizen. But many are not, and therein lie the origins of some of the main dividing-lines in contemporary politics. Identity is closely related to security, since so many of the anxieties that affect both individuals and groups come from feelings of dislocation, physical, social and moral.

Diversity, since it is virtually impossible any longer for anyone to live in closed communities, cut off from the world. Confronting cultures and modes of behaviour different from one's own is an everyday experience in a world of instantaneous communication and global news. Security, identity and diversity are closely related, each with the others. Creating a society in which different cultural and ethnic groups can coexist without serious social breakdown, for example, is a basic part of the security agenda.

No Reversion to Old Labour

Labour must seek to recover the trust of the electorate as the party most fitted to meet the problems and challenges just mentioned; new ideas have be the driving force. A government seeking a fourth term in office has to be ambitious and has to show it has not gone stale. It cannot say, 'Give us more time to show that the policies we have in play will work out well in the end.' It cannot be a party of the status quo, and must expect many of its achievements to be to some degree discounted as they become familiar parts of people's lives.

Should a rejuvenated Labour government remain New Labour? The question is easily answered: it should and must do so. Labour has no chance in the next election if it does not stick to the key principles that have sustained it so far. These could be enumerated as follows.

1 *Keep putting a prime emphasis on the economy* – well, there is little need to tell Mr Brown to do that! Most of the statistics for the UK look good, and Brown never misses a chance to hammer this point home. The growth figure for 2006 was about 2.75 per cent, and is predicted to rise to over 3 per cent in 2007. Productivity per worker, long one of the weaknesses of the British economy, has at last grown to some degree, although not enough to close the gap with the leading countries.

There should be a continuing commitment to an open economy and to the removal of market distortions both nationally and internationally. 'National champions' have had their day. The leading companies from all member states in the EU, for example, are becoming 'Europeanized' – they operate across the EU. According to current trends, by 2009 more than half of the average activity of large companies will be carried out in countries in Europe other than their home base. Any form of support or protection given to a company will hence end up enriching 'foreign' stakeholders rather than the national base.[8]

Job creation should still be in the forefront of policy, and Brown should concentrate upon reaching the target of having 80 per cent of the labour force in work, above a minimum wage that continues to rise in real terms. The New Deal should stay in place. New initiatives should be mobilized to deal with the skills gap and to help further increase productivity, and should be integrated with life-long learning.

As mentioned earlier, some have said that the economic achievements of the past few years are hollow, since the UK economy is floating on a high, and unsustainable, level of debt. However, debt in the UK, at 37 per cent, is lower than in most competitor countries. Of course, should the economy falter in any major way it would have very serious implications for Labour's electoral chances. There are plenty of challenges ahead, because of continuing transformations going on in the world economy.

2 *Do not desert the centre ground!* It is the first and core principle for electoral success. There are plenty of siren voices saying that there should be more divergence between the parties and urging Labour to return to its roots as a firebrand party of the left. Let's open up a bigger division between left and right, they say, and the voters will return. The centre ground, however, is not defined by parties, but by the voting citizenry. When asked where they put themselves on the political spectrum, the large majority of voters put themselves in or near the middle.

The project for Labour should be to continue to shift the centre to the left – in other words, to build up further a social democratic profile for the country. There is now an apparent all-party consensus that there should be strong public services, with the NHS as the centrepiece (albeit reformed and devolved). The Tories now say they will put a healthy public sector ahead of tax cuts as a priority. In principle, it should make it easier for Labour to keep on moving the centre of gravity further leftwards.

3 *It is right to prioritize education.* 'The single most important investment we can make is in education', Brown asserted in his pre-budget speech of 2006.[9] 'Education, education, education' – when Tony Blair proclaimed in Parliament that these were his three priorities, John Major said in response that his own priorities were the same, but not necessarily in that order. It was a nice

point, but in a way there is substance to it. Education, after all, takes various different forms. It is important generically in an economy where unskilled jobs are going to be harder to come by. But we have to invest in early years' education as well as primary and secondary education, decide how to fund the expansion of further and higher education and make resources available for the training and retraining of people of all ages.

4 *Renew and extend the attack on poverty*, recognizing that this is a far more complex issue than many on the left assume. Poverty is not simple deprivation, but takes many different forms. Some experience very short spells, others are unable to escape. A family can have someone in work, yet still be poor. The poverty of seaside towns is very different from that of inner-city areas. Poverty among workers who have lost their jobs as a result of the decline of manufacturing industries is quite distinct from that affecting those working in low-level service jobs. Female patterns of poverty differ from those of most men. The situation of an immigrant who does not speak English and has no skills is quite distinct from that of an indigenous worker who can retrain having lost his or her job. The strategies people use to cope with living in poverty differ widely too.[10]

5 *The need to combat crime or anti-social behaviour is of prime importance.* Having a strong stance on law and order has been and will still be a key factor in Labour's appeal. Crime is a very real problem for many people in our society, and especially for those living in areas of social breakdown. Most forms of crime have in fact fallen since 1997, although how much of this trend is policy-driven is not clear.

Anti-social behaviour orders can be criticized in terms of their effectiveness, but not because they are an intrinsic limitation of freedom. How free am I if I dare not go outside my house in the evening for fear of being mugged? How free am I if I am uneasy about venturing into my local park at all because of the same worry? Sometimes the freedom of a minority has to be limited in order to protect that of the majority in a community.

Yet as far as crime more generally is concerned, Labour policy needs to move on. The government has come to place so much emphasis upon the punishment of offenders – that is to say, upon the criminal justice system – that it is in danger of forgetting the importance of being tough on the causes of crime. Prison works, Tony Blair has said. In Parliament in June 2006, he pointed out that there are '40 per cent more dangerous, violent and persistent offenders in prison than in 1997, despite crime having fallen'.[11]

However, it is far from the case that prison works – at a minimum, the assertion needs to be heavily qualified. Prisons may keep dangerous criminals away from the public for a while, but at some point those people will be released. It is well established in the research literature that prisons are schools for crime, unless a very strong emphasis is put upon rehabilitation. Moreover, being locked up may exacerbate the problems of those with drug or mental health problems, of whom there are many among convicted offenders.

As of early 2007 there is a crisis of overcrowding in Britain's prisons. The country has the highest rate of imprisonment in Europe, with 143 people per 100,000 of the population in gaol. The figure for Germany is 97, and for France 88. A policy focusing mainly on the criminal justice system has run up against its limits. Being tough on crime cannot be equated simply with being tough on the criminal.

A variety of studies have shown that there is an inverse relationship between rates of imprisonment and welfare spending.[12] Countries with the most generous welfare systems have the lowest proportions of people in prison, and the lowest rates of crime more generally. It is easy to see why this should be so. A well-functioning welfare system protects people against extreme poverty and loss of income, as well as cultivating a sense of solidarity with the wider society. In Sweden and Finland, rates of imprisonment have actually declined over recent years. Britain seems to be the only developed country in which increased welfare expenditure (since 1997) has gone along with higher rates of imprisonment, suggesting there is considerable scope for looking in detail at how there could be a more fruitful interaction between welfare reform and crime.

6 *Economic migration must be effectively regulated,* in both a

negative and a positive sense. The UK cannot absorb large numbers of unskilled immigrants, especially if their cultural and linguistic background is very different from that of the indigenous population. On the other hand, the country needs skilled migrants and should not only welcome them but actively seek to attract them. I come back to these issues in detail in chapter 7.

7 *Do not relax on the threat of international terrorism.* The policies Labour has introduced, including the right of the police to hold suspects without charge and to keep them under surveillance, have been widely attacked. This debate revolves to some large degree around the issue of risk. Has the government been purveying a 'politics of fear' in order to force through repressive policies? In other words, has the level of risk to the security of citizens been exaggerated?

My answer to both questions would be no. 'New-style' terrorism is quite different from the terrorism of groups such as the IRA or ETA, with which we have long been familiar. The IRA and ETA have local, nationalist goals; the level of violence they have used to pursue them is limited. The new terrorism is transnational, its aims are geopolitical and amorphous, and its perpetrators are willing to kill thousands if it will further their aims. A 'dirty bomb' – radioactive materials wrapped around orthodox explosives – planted in the centre of London would not kill many people, but would cause mass panic and render the immediate neighbourhood uninhabitable. Larger outrages are possible. The government owes it to citizens to minimize the risk of a serious terrorist attack.

The state and public services will be fundamental areas in which the two major parties will lock horns, so very careful consideration must be given to them. They also form one of the main faultlines between New and Old Labour. Sources of potential division can be minimized if it can be shown that continuing reform will create a more developed public sphere, and at the same time will produce a more equitable society.

Tony Blair talks to Clinical Nurse Managers Louise Molina, right, and Sarah King during the official opening of the first National Health Service walk-in centre at Peterborough, Tuesday, 11 April 2000. On the same day, ten other centres were launched across England.

4

The Public Services: Putting People First

Health is important to all of us, so there are lots of jokes about it, and about doctors too. The same is true of education, a second major area where the state has a big role to play. Having scanned many such jokes, most don't seem especially funny, but all have a point to make.

Walter Mathau: My doctor gave me six months to live, but when I couldn't pay the bill, he gave me six months more.

First man: I tried to kill myself yesterday by taking a thousand aspirin.
Second man: What happened?
First man: Oh, after the first two I felt better.

A boy came home from his first day at school. 'So what did you learn?' asked his mother. 'Not enough. They want me to come back tomorrow.'

Fortunately for us, you could only make the Walter Matthau joke in America. The NHS may have deep problems, but it remains popular, and the joke helps us see why. The other two? Well, it isn't only physical health that has to be handled by the health care system. Education now isn't just for the young, but is relevant to all age-groups: so in place of one day, read a life-time.

What is the State For?

How should we best think of the state and its involvement with public services? On the face of things, the state is easily defined. The state in a democratic society is a body of officials – civil servants – which exists in order to allow governments to put their programmes into practice and provide continuity whenever there is a change of government.

Labour policy documents frequently speak of the need to create an 'enabling state'. It is an important notion, because it defines the state in terms of the empowerment of citizens. The idea is that the state should generate the resources that will allow people to develop their lives for themselves. However, the concept also has clear limitations. It implies that, once having been provided with resources or capabilities, people will be left to fend for themselves. The responsibilities of government would seem to end at the point where they have sufficient means to live autonomous lives.

We should not drop the idea of enabling. Yet we must also recognize that the state has obligations of care and protection for citizens, and that some of these obligations should take the form of guarantees. Without the giving of guarantees (offered in return for obligations of citizens), it makes no sense in fact to speak of a citizenship contract. For example, unemployment benefits are guaranteed for jobless workers as long as they actively engage in looking for another job, or accept skills training.

We should therefore start to think in terms of the *ensuring state*, which includes the idea of enabling, but adds something more. The ensuring state is essentially a regulatory state, where 'regulation' is understood as a means of achieving positive results, not just as a set of restrictions. For instance, rules limiting monopoly actually open up opportunities by allowing open competition in a market. The state provides resources to citizens – above all public services, such as access to education, health care and many other areas – but also seeks to guarantee standards of delivery in these areas too. There are responsibilities for the state 'after enabling'.

One can illustrate the point by reference to privatization.[1] Privatization is not simply an end result – where companies pass from state ownership into the private sector. It is more of a process, which continues after formal control has been transferred. The ensuring state is responsible for the consequences of privatization in several ways. There has to be a regulatory framework within which businesses function, to make sure that they continue to meet their economic and social obligations. Quality controls are necessary. In addition, the state may have the obligation to intervene if there is performance failure, as happened, for example, in the UK following rail privatization.

It cannot be emphasized too strongly that the notion of the ensuring state does not mean a return to the days of the big state. It means almost the opposite. The state itself, and the public services that it coordinates, are subject to reform in order to forge a more open contract with citizens. This emphasis is one of the main differences distinguishing Labour from the traditional left, with its faith in the state as the embodiment of the public purpose and its resistance to state reform.

Moving away from the top-down state means the sharing of responsibilities between government, other agencies (such as third-sector groups) and individual citizens. In a pluralistic society, responsibility for the public good is divisible.[2] This formula will clearly have to be applied, for instance, in responding to climate change. Protection of the environment cannot be done without the state, but is also a responsibility of every citizen, a responsibility that will have to be motivated not only by moral commitment, but by a system of tax incentives and sanctions.

The same is true of business, whose obligations will cover not only restricting or eliminating environmentally harmful products and practices, but also introducing innovations that will actively help combat climate change. Third-sector groups have an important lobbying and watchdog role in relation to government, commercial organizations and the behaviour of citizens – on a local, national and international level. The state has a responsibility at all these levels too, and must also monitor how each relates to the others. The idea of the ensuring state is far more compelling than David Cameron's vague concept of social responsibility, and can also provide a platform for policy.

What is Public about the Public Services?

The public services are at the heart of Labour's programme, and their performance will be one of the major factors influencing the next election. In the light of this point, it is amazing how little effort has gone into defining what the public services actually are. The term is used by politicians and political commentators alike as though its meaning were simple and straightforward. But it is not. 'Public' can mean a mass of people, that is, the citizenry – 'the public'. Public services would then refer simply to services directed to serving the needs of the citizens. This usage cannot be the whole meaning of 'public services' though, because there are many 'private' organizations that serve the needs of the population at large, such as supermarket chains.

'Public' can also mean 'public-spirited', in the sense of services driven by altruistic motives of some sort. There is quite often a tinge of this idea when people use the term 'public services', especially those who speak positively about them. On the political left there is a residue of traditional socialism in this meaning. 'Public' contains the idea of a collectivity, and is hence deemed to be superior to the more mean-spirited world of commercial enterprise, driven as it is by the pursuit of profit. Yet this notion can also be questioned. After all, it is a prime tenet of economic theory that profit-driven enterprise often serves the public good better than economic decisions taken by a higher authority, even where that authority is acting from impeccable motives.

'Public' can also mean 'open' and 'accountable', and there is something of this connotation too in the way in which those in favour of public services speak about them. It implies a close connection between public services and democracy. Those who run the public services are accountable to the public, because their masters are elected by the citizenry and because 'the' public can put pressure on their conduct of affairs. However, members of the public are able to exert pressure upon commercial organizations too, since they are able to pick and choose what they buy in the marketplace.

Finally, 'public' can be a synonym for 'state-provided', or 'largely state-provided', and this is its most generic sense when people talk about public services. It is part of what the term means, but taken on its own it is a dangerous usage. For instance, unions working in the public sector may claim that, by definition, they are representing 'the' public , whereas in fact they might be acting against what is in the public's best interests – for instance, defending archaic work practices.

So let us try and make it clear what we are talking about. I would suggest defining 'public services' in the following way. The public services comprise organizations in which:

1 Substantial funding comes from the state – that is to say, from the tax-payer. The 'state' can be national or local. I don't think it is possible to be more specific about how substantial the funding proportion has to be, and at the edge there are no clear boundaries. Very few services, however, are funded wholly by the state. We have to speak of 'funding' rather than 'ownership', because 'public services' go well beyond those that are actually nationalized.

2 Democratic pressure can be put on providers to influence how the service in question is organized, or how decisions are reached. Such pressure is exerted through national elections and the agendas that parties develop to fight those elections. But it can also be mobilized through the variety of democratic options available to citizens to influence political processes, such as seeing one's local MP.

3 The guiding value is that of the public interest. What constitutes the public interest in any particular context may not be easy to define, and is likely often to be contested. Nevertheless this point is a crucial one. Public services cannot be identified with the state in a simplistic way since what the state does may or may not be in the public interest in a given situation. On the other hand, privatization – turning some services over to commercial deliverers – is not *ipso facto* a betrayal of the public interest, but on the contrary may sometimes serve that interest better.

4 There is a public service ethos which has real purchase, even

if people in public sector organizations have many other motives and concerns too. Research comparing public service workers with those in business organizations shows overall differences in attitudes between the two. In one study, for instance, managers working in the public sector, the non-profit sector and commercial firms were asked about their views of their work. Among sixteen possible goals, public-sector managers placed 'providing a service for the community' first. This aim did not appear anywhere at all in the top ten goals for managers in commercial organizations. Much the same contrast was found between those working in non-profit groups and workers in commercial settings.

A certain sense of commitment to the wider community is intrinsic to public service goals and hence worth including as part of the definition of what the public services are all about. Two caveats are worth making. First, as economists so frequently and correctly emphasize, attitudes and outcomes are not the same things. That is why private providers, driven perhaps largely by motives of personal gain, may in some contexts meet the public interest better than more altruistically motivated groups. Second, for public services to work in an optimum fashion, changes in attitudes might be necessary. Thus 'customer service' was the number one goal in the study mentioned above among the managers in business, but ranked way down among the public sector managers. Yet plainly it should be a major aim of those working in the public services too.

5 Clients in the public services are what I call *citizen-consumers*. In the commercial marketplace, standards are guaranteed primarily through competition. Individuals in this context are more like *consumer-citizens*. A consumer good that is inferior to its competitors and offered at the same price will be forced out of the market. The power of the consumer in this respect is real power. The state is needed, but mainly in order to oversee the general framework of the market, prevent monopolies and provide the means of guaranteeing contracts.

There can, and should be, choice in the domain of public

services too. However, standards normally cannot be guaranteed primarily through choice, as in the marketplace. They have to be supervised in a more direct way by professionals and public authorities. Citizenship takes priority over consumerism, which is why I speak of the 'citizen-consumer'. Choice is not the sole means of voice, because of the integration of public services with the mechanisms of democracy. However, since there are no clear-cut divisions between the public services and other sectors, many overlaps and interconnections are possible.

6 The 'services' provided in the public services include more than just the provision of person to person goods – the sense of 'service' in 'service industries'. They comprise also, for example, the procurement or construction of material goods, such as transport infrastructure or housing. This point takes on a new significance when we consider the rising importance of environmental issues.

According to such a definition, what institutional areas are to be included under the general rubric of public services? Education and health care certainly, even though there is a considerable amount of private provision in both, interconnected with the 'public' elements in complex ways; defence; policing; the law courts; prisons and their administration; major aspects of transport and communications, although the complexities are well illustrated by the railways, with its mixed system of control – as well as the BBC, which has its commercial divisions; the welfare and benefits system; a diversity of agencies receiving partial state funding, including quangos; local services of diverse kinds.

There are different ways in which the public services may be organized to serve the public interest and only looking at the evidence will tell us what is best. Moreover, different countries might choose varying mixtures of provision. For instance, the proportion of students in higher education is everywhere on the increase. In a society (like Sweden) where the proportion of taxation in relation to GDP is elevated, higher education continues to be funded mainly by the tax-payer. In the UK, following the last set of government reforms, those who benefit from going to college or university pay part of the cost, albeit retrospectively. These are contrasting means of reaching much the same goal.

Reforming the Public Services

Why, after nearly ten years of a Labour government, are the public services in this country in some key areas behind those in the best-performing countries elsewhere? Mainly because there was so much ground to make up, and this for three reasons. The historically low level of tax revenue in Britain is one factor. For a long while it stood at about 37 per cent of national income, a considerably lower level than the EU average. It was important to generate more revenue to refurbish and upgrade the public services, as the Labour government has done since 1997. Today, the proportion of taxation in relation to national income stands at about 41 per cent, making possible new investment in the public services.

A second reason is the poor economic performance of the UK in the early post-war period, when it was the 'sick man' of Europe, a situation that lasted for well over two decades. Britain simply was not as rich as most of the other industrial countries over that time and therefore had less to spend upon public goods. The third is the impact of Thatcherism. Some of the innovations made by Mrs Thatcher helped improve the country's economic performance relative to that of other countries. Yet the price paid was a heavy one, since Thatcher's governments allowed the public services to decay. Efforts were made to reform them along market-driven lines, but they were starved of investment. Mrs Thatcher really seemed to believe the adage that anyone over the age of thirty seen on a bus must be a failure.

There is an important lesson to learn from the period of Britain's poor economic performance. It is, namely, that economic and public policy must be considered together, with the aim of achieving mutual benefits wherever possible. In other words, in considering how public institutions are structured – and how best to fund them – we must always give attention to how they influence economic growth and job creation. There are many observers, of course, especially on the political right, who argue that the sheer volume of taxation affects these factors. Low levels of taxation, they say, are needed if a country is to be dynamic economically.

The evidence does not bear out this view. There probably is an upper limit to taxation levels in respect of adverse effects on economic growth. A case in point might be Sweden, which has the highest tax take among the industrial countries, but where GDP per head relative to other countries has dropped over the past twenty years. The other Scandinavian countries, Denmark, Finland and Norway, have high taxation but also excellent rates of economic growth as compared to other mature industrial economies.

For the first two years after 1997, the government stuck to the spending plans of the Tories rather than immediately investing more in public services and other areas. Although the point is arguable, it was the right thing to do because of the need to reassure financial markets that the new government was determined to live within its means. From 1999/2000 onwards, however, large amounts of money were channelled into the public services, especially into education and health care. Quite correctly, the government argued that investment must be coupled to reform and also looked to other modes of funding, including especially private–public funding projects. They have been roundly criticized for their pains, especially from leftist circles. The reasons are at least in some part ideological – anything that involves a transfer of responsibilities from the state to other agencies must be a betrayal of the public services. As I have said, such an assertion is unacceptable.

We must bear this point in mind when considering the government's support (with Gordon Brown in the forefront) of public–private partnerships. What matters is how far these serve the public purpose in an effective way as compared to state provision. They have to be considered in terms of real comparisons, not with a mythical world where state-based organizations are 100 per cent efficient, customer responsive and where they always deliver on time.

The rigid division between 'public sector' (equated with the state) and private provision – drawn by people on both sides of the ideological fence – should be dropped. Mrs Thatcher was as prejudiced in favour of privatization as the Old Left has been in favour of the state. Privatization was thought of by the Thatcherites as a radical solution to what they saw as the inevitable deficiencies of state-owned or state-dominated organizations. There is actually a fluid and changing boundary between the two, which has to be policed by government and other groups.

The privatization of state companies has led to some clear successes, as in the case of British Telecom or British Airways. Where there are competitive markets, and where the privatization process is handled competently and fairly, top-class companies can be created, costs reduced and services to consumers improved. Who would want to go back to a time when it took weeks or months to get a new phone line, and one could have any colour of phone as long as it was black? Yet privatization was far from the panacea that Mrs Thatcher believed and some key privatizations, including that of the railways, were poorly handled indeed. State assets were sometimes sold off for much less than their true value; regulation was often too lax in areas where a full market was difficult or impossible to develop. Labour has had to deal with the consequences of such decisions, not just in the sphere of the railways, but in other areas too. The issue is not re-nationalization, but the creation of an adequate regulatory framework – difficult to do, especially in cases where competition is necessarily limited, as in the case of the provision of water.

The government has tended to argue that whether a given service should remain mainly in the hands of the state, or be turned over to other organizations, should be a pragmatic decision. In my view this is where it has gone wrong, at least in so far as being pragmatic refers only to economic efficiency. The main criterion should not be what is the cheapest, or even what is most efficient. It should be what is in the public interest, which means looking always at a range of criteria.

Considering whether a given service should be privatized should never depend on economic considerations alone. The public interest might be served better by restructuring the system that already exists, or by changing the nature of regulation. As I have stressed earlier, there are generic differences between the public services and the markets sphere. Ideally, we should be looking at mutual learning. As citizens, we want the public services to be efficient, but we also want commercial organizations to act responsibly.

It is in these terms that we should assess public–private partnerships (PPP). The Private Finance Initiative (PFI) has been the main form of public–private partnership deployed in the UK. The 'services' concerned have largely been limited to physical building projects. In PFI, commercial companies fund, construct and own assets, while the state makes a long-term commitment to their use over a given period. PFI schemes make up over 70 per cent of transport projects, the area where they have been most used. However, many schools, hospitals and prisons have either been built or had their plant upgraded under PFI deals.

In comparative studies across different countries PPP/PFI projects on average come out well. Firms in the commercial sector tend to be better managed than those in the state sector, not merely because they are commercial, but because they have been exposed to competition. In a market, unlike in the sphere of the state, badly managed companies will simply disappear. A study of more than forty state projects in transport, carried out in Denmark, showed that in more than 75 per cent of them construction costs exceeded estimates by at least 10 per cent . In half of the cases the figure was more than 50 per cent. In PPPs, the difference between costs and estimates on average is much lower.[3] Moreover, a crucial difference is that in PPPs risk is spelled out ahead of time, since it is borne by the investor. In state projects, when there are big cost over-runs, the rest of the state sector has to absorb the shortfall. A study of the PPPs in the NHS concluded that: 'private–public partnerships are a great improvement upon traditional public sector procurement. Where affordability problems have occurred ... they have mainly been due to central planning.'[4]

Critics worry that the public service ethos will become corroded where state organizations are in partnership with privately owned ones. The evidence leads one to have a more optimistic view. State agencies in the past have often been the opposite of what they should be, especially where the state has had a monopoly – they have been marked by indifference to the needs of citizens, secrecy and unaccountability, quite apart from unacceptable levels of inefficiency. Direct involvement with private sector companies tends to alter these attitudes and practices, as can also be the case where the public sector combines with other non-state groups. Speaking of his own experience with partnerships in local government, Martin Summers has observed:

> [O]ne of the most valuable benefits of opening up what have traditionally been local domains to outside organizations – whether they be commercial organizations, charities, NHS trusts or housing associations – is that there has been the opportunity to see how different means of decision-making perform; thus presenting alternatives to the traditional, monolithic, hierarchical and departmentalised local authority model.[5]

Of course, any project can go wrong if it is poorly managed, and some PPP schemes have turned out badly. PPPs are not intrinsically more or less difficult to manage than orthodox state-run ones. It is often said they are more complicated, but it only seems so because what is involved in them, including risk factors, has to be clearly spelt out. In state projects, these often remain latent, and can rebound badly since it is the tax-payer who has to pick up the bill.

A Crisis in Funding?

All good things come to an end, or in this case taper off. Following the very large sums of money that have gone into the public services, funding is due to flatten out in a couple of years' time. Possible reactions are to say that there must be some belt-tightening, or the knee-jerk reaction of the traditional left: put up taxes.

We should be more radical than either of these solutions imply. In the short term, various spending adjustments could be made. As I suggested earlier, there should be a change in policy as regards crime. So one saving is: don't go ahead with building new prisons, but explore alternatives that are both much cheaper and more effective. Another is: look for a different strategy on defence spending. Also: collaborate more with our partners in Europe; defer a final decision on Trident – the idea that a binding decision has to be taken now does not stand up to scrutiny; contain public sector salaries, which have now risen substantially; introduce a ruthless audit of baseline expenditure in government departments; consider new strategies of tackling VAT fraud and evasion, again preferably in conjunction with other EU members states – it has risen steeply in recent years, and is estimated to be costing the country £12 billion in lost income per year. As of February 2007, the Paymaster-General, Dawn Primarolo, said that there had been a large drop in levels of such fraud, but it is hard to see that it can be permanently contained without action on an EU level, which Britain should push for.[6]

In a recent report, the Institute of Fiscal Studies suggested that Brown should consider putting off the expenditure needed to reach the government's 2010 target on child poverty. This would be a major mistake. As I argue below, countering child poverty should be the driving force of the government's commitment to reducing poverty as a whole.

We should press on in short order with the reform of the state. At the core of the state, there is an essentially unaccountable body, the civil service. More decisive action is needed if the 2004 Gershon Report is to have an effect.[7] When the report came out, with its proposal to slim down public service jobs by more than 100,000, it was said to have 'sent shock waves through every government department and agency in the land'.[8] It was supposed to save $15 billion a year, but remains to be implemented. The Capacity Reviews of the civil service launched in 2005 have reported on departmental capacity in ten main areas. They are a useful beginning, but so far at the moment their recommendations lack bite, and it is not clear how far they will advance the Gershon programme – which should be one key aim.

Gordon Brown might do well to confound expectations by adopting these or parallel strategies. Everyone thinks there is going to be a spending crunch. Well, why not try to turn this into a surplus and spend it on tax reductions for poorer people?

The longer term is where most effort should be concentrated. The reform processes I suggest in this text, desirable in and of themselves, are also directly relevant to funding. Promoting greater innovation in the public services; making breakthroughs in productivity, especially in the NHS; involving citizens more directly as producers rather than just users of services; and expanding the scope of user-charging, which I discuss a little later – these are the ways in which the public services should evolve. All can help stabilize and control the deployment of resources.

Choice and Voice in Education

It follows from my remarks at the beginning of the chapter that the public services cover an enormous diversity of areas. There is no sense in supposing that the same principles of reform will apply to them all. The political debate around the public services has concentrated heavily upon choice and voice, but the nature and applicability of these notions vary widely. There are many regular services where both can be largely left to the normal agencies or mechanisms. For example, it is certainly relevant to citizens that street-cleaning, rubbish-collection and postal services work well, but no one supposes that clients want day-to-day involvement in them.

Choice could be applied in the case of the police. For example, local police officials could be elected, as they are in many American states and municipalities. But much more important in this sphere is voice – the accountability of the police to the public. Corruption has to be kept to a minimum. Uniquely among civil agencies, the police have the capability to deploy violence, and we have to ensure that they only use force when they absolutely have to.

In some other areas, choice is a potentially a big plus factor and quite straightforward. For example, Sweden and Denmark pioneered the use of vouchers for elderly people to choose among providers for home help, supplying meals and other services. As long as their use is carefully regulated, they are both popular and effective. The system also gives incentives for providers to improve the level of service. Vouchers can be used to give poorer families choice over sources of child care and in some other services too.

In schooling, choice operates in quite a different way again. Choosing a school for a child is a decision that by and large has to be stuck with, unless things go badly wrong. It is a vital decision, for this reason, but voice for parents is what counts over the rest of the period a child is at school. Fields of health care that could be opened up for patients to exercise choice, by contrast, could be very wide. Patients in the state system can in principle (and to some extent now do) choose which doctors they see, what treatments they opt for, and where and when they are treated. Those who use private medicine, of course, already have real choice in all these areas, and exercise it.

Introducing choice in education and health is popular. In surveys, over 70 per cent of respondents say that having more choice over the schools to which their children go is 'very important' or 'fairly important'. More people who are on low incomes say that having more choice in education is 'very important' to them than do those on high incomes.[9] Much the same results are found if respondents are asked about health services.

Education and health care are the two big areas where the new Prime Minister will have to take some major decisions. In education, in spite of continuing problems and widespread criticism, by any reckoning the government has a good track record. Thousands of schools were in a poor state of repair in 1997; most have been rebuilt or refurbished. The country stands up well in international comparisons in terms of the use of IT. Teachers' pay has risen well above the rate of inflation. There is far greater diversity in the system, tailoring it much more to the needs of pupils than was the case. More than two-thirds of schools are now specialist schools, the majority of which have improved their performance. Foundation schools have a great deal of independence and manage their own assets. Average GCSE and A-level attainment has risen steeply. The performance of pupils in the schools that had the worst academic records has improved relative to the average.

Should the new trust schools and the further academies that are planned be supported in the future? There is a straightforward answer in my view: they should be. These innovations have been said by many to be a main dividing-line between Tony Blair and Gordon Brown. I hope not. Brown might very well choose to introduce reforms of his own, but he would be sensible not only to welcome choice and diversity, but also actively to embrace them, subject to appropriate government steering.

The impetus to reform should be sustained, but has to shift

direction in some important respects.[10] There are still too many failing schools. In 2006 the regulatory agency OFSTED listed some 650 schools where there are serious problems of under-achievement. Of these, more than 200 were in 'special measures' – the lowest category. There is a reverse gender gap that needs to be closed – girls are outperforming boys by a full ten percentage points in GCSE. While some ethnic minorities are doing very well, others lag well behind. About 30 per cent of children leave school without the skills that employers need: not just those such as good grammar, basic literacy and computing, but also the 'soft' skills so important in a service economy, such as the capability to interact easily with a wide range of people.

Robert Hill suggests 'five big reforms' that could be the basis of the next wave of education policy, and I would endorse these:

1 Extend greater choice and voice to pupils themselves. Listen to what they have to say about how to improve their educational experience. Such an approach will upset traditionalists, but the experience from other countries is that it can have tangible and positive results for educational attainment.

2 Overhaul the curriculum – an issue that the government already has under review. Post-14 there should be a system closer to that which the Tomlinson Report proposed, with a greater range of subjects and skills emphasized than in the current curriculum.

3 Develop school leadership at all levels. School partnerships and federations, which often exist informally, could be more effectively resourced.

4 Involve parents as co-educators. Such a process could be especially important in the case of children from poorer backgrounds. Research shows that the interaction between parents and children in the home has a more powerful impact upon educational attainment than social class as such.

5 Reform school funding, which has grown far too complex.[11]

Further and higher education must brook large. As far as universities are concerned, a major question is whether they should be free to charge students whatever fees they see fit. My view is: yes, this must happen at some point if we are to see a 50 per cent ratio

– and more – in higher education, and if standards of teaching and research are to be maintained. Sizeable amounts of this revenue will have to be set aside, however, to help those from poorer backgrounds.

Going to college or university is different from attending school. It is not obligatory; students choose to go into higher education because of the advantages it brings them. These include major gains in average career earnings, growth in self-confidence and the sheer fun of spending three years or more in a sociable environment where few direct responsibilities impinge.

It is fair up to a point for the taxes of those who don't go to college or university to pay for those who do, since there are benefits which everyone shares. Society needs its quota of doctors, lawyers and engineers. Yet it is also fair for those who gain so much personally from higher education to contribute towards the cost, especially if they only pay their contribution afterwards. Under the government's system, those who don't earn up to a certain level after graduating don't pay back anything at all. Students also are able to borrow at below the commercial rate of interest. The government's scheme is essentially a tax, but tailored to those who directly benefit from higher education.

If universities are able to charge what they like for their courses, will it disadvantage poorer students? Not if sufficient money is put into recruiting entrants from all backgrounds, and is also made available for scholarships and bursaries to support them. It is important to recognize that the preceding system, when higher education was 'free', was a sorry failure in terms of attracting students from poorer backgrounds. In 2000, only 11 per cent of children from the lowest census class went into higher education. Over 80 per cent of those from professional or managerial backgrounds did so. The system actually greatly favoured the affluent.

User-charging: Why it Should be Expanded

User-charging is often thought of as penalizing people, since it means introducing payments for services that should be 'free'. Actually, it accords well with the theme of how public services can come to be 'owned' by those who use them. User-charging helps promote responsible attitudes as well as a sense of involvement. One might recall the old economics adage: no one in the history of the world ever washed a used car. Students have become more demanding and discriminating since they have been required to contribute to the cost of their courses, and quite rightly so.

User charges can contain demand by limiting the frivolous use of services.[12] Health care charges have been in use in Britain for some while – in respect, for example, of prescriptions. It has been a sacred principle of British political life, however, that where direct medical services are concerned, the NHS should be free at the point of delivery. Yet the UK is almost alone in holding to such a principle. User charges for such services are in place in many Continental countries, such as Sweden, France and Germany. In Sweden, patient fees are set at modest levels in order not to deter those who need medical help for seeking it. They contribute only a little over 1 per cent of total funding. France generates a higher proportion of revenue – about 8 per cent – from patient charges, on the basis of payments not fully reimbursed in the public health insurance system.[13] In Germany, the proportion is nearly 10 per cent.

Should there be more fees in the NHS? My answer would be yes – certainly at least to the modest level that exists in Sweden. Charges should be levied for visits to GPs and at the same time coupled to the right to switch GPs at short notice. The principle that the NHS should be free at the point of use is based on the notion that even a small fee would deter some people from visiting the doctor when they need to, especially poorer people. But the whole point of introducing fees would be to deter people from seeing the doctor – those who come for minor or non-existent ailments. In a society where there is no grinding poverty, it is hard to see that a small charge would deter those who really might need treatment.

Before the current system of charging fees to students was introduced, everyone seemed happy that universities were free at the point of use. But in a formal sense they weren't. Students paid fees of £1,175 per annum; and they paid up-front rather than after the event as they do now. In Scotland, students are charged too. In 2005 the sum was £2,145, paid as a graduate endowment.

There is one area where user-charging is bound to leap up the agenda – the environment. A quite radical shift towards environmental taxation and away from income or employment taxes is on the agenda for the next few years. User-charging in this context has potentially a wider application than elsewhere, since many environmental goods have either never been paid for directly by the consumer or properly priced at all.

A prime example is congestion-charging on the roads. A detailed proposal has been put forward by the Institute of Public Policy Research to set up a national system of congestion-charging by 2010.[14] It would deploy global positioning technology, which is already in use for environmental charges for large lorries on motorways in Germany. The technology makes it possible to charge road-users differing rates according to what roads they are using and what times they are travelling. Charges set at the right levels would produce a 7 per cent reduction in road traffic and lower carbon dioxide emissions by over 8 per cent. It could potentially also raise revenue of £16 billion annually by today's prices.

Let me now move on directly to discuss in more detail the NHS – the source of so many of Labour's hopes, but also of some of its major dilemmas.

The Empire Strikes Back: The Fate of the NHS

The NHS is a gigantic organization.[15] By 2010 close to 10 per cent of the country's GDP will be spent on it – up from 6 per cent a decade ago. It will have a turnover by then of well over £90 billion. With figures this size, what happens within the NHS matters enormously to the rest of the economy. We cannot treat NHS reform as though it were in a separate compartment of its own.

The NHS will be one of the main areas of contention in the next election. As in education, the government's achievements in reforming health care are formidable. Pay has risen substantially at all levels. Thousands of new nurses have been recruited, while places in medical schools have risen by more than half. Many new hospitals have been built, mostly using PFI, and even larger numbers refurbished. Death rates from heart disease and the major forms of cancer are down compared to 1997. Waiting times are shorter than they have ever been before. Where choice has been introduced, such as the possibility of having some operations abroad, patients have welcomed it. Innovations such as NHS Direct have been successful. The change in the Tory position means that Labour has won the argument about tax-based funding for health care.

Why then are the Tories ahead in some polls about who can do the best job for the health service? One reason is surely inflated expectations. In an interview with David Frost on 16 January 2000, Tony Blair said that Labour would raise health expenditure to the European average – Brown was reputedly outraged at the time, since he had not been consulted beforehand. Making good the pledge would necessitate spending billions more on the NHS every year. At that point, Labour's plans for the NHS were not fully worked out. The expectations of the public, and those working in the organization, were raised beyond what could be delivered in a short time in terms of standards of treatment and working conditions. In the meantime, there was something of a successful smash and grab by NHS employees in terms of getting higher pay and shorter working hours.

While pay rises have eased manpower shortages, a range of difficulties has resulted. Better working conditions have not been accompanied by sufficient change in working practices. Productivity in the NHS has been rising, but it is at best keeping pace with the amount of cash being put in. The issue is a serious one, and will have to be tackled. It is also one of the factors lying behind the failure of cost control in 2005–6.

The new contracts for consultants and junior doctors have been negotiated without incentives to improved productivity – indeed, some have argued that they will have the reverse effect. Only in the case of the new GP contract is productivity likely to be improved. The Audit Commission uncovered evidence of widespread bending of the rules by hospitals striving to up their ratings. In 2006, 121 NHS trusts overspent their budgets by a total of £372 million, a small sum given the vast size of the system, but a statistic that prompted a barrage of adverse commentary in the media.

These shortcomings will not be remedied by relaxing the pace of

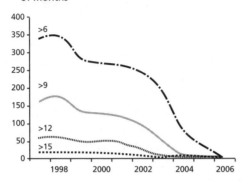

Hospital waiting times have fallen
Thousands of people waiting a number
of months

Figure 4.1: There have been continuing improvements in the quality of health care

reform, or by supposing that one can 'return power to the front-line professionals'. Increasing patient choice can help stimulate productivity, but so also can more effective and selective incentives for medical staff. The use of commercial providers does not *ipso facto* represent a betrayal of the public purposes of the NHS, for reasons mentioned earlier. In any case, the NHS is far more dependent upon commercial services than many on the left care to admit. Most GPs work in private partnerships. The chemists where patients go to get their prescription drugs are commercial companies, as are the firms that make the drugs they use.

If ever the trite phrase 'at a crossroads' meant anything, it applies to the NHS as of the year 2007. Two possible futures stretch ahead. One is of a service where reforms are successfully resisted, and an un-modernized NHS, characterized by monopoly and the dominance of producer interests, consumes a high proportion of the nation's GDP. There would be major consequences for the economy as a whole, since productivity is likely to remain static in such circumstances, while that of the business sector will continue to rise.

The other would be of a transformed NHS, up to the standards of best practice in other countries. We can only sustain the values of the service – a nation-wide system, in which effective treatment is available for all – by thoroughly transforming how health care is delivered. It is the pathway towards a service that is attuned to the needs of a post-industrial society, characterized by pluralism, areas of competition, improved primary care, where patients have responsibility for, and involvement in, their health needs, and where they feel like valued clients. These are in no sense unrealistic aims, but they will demand political courage to achieve. According to how different rankings are calculated, the NHS is between number 18 and 24 in terms of international comparisons of health systems. It is a poor performance. If the 'Empire' successfully blocks further transformation, the service will stay right down there, increased expenditure or not.

Most of the social and economic changes that brook large in this book impinge directly on health care, and only a diverse and flexible system, with most decision-making devolved, will be able to cope.

They include, first of all, globalization. As a result of IT-based outsourcing, some medical services, including certain types of operation, can be provided remotely. The areas they cover will expand, even in the near future. Second, the advance of science and technology will radically affect medicine. Genetics will allow the prediction of the likelihood of future illnesses in currently healthy people, and may generate new preventative treatments. Other influences could be automation, robotics, imaging, minimally invasive surgery and nanotechnology.

Third, everyday democratization (see chapter 9) is rapidly changing the relationship between patient and doctor, as the public becomes better informed about health and illness. There are already situations where, because of information freely available on the internet and other sources, patients know more about their illnesses than the GPs they go to see. Fourth, lifestyle change, which I discuss extensively in chapter 6, has become immediately relevant to health care issues. Some of the major chronic diseases are lifestyle related. There are major implications for public health, as well as for health inequalities. Fifth, the changes that have made large-scale, top-down systems dysfunctional in other areas of society and the economy also apply in the area of health care. The future lies in flexibility, adaptability and the ability to innovate.

The health economist Nick Bosanquet has compared the situation of the NHS in 2006–7 to the British economy in the era of stagflation – a 'stop–go' scenario. A surge of spending has been followed by a 'stop' or slow-down that threatens the very reform process. From 2008, as elsewhere in the public services, there will be more limited state spending, potentially setting up an even bigger confrontation between the public's expectations and what can be delivered. In 2006–7, the NHS will spend £84.4 billion. There will be a spending increase of 3.5 per cent, as a result of efforts to deal with deficits, followed by three years in which spending will increase by 2 per cent a year in real terms.

As of the end of 2006, 175 NHS organizations were in deficit. A smaller group had 'super deficits', amounting to £15 million or more. In 2007 they will all be covered by resources that have been put into a contingency fund. However, value for money will not come from a system that effectively depends at the bottom end on subsidies and windfall payments. Recent research shows clearly that reforms have slowed, just when they should be accelerating. The government's aim is that by 2008 all acute and mental health trusts will have reached the stage of being able to apply for foundation status. However, it looks as though only between 100 and 140 will have foundations by 2009. Ways have to be found to accelerate the process.

Independent sector treatment centres – ISTCs – have been highly successful. Waiting times have been brought down radically and quality of patient care improved. Local providers have been stimulated to improve their performance. However, there has been considerable resistance from some local managers, who do not see ISTCs as proper partners. Some have struggled to get referrals. If the ISTC market is prevented from growing, it could ultimately wither on the vine, yet it is needed to drive up general standards, as the experience of other countries shows.

Like the UK, most countries have a private system working alongside, but largely separate from, the state-based one. Some states, however, have moved to allow the two directly to compete. In France, which has a social insurance system, patients have a choice of private or state-based care: private clinics provide 40 per cent of health care, but they account for only 22 per cent of costs, revealing their greater efficiency as compared to the state sector.

In a comprehensive and comparative discussion of health care, Michael Porter and Elizabeth Teisberg argue convincingly that what they call value-based competition based on results, rather than the use of targets, is the main way to improve efficiency of patient care.[16] Performance-related pay will only serve to raise costs if providers have to comply with targets with no such competition. Porter and Teisberg are equally harsh on those who believe that any form of competition undermines the values that should underlie health care: '[S]ome observers assert that a benevolent monopoly ... will avoid the duplication and inefficiencies of the current system [in the US]. But history tells us that monopolies that are truly benevolent and effective are rare.'[17]

Value-based competition complements choice, although there are various ways in which state-operated systems can be organized to generate it. In Singapore, with a small population, the health care system has been divided into two provider groups. Each is autonomous and they compete intensively for patients. In Sweden, which has radically decentralized its health care, performance data are published on all of the country's hospitals. In tertiary care, the university hospitals in the country compete both on quality and price.

Bosanquet and his colleagues suggest several ways in which reform should be re-invigorated, promoting greater pluralism, choice and competition.[18] The commissioning role of Primary Care Trusts should be upgraded, with the brief of securing the best value for the patient in their area, no matter what providers are used. A voucher system should be introduced for primary care services, which an individual could take to any approved provider. New forms of PPPs should be introduced where the provision currently offered by the NHS is clearly inadequate, as in audiology. In the longer term, there should be a smaller, better-supported workforce in the HNS in order to make productivity gains.

The NHS has in fact already become more distant from its political masters than it was. A range of independent bodies now controls decisions that were once in the hands of the Department of Health. They include the Health Care Commission, responsible for quality inspection; the National Institute for Clinical Excellence, which takes decisions about rationing; the Appointments Commission, which handles recruitment; and the NHS Confederation, which deals with pay negotiations.

How might Brown create headline news on the NHS? After consultation with the public, he might think of making a Declaration of Independence. He could announce that the NHS will be run at arm's length from government in terms of operational management, and suggest how, and also turn over most aspects of regulation and inspection to independent organizations, including the production of statistics of health care, so that public confidence in their impartiality is restored.

Choice and diversity: do they serve to accentuate inequality rather than the opposite? Perhaps no battleground in the area of public services is more contested. Yet the evidence on the issue is rather clear. The more affluent find ways of exercising choice, even where, formally, none is on offer. People at the bottom, who lack both material and symbolic capital, do not have such an option. Any measures that introduce real choice, and voice, for them must help break down barriers to their life-chances.

In the next chapter I turn more directly to the issue of inequality. First, of all, however, I consider the question of how social democrats should view markets in terms of their impact on the wider society.

Gordon Brown prior to receiving his Honorary Doctor from Newcastle University, Monday, 8 January 2007. The university was honouring a list of high-profile campaigners against world poverty.

5

We Can Have a More Equal Society

Social Problem	New Labour	Conservative
The unemployed	Get people into jobs	Let them suffer
The poor	Provide more income	Let them suffer
Criminals	Address causes of crime	Let them suffer
The sick	Put more money into the NHS	Let them suffer
Those living on welfare	Offer resources for people to improve their lives	Let them suffer
Cost to the tax-payer	£100,000,000,000	£0

In the interests of humour, it's all a bit exaggerated, but you get the picture. The column on the right only applies to the Tories before David Cameron came along – but how far will they really be able to change? And the policies on the right-hand side would actually cost the country more than the ones on the left, because of the destructive social and economic consequences they would have (and have had).

Why Social Democrats Must be Market-friendly

The left has always been suspicious of markets. It is an emotion engrained in its history, since its very origins were bound up with the critique of capitalism. The revolutionary left wanted to put an end to capitalism altogether, and tried out this project on a grand scale. Not long after the Second World War, about a third of the population of the world lived in communist-led societies. How far market mechanisms were eliminated in practice varied. Some communist countries preserved a considerable amount of private property in agriculture, for example. In the two biggest, Russia and China, property in industry and agriculture was almost wholly expropriated by the state.

It was a grand experiment, and it failed. The state turned out to be a worse enemy of the people than markets ever could be. Moreover, the command economies only worked as well as they did because people found ways round the state's dictates. In the Soviet Union and China, 'favours' replaced money, since there was very little on which to spend money anyway.[1] What mattered was using contacts, often with state officials, to get everyday tasks carried out. Price signalling done in an informal fashion introduced sufficient flexibility into the system to enable it to survive, but it was a highly cumbersome way of doing things. The whole edifice crumbled as the international economy became globalized, and economic transactions became quicker and more complex.

Economic globalization also put an end to Keynesianism in the West, with large implications for social democracy – it was the end of the 'first way'. Keynes was a liberal, but his theories were the foundation of post-war social democracy, because they found a clear role for the state in a mixed economy. The role of the state, put crudely, was to manage demand, in such a way that full employment could result and a repetition of the disasters of the 1930s avoided. Demand management was only able to work where nations could directly control much of their economies; it started to dissolve once this condition no longer applied.

Some of the main traditions on the political right in the past had as many objections to markets as did the left. The radical right saw the market economy as corroding the moral traditions upon which society depends. Christian Democrats, on the other side of the ideological divide from social democrats, also had their reservations about the market. They always wanted protection for people, provided not so much by the state as by religious and voluntary organizations. It is this tradition that helped breed today's compassionate conservatism.

When the right learned to love markets, it was a major turn-around. In the late 1980s it also seemed the final victory, since the left was in retreat everywhere. Those countries that stayed nominally communist either embraced markets, or remained isolated and frozen in time, like Cuba or North Korea. Social democrats started to look for different approaches from the past, as charted in this book.

Markets still produce some of the consequences that Marx listed. Unless properly steered, they lead to periods of boom followed by depression; if not regulated, they create monopoly; they can reduce human contacts to commercial ones; there are some areas where market mechanisms will not work – the Stern Report (see chapter 6) calls climate change the biggest market failure ever; and if there isn't major intervention, they can create unacceptable divisions between the rich and the poor.

Yet social democracy today must be market-friendly. It is a trite, but valid, observation that the market makes a good servant but a bad master. The left shouldn't forget that the same applies to the state!

Why should we nowadays be friendly towards markets? First, because markets, and capitalist enterprise more generally, are the keys to economic efficiency and thus to prosperity. Markets send millions of pricing messages everyday to producers and to consumers. The idea that all this could be controlled centrally, and thereby provide for human needs better, as in the case of communism, turned out to be a cruel myth. Even nationalized industries in democratic societies tend to be inefficient.

Second, markets are intrinsically connected to freedom in the sphere of consumption. In a competitive marketplace, producers do not make the decisions about what to produce: consumers do. No capitalist can succeed if others do not buy his or her products. Producers try to shape tastes through advertising, but the appetite for the product has got to be there.

Third, market enterprises do not make laws and they do not possess armies. Of course, big business may try successfully to influence governments to take decisions they see as in their interests, but businesses cannot wage wars in the way in which states can and regularly do. Fourth, market competition (in principle) both holds prices down and provides a laboratory for new ideas to be tested out. Markets provide an 'evolutionary environment' in which 'experiments' can be tried – thousands and thousands of them. Those rejected by consumers perish, but there are always new ventures coming along.

Fifth, the outcomes of market relationships can be quite different from the motives that drive capitalist organizations themselves. The left has long had its doubts about Adam Smith's invisible hand, but there are quite plainly many circumstances where it applies. That is to say, business firms have to make a profit if they are to survive, but the outcome of the seemingly antisocial profit motive may benefit the public interest, and may do so more than the activities of other organizations where altruistic motives are more prevalent. So – to repeat a theme of the preceding chapter – it won't do to criticize capitalism (or privatization) simply by saying that public goods shouldn't be provided by people driven mainly by their desire for business success.

We can only get so far by talking of 'the market' as such. There are three main types of market – product markets, capital markets and labour markets – and they obey somewhat different principles. Let us deal with labour markets first, since they are discussed at many other points in the text. For economists, labour is simply one 'factor' of production. But 'labour' refers to people's lives, their hopes and aspirations. There is competition in labour markets: between workers for jobs, and between businesses to hire the best employees. Only the most ardent Thatcherite would hold that labour markets should be completely unregulated, apart from health and safety. For social democrats, there are many areas where workers' rights are important; but the fundamental question is to find a balance in regulation between job creation and social protection.

Flexicurity plus a decent minimum wage is the best means. It is in the interests of workers, because more jobs are available for them than if passive unemployment benefits are in the forefront. However, as I argue below, flexicurity is not enough. We should look for every means possible of minimizing the shock of losing one's job, especially for older workers. Yet transitions between jobs are by no means always negative. The idea of having a job for life only appeals to a minority of the younger generation. The point of policy here is to help ensure that transitions are as far as possible fruitful for the individuals involved.

This example already shows how complicated the relation between markets and regulation can be. To be market-friendly can't mean just bluntly 'being in favour of markets'. Flexicurity is pro-market in the sense of not standing in the way of job creation. It helps business in the sense of providing for the retraining of workers. At the same time, it is aimed at curbing the effects of capitalism and helping to humanize it.

Corporate Responsibility Must Become Real

These relations are even more complicated in the case of product and capital markets. There are many circumstances in which it is in the interests of the centre-left to make such markets work better. Enforcing anti-monopoly legislation is one of these. Competition is almost always in the interests of the consumer whenever market conditions apply.

The centre-left these days tends to rely upon supply-side measures in seeking to intervene in the economy. It makes obvious sense, as discussed earlier, to put a major emphasis upon education, although of course there are wider goals involved than only economic ones. However, I don't believe that this position can any longer be regarded as sufficient. I'm not suggesting a return to traditional economic intervention or the preservation of national champions. But we should foster a model of responsible capitalism alongside that of the ensuring state – a capitalism responsive to the needs of citizens. As in other areas, this idea means sometimes cultivating markets and sometimes curbing their influence.

Businesses are the wealth-producers, but there is no way that they can work on their own. They depend upon a whole range of social goods generated by the state or in civil society, including today an educated and adaptable workforce, a framework of corporate law, protection against crime and many others. In the

1980s and 1990s, partly because of the triumphalism that came along with the fall of communism, there arose the cult of the business hero. It seemed as though the CEOs of the big corporations had special insight into the future, acting as swashbuckling adventurers like the explorers of unknown territories in the past. It was as though they owed nothing to the wider society. Getting on better terms with those working in the business world (which the left was only just learning about in the mid-1990s) sometimes meant accepting the self-definitions of business leaders themselves, no matter how self-aggrandizing. New Labour was by no means immune from this tendency.

It all looks different now. Two or three years ago *The Economist* carried a front cover headed 'The Death of the Business Hero', and it was an appropriate phrase. Some of the erstwhile heroes have fallen from grace altogether, having made disastrous miscalculations – there were many examples during the period of the dot.com bubble. Big business at this point became a hazard to itself, threatening to undermine its 'licence to operate'. Surveys showed big changes in public attitudes over time. In the 1960s, 60 per cent of the population agreed with the statement, 'The profits of large companies help make things better for everyone who uses their services.' By 2003, the proportion agreeing had fallen to 27 per cent.[2] In 2003, 61 per cent of respondents agreed with the statement, 'Large companies don't really care about the long-term environmental and social impact of their actions.'

The social and moral context of business is changing, and government should pull out all the stops to push the changes in the right direction. Companies that don't take their social and environmental obligations seriously will face increasing threats from consumers and NGOs. Since these obligations have to focus upon consumer behaviour itself – lifestyle change – the role of business becomes even more crucial. Climate change is likely to dominate much of the political agenda over the next few years and beyond. Business will have a vital role in developing new technologies to reduce emissions, but also to help in adapting to the effects of warming. The potential implications for insurance, for instance, are staggering. Insurance companies will have to work closely with government to cope with them.

Of course, there will be – already is – a lot of posturing on the part of companies trying to give a green hue to what they do. But a new generation of business leaders is needed to take on the challenge, and in a hard-headed way. They are emerging. Terry Leahy, the CEO of Tesco, the biggest retailer in Britain, stated in January 2007 that he accepted that the social and economic consequences of climate change would be 'stark and severe'.[3] He announced a series of sweeping alterations in how the supermarket chain will operate. Tesco produces two million tonnes of carbon a year in the UK. The company has committed itself to putting labels on all the products it sells. Customers will be able to compare the carbon costs over the whole range of the 70,000 Tesco products. The firm has committed itself to cutting by half the amount of CO_2 used in its distribution network within five years. All food products coming into Britain by air will be visibly marked as such.

The other big supermarket chains are doing likewise, here and elsewhere. Walmart in the US, the parent company of Asda in Britain, led the way. The corporation made a pledge in 2005 to turn over completely to renewable energy, create zero waste and slash its carbon emissions. Asda is following suit; Sainsbury's, Marks and Spencer and others have announced parallel measures, some companies being rather bolder than others. It is important to recognize why all this is happening. It is in part as a result of enlightened leadership. But in addition, the companies have come to see that there could be major business opportunities, as public consciousness of green issues increases and tastes start to shift. It has also been driven both by government intervention and pressures from NGOs. In 2006 the biggest four supermarkets were asked by the government to do much of what they are now doing. Marks and Spencer's 'eco-promise' plan, introduced last year, comes with endorsements from Greenpeace and the World Wildlife Fund.

Similar pressures – and opportunities – face an overlapping industry, the food industry. Putting salt and calorie counts on the labels of products, which producers are now obliged to do by law, is only one aspect of the changes the industry will have to face up to. Rates of smoking were brought down in some part by strict controls on advertising (banned altogether in some countries) and by the compulsory posting of health warnings. Food is next in line, given the severe health implications if dietary habits do not change.

But what of capital markets, in some ways the leading edge of modern capitalism? When those on the left speak of capital having 'broken free' from social control, it is these markets they really mean. Here is capitalism at its most globalized. Vast sums of electronic money swirl around the world; transactions can take place instantaneously, from any part of the globe to any other. In the City, the top traders can make salaries of millions a year. Since many jobs are thereby created, should government just stand aside and leave them alone to get on with it? I don't think so. First of all, as I say below, corporate leaders should accept that with wealth should come citizenship obligations.

Equally, though, government, in combination with consumers and NGOs, has a responsibility to patrol the wilder edges of high-tech capitalism. Enron in the US was a financial services company – it produced no physical products. The straits into which the company got itself, however, affected many aspects of peoples' real lives – including the power black-outs in California in 2001. Regulation has since been tightened up in the US, and is in some respects now well ahead of what is in place here.

In conjunction with its creation, the Financial Services Authority, government should have a close monitoring watch on the role of derivatives and hedge funds. The American financier, Warren Buffet, famously described derivatives as 'weapons of financial mass destruction'. As the whole world knows, no weapons of mass destruction were in fact found in Iraq, and the same may turn out to be true of financial WMD. Yet pensions funds in the US and here have started to invest in hedge funds, a worrying development because no one quite knows what possibilities of meltdown there are. Hedge funds in the US have already experienced several smaller implosions.

The collapse of Long Term Capital Management in 1998 was a warning of things to come, although also to some degree a learning experience. Amaranth Advisers, a hedge fund company in the US, recently lost $6 billion in a few days as a result of the activities of one trader. Hedge funds are far less regulated than more orthodox investment mechanisms, nationally and internationally, and the overall amount of money in them continues to rise. When LTCM went under, about $300 billion was invested in US-based hedge funds. In 2006 the total had risen to £1 trillion. London has become the biggest centre of hedge funds after New York. The funds in this sector comprise only a fraction of those in other investments, but in the London markets this has grown fivefold over the past eight years.[5]

Keeping an eye on hedge funds should not mean simply adopting the hostile attitude that the left has traditionally had towards most forms of financial capital. One should have an open mind. It can be cogently argued that, rather than being a source of systemic risk for capital markets, hedge funds have the opposite effect. They diversify the portfolios available to investors, and thereby in principle generate resources that might not exist otherwise; and they may actually have a 'fire-fighting' role, reducing systemic risk.[5] There was a clear learning process in markets after the collapse of LTCM. In 1995, LTCM was leveraged at 28:1. In 2006, in hedge funds in the UK, leverage was on average 2.4:1.

Tax: Should We Be Paying More?

Given the need to continue investing in the public services, should Labour be considering further increasing tax rates, especially income tax, the greatest revenue-earner? Many on the left would answer 'yes'. Citizens, it is said, will pay more tax if the way in which their money is spent becomes more transparent. They will also support hypothecated taxes if such taxes are strictly kept for the purposes for which they are designed.[6] I am certainly in favour of hypothecated taxes in specific areas – including for some forms of environmental taxation. A greater emphasis upon green taxation has to be a feature of the next few years, given the central importance of controlling climate change. The proceeds of road-charging, for example, might be linked directly to spending on improving public transport, as has happened in London.

In talking of taxation more generically, however, we should concentrate upon the tax *take*, and how effectively it is spent, not upon formal tax rates. The tax take in turn is influenced in a fundamental way by what the consequences of fiscal practices are, and by their interaction with other aspects of economic institutions. Taxes influence behaviour (quite often, as in the case of environmental taxes, we *want* them to influence behaviour). Taxation has risen to a higher proportion of GDP not mainly because of increasing tax rates (such as the increase in national insurance), but because of success in generating good growth rates and in furthering job creation.

The challenge will be to discover as many policies as possible that help reconcile economic growth and social justice – as tax credits have done, by increasing the incomes of the working poor and helping people into work. Consider, for example, one of the big difficulties facing the country – the fact that the bottom 30 per cent of children in the education system fare badly in terms of literacy and functional skills. Changing this situation would increase the fund of human capital, reduce social divisions, improve life chances and help job creation – all of which would impact positively on public service expenditure at the same time as it has much more profound social effects.

Improving the public services, or some main parts of them, especially education and health care, can itself have major economic multiplier effects. Just as the interaction of fiscal measures with economic performance crucially affects available funding for the public services, the same is true in reverse. How far the public services are efficiently run, and how far they reach their goals, vitally affect the state of the economy, as well of course as overall well-being.

Having a high proportion of people in work (above a decent minimum wage) is a crucial factor in welfare. An 80 per cent participation ratio, other things being equal, would be the equivalent of a cost injection into the public services of £20 billion a year, taking into account increases in tax revenue and the lower level of welfare payments that would result. Helping more disabled people get into work, for example, clearly reduces strains on welfare benefits and well as having a positive outcome for those involved. The same applies to policies aimed at persuading those over 60 either to stay in work or to come back to it. In Finland, for instance, as a result of policy innovations of this sort, the proportion of older men and women in work has risen to 64 per cent. In the UK it is only 33 per cent.

Policies affecting women will be central to the effectiveness as well as the economic viability of the public services. A high proportion of women are in part-time work, many because they want to be, but also because of lack of opportunity. Schemes that make it possible to move from dead-end jobs into managerial positions could play an important role – at the moment, most have been developed by businesses themselves rather than by the state. Women who do not have consistent paid employment tend to have inadequate pension provision later on and hence become heavily reliant upon public revenue – not a good situation for anyone.

Well, after all this, should Labour under Gordon Brown be thinking of putting up taxes? Short of some currently unforeseen circumstance: no, if this means raising tax rates in order to generate more revenue. The 'no' will need to be a big no, because the Tories will paint Gordon Brown as bent upon siphoning more money out of people's pockets.

The change-over to more green taxation – the biggest change looming – should be as far as possible revenue-neutral, as the Liberal Democrats have proposed. Increases in environmental taxation should be accompanied by tax reductions elsewhere, especially those that would help poorer groups, and particularly where they involve incentives to work. The growing prominence of environmental taxes will create difficult problems, which will need very careful overall tax planning, and determination, to cope with. At the moment, investment in sustainable energy resources, for instance, stands at a low level. Tax incentives and sanctions designed to encourage citizens to become more environmentally conscious may generate new net revenue, but by definition that revenue will decline as behaviour change actually occurs. Should a major technological breakthrough of some sort occur, say with pollution-free electric vehicles in terms of battery life, or nuclear fusion, it could not only fundamentally alter the environmental field but also have major effects on revenue-generation.

A report published by the Institute for Fiscal Studies in November 2006 showed that the share of national income and overall tax receipts received by the government from green taxes was actually lower in real terms than was the case when Labour came to power in 1997.[7] Revenue from green taxes fell from 3.4 per cent of national income in 1997 to 2.9 per cent in 2005. This situation did not come about because such taxes had been used effectively to change consumers' behaviour; indeed, the volume of carbon dioxide emissions rose over that period. It is explained largely by the decision – taken under pressure from groups that blockaded petrol stations – to discontinue the annual fuel duty escalator in 1999. Since that point, revenue per litre on fuel has dropped by 17 per cent. The halving of the rate of Air Passenger Duty in 2001 had a further adverse effect (although it has just been increased again). On the other side, the Climate Change Levy was introduced and various other green-type tax adjustments made, including a steep rise in Landfill Tax.

Striking a balance between the different components of social and economic policy will determine the future shape of public spending. I don't think it is possible to be too prescriptive about what the proportion of tax in relation to national income should be. Developing flexibility in the fiscal system will be most important in a world of rapid change, where the outcomes of such change are not predictable.

Towards a New Egalitarianism

Britain remains a society with too many inequalities, too many barriers to opportunity for those at the bottom, too many lives damaged or foreshortened – as exemplified by the health statistics. 'Not enough redistribution!' say some. If only things were so simple. Redistribution there must be, but much more besides.

We can define the pursuit of social justice in a post-industrial society in terms of a number of priorities: the fight against poverty, above all child poverty; fair and equal access to education; jobs for those able to work; a welfare system in which clients are empowered; redistribution of income and wealth where they inhibit the realization of these goals.[8]

Average income in the UK has grown substantially since 1997, having risen by 2.4 per cent a year up to the end of 2005. London has seen the highest rises. However, if differences in house prices are taken into account, there is far less variation between London and other areas in terms of spending power. There has actually been considerable redistribution, towards pensioners (a term I dislike for reasons mentioned below), single parents and children. The proportion of older people living in poverty is now less than the average for the population as a whole.

In 1997 there were 13.8 million people living in poverty as measured after housing costs and 10.2 million measured before housing costs.[9] These numbers have fallen to 11.4 million and 9.2 million respectively. One-fifth of the population now lives below the poverty line (60 per cent of median income) compared to almost a quarter in 1997.

The government failed to meet its declared target of reducing child poverty by a quarter by the end of the financial year 2005. Although 700,000 children were lifted out of poverty, reducing the overall number to its lowest level since the late 1980s, this figure was 100,000 short of the target set, assessed before housing costs, and 400,000 including housing costs in the measure. The reduction in child poverty has been achieved mainly through tax credit policies, which have helped get more people from vulnerable households into work.

A renewed egalitarianism will mean significant policy change. Re-energizing the quest to reduce child poverty should be the main driving force, since so much else hangs on it. This should be the 'flying wedge' of a wider War against Poverty. If current polices are maintained, child poverty by 2010–11 – the target date to reduce it by half as compared to 1998–9 – will in fact not differ much from its current level.[10] Like other forms of poverty in Britain, child poverty is a relative measure. The income from tax credits and other benefits for poorer families would be offset by the level of increase in earned income.

There are several possible policy packages that could be introduced to meet the 2010–11 target. The Child Tax Credit or Child Benefit could be increased substantially, or a mixture of both. There could be an extra premium for large families and also Working Tax Credit for couples. Donald Hirsch argues that the best package would be one that increases the child element of the Child Tax Credit, combined with paying higher Child Benefit for families having three or more children.[11] This policy, other things being equal, would allow the 2010–11 target to be met, at least in terms of incomes before housing costs.

The most thorough recent discussion is the 2006 Harker Report, which the government has said it broadly welcomes.[12] It makes a large number of detailed points. Other agencies and programmes that impinge on child poverty should clearly signal when this is so. Jobcentre Plus will necessarily play an important role, since it is charged with getting unemployed or economically inactive people back into work. There is a New Deal for single parents, but parents taking part in welfare-to-work schemes are not automatically identified as such. Job-seekers should be seen in the wider context of their family so that flexible programmes of support can be built that are tailored to their needs. Moreover, many children in poverty live with parents who have no contact with welfare-to-work schemes, perhaps because they are in low-paid jobs. Helping the partners of low-paid spouses to get into work could play a crucial role in lowering child poverty.

The net cost of meeting the set targets is difficult to assess, since the state of the economy, and policies put into play elsewhere, will have a major influence. Hirsch estimates the cost at £4.3 billion, but this is a gross not a net figure. The net cost could be much lower if policies in other areas (such as early years' education, improvements in child care services and so on) are modified to have an impact on child poverty.

The government's target of 'eliminating' child poverty by 2020 has not yet been clearly defined. Three countries in Europe have managed to achieve child poverty rates of just 5 per cent: Denmark, Norway and Finland. Such a rate could be treated as equivalent to abolishing child poverty, since it is probably as close as a society could ever get. But even achieving a rate of below 10 per cent by 2020 would represent very considerable success in terms of British society. The 2020 target should in fact be thought about now, not just left until we see what progress has been made by 2010–11, since more deep-lying changes might be needed to achieve it. Mike Brewer shows that meeting a target of 5 per cent child poverty could be done through a mixed policy package, involving the use of price indexation for family earnings and large increases in child credits and benefits.[13] However, the issue should be approached from a much wider policy perspective. In other words, much will depend upon other means that can be found to reduce poverty and inequality more generally.

Those on the traditional left seem to think it is easy to reduce inequality and poverty. You take money from the rich and give it to the poor. Yet the rich, however defined, are only a tiny minority. If they are to be taxed more, it should be for other reasons than simply a little more redistribution. It would do virtually nothing to alleviate the deep structural problems that make the UK so unequal. What follows are sixteen policy areas that could make a

Box 1   The new egalitarianism

1 Concerned not just with social justice but also with economic dynamism. We know that the two can be closely reconciled, although there are trade-offs.
2 Traditional redistributive mechanisms stay in place, although in modified form. For instance, progressive taxation is still highly important, but is altered where known to compromise economic needs and job creation.
3 Some policy orientations have to be towards the long-term poor and the genuinely excluded; but we have to be especially concerned with transitions, most notably with transitional labour markets.
4 Policies that benefit more affluent groups are important if they have the effect of consolidating commitment to the welfare system.
5 Gender-sensitive policies are crucial, not only to continue to improve the economic position of women, but also to help men in vulnerable categories.
6 Emphasis upon activating labour market strategies.
7 High standards of social and economic citizenship demanded of the top earners.
8 Reducing child poverty has a particularly central place.

difference. I include the rich among them, but only as one of the categories.

1 Make reducing child poverty a driving force, as just mentioned.

2 Traditional redistributive mechanisms should stay in place, but be adjusted if they compromise job creation. Progressive income tax is still a major means of reducing inequality: pre-tax income is much more unequal than post-tax income. All fiscal policies should be assessed in terms of their consequences for redistribution as well as whatever other goals they are introduced to help achieve. Congestion-charging and parking charges in cities, for instance, can be designed to have a progressive content – many poorer people do not own a car; the proceeds can be channelled into improving public transport; drivers of larger cars can be made to pay more. Each of these principles is already built into charging schemes in London and could be generalized.

3 Active labour market policy (the New Deal and welfare to work) is highly important in reducing the disruptive effects of job loss. But because of rising levels of technological change and international competition, we need to explore policies that will help workers even before jobs are lost. As Günther Schmid has said, current policies are like throwing people into a pool to see if they can swim, only helping them once it is clear they can't. Far better to prepare them beforehand.[14]

Possibilities include the use of vouchers for in-work training for those in vulnerable industries, as part of an agreement to accept lower wages for a period. Such schemes, usually involving employers, unions and government, are already being pioneered in some European countries.

Losing a job in an industry where one has worked perhaps for many years can be a highly traumatic experience. In Austria, work foundations have been set up to provide a network of resources for workers who become redundant. They are based upon partnership between employers and unions.

Where a company is forced to lay off large numbers of workers, those who stay in their jobs make a contribution to the foundation as a gesture of solidarity. The company makes a larger overall donation. Those who lose their jobs contribute half of their redundancy payments. The state provides support also for retraining and job search. Somewhat similar proposals are being tried out in the US too.[15]

4 We should be starting to think of the possibility of employment or wage insurance. In 2001, two American economists, Lori Kletzer and Robert Litan, wrote an article proposing wage insurance as a means of helping workers adjust to the effects of job redundancy.[16] It will be difficult for political leaders to persuade workers of the benefits of economic globalization if some actively lose out from the process. In contrast to unemployment benefits, wage insurance only comes into play once a worker who has been laid off finds another job.

   Two-thirds of workers who lose their jobs through international competition earn lower wages when they find new work. Wage insurance would replace a substantial proportion of lost earnings for up to two years. A pilot version already exists in the US. Under the programme workers have to show that they lost their jobs as a result of trade competition, be over the age of 50, make less than $50,000 in a new job and be re-employed within six months of being made redundant. Wage insurance would provide an incentive to search for work and also soften the impact of job loss. A version has been set up at the EU level in the shape of a 'globalization fund' to be spent in much this way.

5 Contesting ageism and generating more job opportunities for older people can make a major impact on poverty and inequality. Older people on average have become better off since 1997, but 17 per cent still live below the poverty line. We should aim to get to 60:60 – 60 per cent or over of those over 60 in work, in full-time or part-time jobs.

6 A minority of the poor lives in embedded poverty, and is the

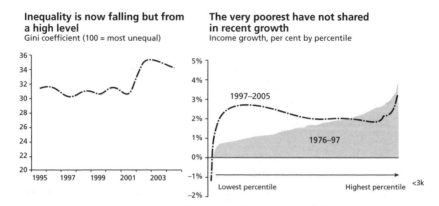

Figure 5.1: Growth has benefited the poor but a challenge remains to reach the very poorest

hardest to reach with current strategies. People in these circumstances often have to face multiple hardships. They may have few skills, have problems with drugs, fall into a life of criminality and find it hard to sustain lasting relationships. The experience since 1997 shows that orthodox policies, whether based on benefits or tax credits, tend to have little impact in such circumstances, partly because of low levels of take-up. Various further approaches can be tried, however. One is through intervention targeted at very young children. Research shows that what happens to children as early as the age of 2 or 3 can establish behaviour patterns that are thereafter very difficult to break.

Propensities to addiction can be laid down early in life too. Addictive behaviour later on tends to produce a deteriorating cycle in ability to cope. Policies here have to include the targeted provision of counselling, support groups and specific medical treatment.

A further significant factor is housing. A great deal of progress has been made in reducing the numbers of rough sleepers. About 50,000 people nationally, who might otherwise be on the streets, are living in hostels or temporary accommodation, but these people cannot find more permanent homes. There are also large numbers of 'hidden homeless', who are sleeping on the floors of friends or family members, as already mentioned. These are often circumstances in which problems such as drug-taking and criminality become compounded.

Not enough cheap homes are being built in the country at large to meet demand, not just among the homeless but for workers whose families live in cramped conditions. There are clear knock-on implications for the economy. If workers can't move to where the jobs are because rents or house prices are too high, then productivity and growth will suffer. The government has invested millions in repairing existing council houses; but at this point more social housing is the only feasible solution for those at the bottom.

A short while ago the government announced proposals for a new agency to oversee urban regeneration. It will look for new ways of using commercial, voluntary and local authorities to develop investment and building programmes. It will also concentrate on upgrading what the government calls 'failing estates'. The agency will apply rigorous environmental standards, it is said, in pursuing its work. It is too early to say what difference the changes may make.

7 It is worth thinking further about asset-based schemes.[17] Research shows that even owning a small amount of capital can make an important difference in life. People who own assets at the age of 23 on average earn more ten years later than those without them, even when income, class and gender are taken out of the equation. The government's current Child Trust Fund pays £250 to every child at birth. Children from poorer backgrounds get double that sum. The fund is topped up when the child is 7, with, again, more money for poorer children. The child cannot touch the money – nor can the parents – before he or she reaches the age of 18. Depending on how it is invested (the government provides investment advice) and what happens economically in the interim, the sums could be quite large when they are taken up. Surveys show that poorer parents like the scheme, and approve of the fact that the money is locked up for a long period.

8 Poverty is an endemic condition for some, but there is also far more movement in and out of poverty than we used to think. The condition depends upon how long it is experienced, what happens between spells of poverty and at what time of life a person falls into poverty. We should recognize that much poverty is 'biographical'. People fall into poverty through specific life-events and episodes, such as divorce or the break-up of a relationship, leaving the parental home, illness or, of course, losing a job. Since the job–marriage–children progression is less stable and predictable than in the past, the biographical nature of poverty has to be taken very seriously. It follows that we should not concentrate policy only on those who are poor at any one time.

We must often focus upon those *above* the poverty line, given known factors that might cause them to drop below it, or which might lead individuals to drop back into poverty again, having once escaped from it. It is important also to consider policy relevant to those in low-paid jobs – any interventions that help people stay in work are important. Men in low-paid jobs who have been in work continuously for five years or more, even if they lack qualifications – are 80 per cent more likely to move out of the low-pay category than those who have held their jobs for less than two years.

Single parents on average are more likely to leave a job than others in the workforce. The government is currently evaluating a project aimed at helping them stay in work and advance their careers. Those moving into work via the New Deal will have an adviser to whom they can turn in order to avoid some of the most common problems that cause new jobs to be short-lived; and there are proposals to pay financial incentives to encourage staying in jobs.[18]

9 Since there is so much movement in and out of poverty, a key set of policies will be those that help ensure that people can deal with transitions in their lives, and wherever possible make something positive of them. Labour policy-makers should pay attention to the newly developing theory of transitional labour markets (TLMs).[19] The intersection between

work and the family has become more complex now that so many women are in the labour force. Improving work–life balance is a major task for political strategists. There is a further conceptual step to take, however, especially if labour market policy is to be integrated with positive welfare or well-being. The relationship between work and non-work has grown much more complex than it used to be: it has become much more open and malleable. Being able to take advantage of transitions – losing one's job, falling into poverty, getting divorced or becoming disabled – rather than being brought down by them, becomes extremely important. We should start to think of policy much more in terms of the life-span, rather than just in the here and now. As far as the labour market is concerned, this means seeing employment in a very different way from the past – as a temporary state or current expression of long-term employability.[20] A guiding ideal, for both sexes, might be a thirty-hour working week over the entire career of the individual, with varying sorts of interruptions, career breaks and perhaps part-time work across that time.

10 Improving the economic situation of women remains crucial to reducing overall inequality, although the pay gap as such has closed considerably over the past few years. The Women and Work Commission found that the gap between the pay of men and women working full-time in 2005 was 17 per cent in terms of hourly pay rates.[21] Women's patterns of employment used to be quite dissimilar to those of men. Many women never thought in terms of a career – the ambition to better oneself and one's family through a series of promotions at work. Now the majority of young women do. But there are several reasons why women still tend to lose out in the job market, all of which could be eased by policy intervention. One is what happens following the birth of a child. Women who go back to their jobs soon after having a child lose out far less in terms of promotion chances than once was the case, showing that legislation and moral pressure on employers is effective; but the pressure needs to be kept up.

More women than men work in low-level service jobs,

such as at supermarket check-outs. Their chances of promotion are low, although they do not necessarily live in poor households, since they may be secondary earners. The state should encourage employers to alter this situation, perhaps with the use of tax incentives. The lead is being taken by some big companies in the US, which have introduced schemes making it possible for women to move into management.

11 Many older women live on state pensions and/or work as carers for others, usually informally. Because they have had few opportunities to build up savings, their position is especially vulnerable. Two-thirds of those claiming Pension Credit are women. At the moment 85 per cent of men have entitlement on retirement to a full Basic State Pension, compared to 30 per cent of women; only 24 per cent of women have that entitlement on the basis of their own contributions. The government has introduced a new contributory principle, but it will not do much in the immediate future to help. The pension system, moreover, remains extraordinarily complex; it must baffle many of those it is designed to help.

12 Lifestyle changes are starting to influence inequalities a great deal – not just reflect them – especially in the field of health, but in other areas too (more on this question in the following chapter). The remedies here will have to be behavioural rather than simply economic. It has been found, for example, that improving the diet of children with special needs, combined with exercise, significantly improves their attitudes and attainments.[22] Restlessness, anger and erratic attention span all improved after a seven-month programme.

13 Education can be a way of overcoming disadvantage; but it also can be a means of sustaining or consolidating it – at all levels of the school system and into higher education. Giving an effective choice of school to parents from poorer backgrounds must be backed by further policy strategies. One indicator of under-privilege is entitlement to free school

114

meals. Only 3 per cent of pupils at the best-performing state schools fall into this category – showing the extent of 'middle class capture', but also revealing plainly that the pre-existing system did not produce equity. The average nationally is 17 per cent.

The government has made some recent innovations to try to reverse this situation. The new school code announced in January 2007 suggests introducing a lottery system of admission, to stop parents gaining admission for their children by buying houses nearby. Some city academies already operate 'random allocation' policies, ensuring that some children from poor backgrounds get a place. The new code is mandatory and will cover anyone applying to state schools in 2008. But it is clear that further policies need to be explored.

14 Labour has largely left the private schools on one side. The overall thrust of policy has been to try to improve the state sector sufficiently so that the gap between the state and private sector will be closed. Gordon Brown has said that he wants to increase spending on state schools per pupil until it reaches that of private ones. It is an entirely laudable intention, but it can't be realized overnight. Some effort has been made to put more obligation on private schools to show social responsibility. The policies have worked to a degree, since a few schools have made such gestures as trying to extend their scholarship schemes. Yet without further innovation being made, the private schools will surely find means of keeping ahead.

The private school system in Britain is quite different from that found in most other countries, where most private schools are denominational. Here, it is quite explicitly geared to providing educational advantages for the sons and daughters of those who are already advantaged. And it works: 48 per cent of students at Cambridge University attended a private school, and 45 per cent of those studying at Oxford, although only 7 per cent of the population as a whole are educated in such schools. The best private schools provide an excellent education and there can be no question of reducing the inequities they sustain by trying to level down. But what we could do is to open up access.

The government has been reluctant to support the scheme pioneered by the philanthropist Peter Lampl, but in my view it should show more interest.[23] The Belvedere School in Liverpool is a private school. Lampl has given sufficient funds such that the school can operate blind-needs admission. In other words, anyone who qualifies for entry is guaranteed a place, regardless of his or her family's financial circumstances. The scheme has been a remarkable success, with children from a wide variety of backgrounds represented. Lampl asked for state support to help extend the scheme to some other schools, but none has been forthcoming so far. David Willetts, the Tory Shadow Education Secretary, said in May 2006 that the Tories would back such a proposal.

15 As far as university entrance is concerned, we could look at a variant of the scheme originally introduced, somewhat surprisingly, in Texas in the US, and now taken up in France. In 1997 the State of Texas introduced a policy whereby all students graduating in the top 10 per cent of their class in high school are guaranteed university entrance. As a result, the proportion of students from poorer backgrounds and minorities has steadily grown. The evidence thus far shows that students admitted in this way perform as well academically as those accepted in the usual fashion. The idea is easier to apply in France than in the UK, because of the centralized and standardized nature of French higher education. However, either the government, or universities themselves, could agree to try out a similar scheme in a city or region.

16 Finally, what about the rich? What about the fact that the salaries of corporate leaders have been pulling away from those of their employees? What about the city high-flyers making millions in salaries and bonuses? Should Labour, as Peter Mandelson once remarked, be 'relaxed about people getting filthy rich'? No! Labour can no longer be against entrepreneurs, the driving forces of economic success. But

becoming wealthy should carry with it social obligations, and every effort should be made to enforce or encourage the acceptance of these. They include the obligation to give something back to the society that has helped nurture them; to pay taxation in full and not seek every way to limit it; and to encourage social and environmental responsibility within their companies.

For several decades after the Second World War the ratio of the earnings of top executives to average income was stable. In the 1980s, it began to accelerate away and hasn't stopped doing so since. A large part of the explanation is the granting of share options and generous pension arrangements. These changes have been further highlighted by the dubious practices that have gone on around them. Senior managers in several countries have been convicted of illegally manipulating their payments – for example, through insider knowledge or influencing the timing of when their options are issued.

There is no official richness line in the same way as there is a poverty line. Let's say arbitrarily that 'the rich' are the top .05 per cent of income earners. To them, the same theme – no rights without responsibilities – should apply as to the rest of the population. Are high earners in the City and the corporations living up to their citizenship responsibilities? These obligations include tax.

Labour should consider introducing a wealth tax, such is found in a range of other countries. Wealth is more unequally distributed than income, with a high concentration in the hands of a few. Writing about the US, the economist Edward Wolff has suggested a system based upon that used in Switzerland.[24] Assets would be taxed annually, with a steeply progressive scale. Those with assets under a specific threshold would not pay, with steeper rates cutting in at, say, £1 million in assets. Wolff's system would generate about 1 per cent of total revenue – more than would be achieved in the UK if income tax were raised to 50 per cent for people earning over £100,000. It would be easy to administer, Wolff says, because it could be fully integrated with personal income tax. According to his calculations, it would be neutral in terms of wider economic implications. The proceeds of such a tax if implemented here should not go into the Treasury coffers, but be devoted to a specific purpose – for example, helping children from underprivileged backgrounds get into higher education. A possibility is that it should be bracketed to philanthropy. Those contributing substantial sums to charities could be absolved from the tax.

Reducing tax evasion and closing down the loopholes that make possible widespread tax avoidance should be priorities – as far as possible on an international as well as a national level. The Tories have talked about abolishing inheritance tax, but the strategy should be to make it more progressive. At present only 6 per cent of inherited wealth is taken in tax. A steeper rate at the top (plus, again, keeping control of loopholes) would both be fairer and generate more revenue.[25]

Philanthropy is clearly one of the main responsibilities of high earners, since they should give back to the society that has helped them realize their opportunities. In the US, top earners in effect pay a voluntary tax on their earnings, and very large numbers accept the obligation. Some prominent figures have given away virtually all their fortunes in their life-times, especially towards the end of their lives. There is not the same culture of philanthropy in this country, and in spite of the introduction of tax incentives, not yet the same level of tax breaks. We should be making every effort to change the moral culture of the rich and seek ways of shaming those who reward themselves to the detriment of those who work for them.

In September 2006 the top managers in Siemens, the large German electronics firm, were awarded a pay rise of 30 per cent. The company is in the middle of restructuring, and many workers stood to lose their jobs. Most of the rest of the workforce had accepted pay reductions in previous years through agreements reducing their formal hours of work. There was widespread outrage. As a result, the executives announced that they would donate their pay rises to assist Siemens workers who stood to lose their jobs. A report of this episode in *The Economist* says that such a thing couldn't happen here: in Britain, the senior management might indeed have been praised for keeping the company on an even keel when it faced increasing competition from overseas.[26] If so, it's our business culture that needs to change. What kind of society is it in which business leaders feel no solidarity with their workforce?

It is sometimes said that the very high levels of corporate pay reflect the fact that business leaders have to be rewarded because they take greater risks than their employees. But the reverse is usually true, since those who fail are almost always covered by redundancy packages. 'We must show that ... we will be a party that is for working people, not rich and powerful vested interests' – who said this? Not Tony Blair, not Gordon Brown, but David Cameron. Labour should take note.

Tony Blair exercises on a rowing machine at the YMCA in central London, Tuesday, 25 April 2006, during a visit to promote exercise in society.

6

Changing Lifestyles: A New Agenda

Mrs Pankhurst's advice to Keir Hardie, the first ever leader of the Labour Party: Votes for women, chastity for men, prohibition for all.

Phyllis Diller: Health is what my friends are always drinking to before they fall down.

A man goes to the doctors for a medical check-up. The doctor examines him and says: 'You're as fit as a fiddle. You'll live until you're 90!'. The patient says, 'But doctor, I am ninety.' And the doctor says, 'I told you so.'

The temperance movement has been long forgotten, and it is hard to see Mrs Pankhurst's thoughts inspiring many people today. Yet if temperance means moderation, it is certainly needed. Binge-drinking is becoming a major health problem in the UK, and is not especially stigmatized. Alcohol is one of the respectable drugs, and indeed seems to have beneficial effects if taken in moderation. The habits we follow in our lives are likely to have much more effect upon our health than anything doctors do.

David Cameron has had quite a bit to say about well-being. Labour should not cede the well-being agenda to the 'New Tories', but on the contrary develop it in a more rigorous way than the Conservatives are likely to be able to do. This task means looking more closely at the idea of welfare, where Labour's thinking to date has remained fairly conventional. The welfare state was originally defined mainly as a safety-net. It served to pick up the pieces when things went wrong in peoples' lives. If you lose your job, fall into poverty, become ill or pass retirement age, the welfare system is there to help you.

These forms of social protection, of course, are extremely important, and explain why the welfare state has been popular for most of its existence. Yet welfare here is defined in quite a narrow and also negative way. In a society of more open lifestyles, where lifestyle choices have major economic as well as political implications, we need a more positive definition of welfare. In this chapter, I concentrate on four areas where such a notion is directly relevant, although I discuss the first two only briefly. These are disability, ageing, health and climate change. A distinctly mixed bag, one might say! But not so: what they share in common is that, to cope with them, policy must be interventionist, rather than just of the safety-net type; and that in each case positive outcomes will presume lifestyle change.

The title of this chapter is deliberately ambiguous. Lifestyles for many are changing quite radically; but lifestyle change has also become a prime political goal. It is a basic response to climate change, to which I devote a sizeable part of this chapter.

From Negative to Positive Welfare

The burgeoning debate on happiness among economists seems to me a marker of the importance of issues of lifestyle today.[1] Happiness is plainly a positive condition, not just the absence of negative ones. It is another word for well-being, but with a sharper edge. Happiness can be precisely defined, according to some, since expressed feelings of happiness correlate with defined states of the brain. It may be so, but happiness seems to me still a complex notion and, moreover, not the only, perhaps not even the prime, measure of a satisfying life. Alan Bennett summed up this point when he wrote: 'I'm not happy, but I'm not unhappy about it.'[2]

Instead, I propose to speak of *positive welfare*.[3] Welfare should be redefined in terms of personal autonomy and self-esteem, as desirable qualities of the good life. The cultivation of these qualities allows individuals to adapt to change and to make the most of their opportunities in different areas of their lives. These aims might seem vague, but they are not. Autonomy – the capability to take independent decisions and act on them – is a vital quality in many areas of life, including, for example, the job market.

Lack of self-esteem has been shown to be bound up with a range of social problems, including poverty, crime and poor health among others. Low self-esteem limits autonomy of action and the capability to better one's life circumstances; but it can also actually produce self-damage or aggression towards others. Many forms of behaviour that centre upon addictions, including eating disorders, self-mutilation, drug-taking and alcoholism, relate to low self-esteem and lack of a stable sense of self. In terms of working days lost, the cost of treatment, criminal punishment, working life cut short and welfare expenditure, these problems cost the country billions, quite apart from the despair they can reflect.

William Beveridge was the intellectual founder of the British welfare state. We should turn his five 'negatives' into positive guiding ideals of welfare. Beveridge's five 'Giants' to be slain were Want, Disease, Ignorance, Squalor and Idleness. In place of Want, we should put personal autonomy – the capacity to open up life-opportunities and make use of them. Rather than concentrating only on the avoidance or treatment of Disease, we should have a model of active health as a life-goal. Instead of Ignorance, in today's society we must stress education as a positive virtue, and one that should be a continuing part of life.

No one should live in Squalor, to be sure; but put positively, we should want a society in which everyone can share in the prosperity that economic growth and technological advance can offer. Idleness, finally, can sometimes be a virtue in itself – if it means the capacity to relax, or even daydream – as Bertrand Russell pointed out. 'Everyone knows', Russell wrote, 'the story of the traveller in Naples who saw twelve beggars lying in the sun ... and offered a lira to the laziest of them. Eleven of them jumped up to claim it, so he gave it to the twelfth.'[4] Yet involuntary idleness – unemployment – remains one of the prime sources, not only of poverty, but also of loss of self-esteem and of unhappiness.

As a positive value, we should replace it with the capacity and willingness to work, as well as to deploy initiative in the work environment. And we have to add another value, which never even crossed Beveridge's mind. Combating climate change is usually thought of purely in a negative way – as limiting the harmful

Box 2 The traditional welfare state

1 Policies are 'after the event' – picking up the pieces after things have gone wrong. The welfare state is essentially a collective insurance system, based upon the idea of a safety-net.

2 Apart from the fields of education, and to a lesser extent health, the welfare state is not seen as a generative agency. This orientation is partly because lifestyle is not seen as problematic – behaviour and many structures (such as gender roles) are dictated by custom.

3 The welfare state is designed to increase cohesion, but above all through the reconciliation of classes. 'The' social problem is the problem of class conflict, centring upon the division between the manual working class and other major class groups in society.

4 The welfare state develops primarily through the extension of rights. T. H. Marshall quite correctly distinguished three successive 'layers' of rights: legal rights (such as freedom of speech), political rights (universal franchise) and economic rights (unemployment insurance and so forth).

5 Producer interests tend to dominate over those of clients, who by and large have to 'take what they are offered'. 'Doctor knows best' mentality predominates in most spheres. Citizens assumed to be largely passive as recipients of services.

6 Policies oriented to here-and-now problems as they occur in people's lives, but overall life-span presumed to be stable and predictable. Pensions are built around these assumptions, but so are most other policies.

7 Education has a central place, but is understood primarily in terms of primary and secondary education, and in terms of its extension to groups whose access was restricted.

effects it will cause. Yet there should be positive values involved too. What should our relationship to nature be? What sort of lives do we most want to lead?

Today I believe we should be talking of the imminent end of the welfare state in its traditional sense. Of course, safety-net provisions are still needed. But even they will have a more activist dimension than in the past. The welfare state is becoming a *social investment state.*[5] Do we need such a notion in addition to the ensuring state? Yes, I would say we do, since they are complementary ideas. 'Social investment' refers to the means whereby economic dynamism and social justice are brought together. 'Ensuring' concerns the state's responsibilities in coordinating the variety of agencies needed to help pursue these twin objectives.

Two Examples: Disability and Ageing

A positive welfare approach should be interventionist or pre-emptive instead of mainly remedial. Interventionism means seeking to tackle social problems at source rather than only providing an insurance mechanism for when things go wrong. Take disability as an example. The disabled used to be called the 'handicapped'; the label implied an inevitable incapacity. A disabled person could become reduced to the status of a bystander to normal social life – the 'does he drink tea?' syndrome.

Labels, and the attitudes that go with them, can quite often be taken over by those to whom they are applied, producing or reinforcing feelings of lack of self-worth. Many disabled people could lead more active and satisfying lives than they do, and it should be our aim to expand these possibilities as far as possible. Those who want to work should be able to do so. The category of people currently classified as disabled includes significant numbers whose problems are as much mental as physical. The wider availability of therapeutic services is one way in which such people could be helped to stand on their own two feet again.

Using a broad definition, there are eleven million disabled children and adults in Britain. A lengthy report from the government's Strategy Unit suggested a number of ways to improve the quality of their lives – and allow significant numbers to enter the workforce. Its recommendations included helping disabled people to achieve a higher level of independent living by providing them with an individual budget, which the recipients decide how to spend. Greater support during childhood and adolescence would provide the individuals with the resources to help develop their potential. Against this backdrop, a range of provisions could be set in motion to help disabled people get into work and progress in their careers.[6]

Does putting positive welfare in the forefront mean relapsing into a 'soft' agenda, or making impossible demands on the public purse? No, it does not. Disablement again provides a good example. At the moment there are many people outside the labour force who want to be in work, but who are dependent upon state benefits or other forms of support. Their entry into the workforce would be both a positive outcome in terms of their own self-fulfilment and at the same time functional for the economy.

Consider now the 'ageing society'. The term is really a misnomer. What is actually happening is that the lifestyles of older people are merging with those of younger ones. Older people are in effect getting younger – less and less confined to an old-age ghetto. Labour has not properly woken up to the importance of these changes, having concentrated most of its concern upon the issue of pensions. We should forget altogether the term 'pensioner', which the government uses liberally in its pronouncements, but which suggests someone inherently dependent, who has to be provided for by the rest of the community.

In my view there should be no fixed age of retirement, but flexibility in when people give up paid work. Older people should have the right to work like anyone else, subject to the same provisions of competence and dedication. The very term 'pension' should ultimately disappear; pensions should be like any other type of investment for the future. Ageism today is as big a problem for the society as sexism was – and to some extent still is. Older women suffer from both. Having a higher proportion of older people in work is essential if members of the younger generation aren't to lose out all round, so the persistence of ageism hardly helps them. Incentives and the right material conditions are required, since many older people who are not working say they want to do so.

To be sure, ageing poses many problems for our society; but it is itself part of the solution to those problems. No one should be considered as unfit for work simply by virtue of having reached a certain age. It is not as if having more older people in work will take jobs away from the younger generation. The issue is exactly the reverse. It is in everyone's interests to provide job opportunities for older people and to ensure that ageism doesn't prevent them from performing well in those jobs. Ageist stereotypes are not just a problem affecting those among the younger generations who hold them; like all stereotypes, they can be taken over by those to whom they refer, reducing people's self-esteem and perhaps in the end their actual capacities.

We know that many illnesses or disabilities once widely thought to be intrinsically associated with ageing are actually strongly lifestyle-related. For instance, women on average live longer than men. It is possible that this difference is influenced by genetic factors, but at least a proportion comes from variations in lifestyle. Men on average smoke more than women, drive more carelessly, don't watch what they eat and go to the doctor's less often.

More is known about ageing and the brain than even ten years ago, because of the development of new scanning technologies. The belief that brain cells die as one ages has been shown to be false. If we standardize for diet and lifestyle, there is actually very little decline in mental abilities between the ages of 20 and 70. The brains of healthy people in their 80s are virtually as active as those of individuals in their 40s, as functional magnetic resource imaging shows.[7]

Only 7 per cent of people over 65 in the UK live in retirement homes and hostels. The vast majority live in the community, and want to do so. Physical fitness, good nutrition and mental activity not only prolong active life very significantly; they also have positive effects on a person's self-esteem and self-image. New terminologies are needed. 'Senior' and 'senior citizen' are a lot better than 'pensioner', but they still have a patronizing ring to them.

A ten-year study on ageing in relation to lifestyle came up with important results. More than 2,000 men and women from nine different European countries were studied. Baseline measurements of diet, lifestyle and health were taken regularly from 1989 to

1999. Having a low-quality diet, smoking and being physically inactive each individually led to significantly increased mortality risk. An especially significant finding, since replicated in other research, was that the net effect of a healthy lifestyle on ageing is likely to go together with what doctors call 'compressed cumulative mortality'. In other words, the period towards the end of life when someone is either frail, ill or both is shortened – a very important outcome not only in terms of limiting suffering, but because of the high proportion of medical costs that are incurred during the last few years of life.

Older people, and especially the frail elderly, consume a large proportion of the resources of the NHS at any one time – as well as depending upon informal systems of care in the family and other groups. There is a joke in which someone who doesn't bother much about his health says of those who do: 'Someday all you health nuts are going to look pretty foolish, lying in hospital dying of nothing.' Yet perhaps it is not quite as silly as it seems. Everyone dies of something, but perhaps the numbers of the frail elderly could be radically reduced, especially if chronic illnesses could be tackled, since these certainly help explain why so many elderly people are also frail.

Lifestyle and Health

Health is a key area for interventionist policy. Can such policy be developed without undue intrusion into areas of personal freedom? Yes, because freedom should always be defined, as I suggested earlier, in terms of substantive freedom, or autonomy of action. Obesity, for example, especially in children, has great consequences for later health. Taking quite draconian action against its causes – the high carbohydrate and sugar content of foods, advertising directed towards children promoting such foods and failure to take exercise – is not difficult to justify. Much the same applies among the adult population, except in a more conditional way.

We know that policy-making can change how people behave – there are many examples, including the wearing of seat-belts, reductions in rates of smoking and the successful development of a market for hybrid cars. Quite often, legal intervention is needed against manufacturers, as happened for instance in the case of smoking, and as is starting to happen also in the food industry. Thus the New York City Health Department has recently banned trans fats in all bar and restaurant menus. Trans fats are believed to be linked to heart disease and are certainly connected to obesity.

The example of Finland shows how habits can be changed by concerted policy intervention. In the 1960s Finland had one of the highest rates of heart disease among men in the developed countries – especially pronounced in North Karelia, in the eastern part of the country. Dairy-farming was the main industry in the region. Consumption of high-fat dairy products, such as whole milk, cheese and butter, as well as red meat, was part of most people's daily diet. Smoking was also more widespread than in other regions. A concerted programme to induce people to eat more healthily was introduced, with local debates about health issues featuring prominently. Finland was the first country to ban smoking in public places. Those running the campaign worked with food producers to persuade them to develop low-fat foods and reduce salt levels in their products. By the 1990s the incidence of heart disease had been reduced by 75 per cent, with similar results for high blood pressure, obesity and diabetes.

A positive welfare agenda means widening the debate on the NHS and especially its longer-term future. My earlier discussion of the NHS stuck mostly within the parameters of how it is currently organized – plenty enough to worry about there, one might think. Yet even more profound issues loom at some point in the near future. The NHS was and is a major element of the traditional welfare state. It was and is, above all, concerned with the treatment of individuals who have fallen sick or require treatment of one kind or another. As some observers have remarked, it might more properly be called a National Sickness Service.

Beveridge assumed that calls on the NHS for treatment would actually decline over time, reducing costs or at least keeping them stable. In fact, costs have spiralled, because of factors such as the rise of new treatments, some of them very expensive, and rises in labour costs and in patient expectations. But the main reason is that the decline of serious infectious diseases has meant that other health conditions have come to the fore, and nearly all of them are in some way lifestyle-related.

'The problem with the NHS', it has been said, 'is that it is too focused on the hospital as an institution', and too much on after-care to the detriment of prevention.[8] The government has plans to shift the emphasis of health care in a more preventative direction, but not a great deal of progress has been made. David Boyle and his colleagues point out five problems that are frustrating progress towards a 'National Wellness Service':[9]

1 The professionals in the NHS have too much influence and have not grasped the changing nature of patients' needs in a quite different type of society from the past. The fact that people go to see the doctor only when they have fallen ill encourages them to be dependent upon the health service rather than taking more responsibility for their own health. It could be argued that most admissions to hospitals express a failure of health policy. Problems are often not spotted or reported early enough, either by the patients themselves or in primary care.

2 Lifestyle change is outflanking the capability of the pre-existing medical system to cope, a situation likely to worsen as the longer-term effects of unhealthy lifestyles begin to show themselves. In spite of some high-profile attempts to change it, hospital diet oddly enough often reflects these very problems, contributing to the situation the health service is supposed to help resolve.

3 About 80 per cent of illnesses which land people in hospital now are chronic ones. The NHS was originally established to deal with quite different patterns from those pertaining today. Every day thousands of patients go into hospital who are neither very ill, nor in need of the specialized services hospitals can provide, but because there is nowhere else they can go for care.

4 With increased mobility, neighbourhood networks have quite often become less supportive than they were in the past. Those who lack social networks face health risks as high as those associated with smoking. As it is currently organized, there is

very little the NHS can do to alleviate such difficulties. Most harmful lifestyle habits are addictive. The health system can tackle some of the more pronounced forms of addiction, such as anorexia, when they threaten entirely to undermine someone's health, but not those that are more generalized. For instance, a person's health can be affected by stress that comes from workaholism.

Box 3 The post-industrial welfare society

1 Policies are based on preventive welfare and investment in human capital. Safety-net approach remains in place, but integrated with more generative policies. Policies are oriented towards positive life values.

2 Lifestyle change becomes a core concern of the welfare system. Incentives and sanctions are deployed to help secure positive outcomes. These have to be shaped through orthodox democratic mechanisms and should be geared to substantive freedoms.

3 The welfare system is designed to increase solidarity, but above all through helping to reconcile cultural and lifestyle diversity with overall social cohesion. 'The' social problem is that of creating this balance, and ensuring the full participation of minority groups.

4 Rights go along with obligations or responsibilities in virtually all areas of the welfare system. However, once stabilized, rights cannot be just taken for granted. They might need to be reformed, and also can come directly under threat (such as freedom of speech).

5 The clients of the welfare system are empowered through a series of mechanisms, such as availability of information, personalization of services and choice.

6 Policies are oriented towards transitional problems in people's lives, many of which are unpredictable, but which also are often actively taken decisions. Policy aims to invest in people's capabilities and, where possible, has a long-term perspective.

7 Further and higher education become of great economic and social importance, as well as learning across the life-span.

5 Making progress with these problems will be very difficult. Yet without a different orientation, it is hard to see the NHS standing up to the new strains that will be put upon it. There are major changes going on that could help generate quite radical transformations in health care. One is the growing use of complementary medicine, for example, much of which is preventative rather than curative; much of it also emphasizes the need for holistic treatment that looks at the person's way of life. Complementary medicine is now used in a routine way by about half the population. Virtually all takes place outside the NHS, indicating that more people are accepting wider responsibility for their own health. Unfortunately, at the moment it is heavily class-biased, with poorer people making much less use of such treatments – at the same time as they follow less healthy lifestyles.

Avoidance and management of chronic illnesses depends more upon what patients rather than what medical specialists do. It is puzzling that Labour has not put more stress before on personal responsibility in the health field, given the strong emphasis upon responsibility elsewhere. Perhaps this is another expression of the hold the NHS, as it is currently set up, has over political thinking. Assuming greater responsibility for one's own health should be a fundamental part of active citizenship, but needs to be matched with the right responses from government.

The health service at the moment focuses more on disease than upon patients, while patients in turn are expected to be passive and grateful for whatever attention they receive. These are not the right traits for dealing most effectively with chronic disease, where more active life management on the part of the patient is often crucial. There are some programmes in existence that seek to harness the capabilities of the patient together with those of health care workers. The Expert Patient programme, for instance, offers training to volunteers with chronic health conditions in conjunction with local Primary Care Trusts. The project has been notably successful in reducing demands for hospital care. A similar programme in Michigan in the US reduced periods of hospitalization for diabetes patients by 45 per cent.[10]

The government has frequently spoken of the need for the personalization of public services, including health, but without new initiatives such as these the trend seems to be towards the opposite. GPs see each patient for an average of ten minutes at a time. In larger practices it is hard for patients to maintain a relationship with a single GP. In hospitals, many patients never see the same specialist more than once.

Putting more money into conventional health care will lessen some of these strains, but they will only build up again. Much more thinking should go into what a National Wellness Service would be like, and how far it could relieve some of the pressing problems of the NHS. Most breakthroughs in health in the past have in fact come from improvements in public health rather than in health care as such, and the same is likely to be true again.

Climate Change, Lifestyle Change

Lifestyle change is at the heart of the environmental agenda. When we think about it globally, as we obviously must do, such change will have to be of a far-reaching kind. In British terms, devising a set of tax incentives and more punitive fiscal sanctions will be a major test for a Brown-led regime. Labour should put an arm-lock on the climate change agenda, and indeed as far as possible foster a cross-party consensus about it.

It is a welcome innovation to have a serious and detailed report on climate change produced by a mainstream economist in the shape of the Stern Report, commissioned by Gordon Brown. Nicholas Stern is a scholar of impeccable reputation and certainly no scaremonger. Since economic considerations are the main reason why there is so much foot-dragging in taking action against climate change, his emphasis upon the sheer economic costs of a failure to respond has a great deal of force.

It is now virtually certain that the stocks of greenhouse gases in the atmosphere – carbon dioxide, methane, nitrous oxides and other harmful gases – have risen as a result of human activity. Before the industrial revolution, the concentration of these gases in the atmosphere was about 280 parts per million (ppm) CO_2 or

CO_2 equivalent (CO_2e). Currently the figure is 430 ppm CO_2e. As a result, the world has warmed up by over half a degree Celsius. Given the stock of greenhouse gases already in the atmosphere, it will increase by at least another half degree over the next forty years. If nothing changes, the stock of greenhouse gases could increase by 300 per cent by 2100. According to climate change modelling, this situation would give a 50 per cent risk of a temperature rise of 5 per cent, the consequences of which could be devastating.[11]

Warming will have its most severe effects in the developing world, and preparing to contain those effects has henceforth to be integrated within major development projects. Many of the most severe effects will involve water. The melting of the glaciers and polar ice will increase the risk of flooding in low-lying areas and later substantially reduce supplies of water. About a billion people in the world will be directly affected by these changes, mainly in the sub-continent of India, parts of China and Latin America. Crop yields will suffer in more tropical areas, especially parts of Africa.

In the developed parts of the world, which are mainly concentrated in the north, warming might initially have some small beneficial consequences. However, the harmful ones will radically outweigh them, especially as climate change advances further. A temperature rise of 2 per cent could lead to a 20 per cent drop in water supplies in Europe. Climate change will bring more disruptive and extreme weather everywhere.

At the time of writing, the UN's Intergovernmental Panel on Climate Change is about to issue a vast new report surveying the current state of the evidence. Some of the content is already available. The report says that the possibility that observed trends towards warming are the result of natural factors, and not greenhouse gases, is less than 5 per cent. Under a 'business as usual' scenario, temperatures could increase by as much as 5.8°C by 2100. Temperatures will continue to rise by 0.1°C each decade even if all sources of emissions were frozen today.

There are feedback effects that could add further to temperature rises. For instance, forests, oceans and the soil could become less able to absorb carbon dioxide. It is even possible that such feedback effects are happening now. Since 2001 there has been an unanticipated surge in the level of carbon dioxide in the atmosphere. The science report is the first of three weighty IPCC reports due to be published this year. The IPCC Chairman, Rajendra Pachauri said: 'I hope this report will shock people and governments into taking more serious action, as you really can't get a more authentic and a more credible piece of scientific work.'[12]

The economic costs of increased warming, for individual countries and the world as a whole, will greatly outweigh the benefits if no significant progress is made in checking it. According to the Stern Report, the adverse economic impact of climate change is likely to be worse than was thought a few years ago. The costs of the 'business as usual' scenario would quite soon outweigh the economic benefits. Even in the relatively short term they could have effects on world financial systems. For instance, more unpredictable weather conditions could directly affect the insurance industry, with wider consequences for financial markets.

Climate change has been brought about by economic development. However, Stern argues, regulating the effects of climate change 'is feasible and consistent with continued growth'.[13] This is a crucial conclusion, and I believe a correct one. The pollution of the atmosphere is closely related to levels of GDP. The developed countries have produced about 70 per cent of the total. From the present point onwards, the developing world, or parts of it, will accelerate their share of emissions, because of their very rapid economic growth and because they have become responsible for much of the world's manufacture. Technological change, however, has potentially changed the nature of the equation. With the right policy choices, it is possible for both developed and developing economies to reduce carbon levels while sustaining economic growth. Economic growth will in fact move into reverse at some point under the 'business as usual' assumptions.

The Free-riding Dilemma

The Stern Report doesn't concentrate mainly upon policy programmes, but the problems we face are daunting. One of the biggest issues to overcome is that of free-riding. There is first of all the potential free-riding of the generations – that is, of the present generation on future ones. The temptation for governments and ordinary citizens is to put things off. Why should we worry too much when the worst effects of climate change will happen way down the line?

Then there is the possible free-riding of some nations on others. Those in the developing world, for instance, might simply say to the developed countries: 'You created the problem, you resolve it' – in fact, this attitude is already common. Among the developed nations, one or more countries might simply decide to let others make the needed changes – this has been essentially the stance of the Bush administration in the US, the biggest polluter of all. Individual citizens might do the same, especially if climate change legislation lacks teeth – 'Let others give up their gas-guzzling cars, I'm not going to.'

Finally, in spite of the compelling nature of the scientific evidence, there is still scepticism, especially pronounced among those who believe that combating warming will compromise economic prosperity. The Competitive Enterprise Institute announces on its website: 'They call it pollution (CO_2). We call it life.' Global warming is a situation where it is impossible to prove with 100 per cent certainty that the risks are real, since we are anticipating a future situation that we want to avoid.

How can we limit the possibilities of free-riding? There are in fact various ways. International agreement involving all countries is the prime one, as political leaders come to recognize that no one will escape the harmful, potentially devastating, consequences that would come from ineffective action. The Kyoto experience thus far shows, however, that this point has not yet been reached, since some countries, including the US, have not signed up. Those that have must keep up the pressure on the ones that have not, which will become easier to do the more the evidence accumulates, and the more visible the manifestations of global warming become. Since we need to go well beyond the Kyoto agreements, we have to work as rapidly as possible towards a global consensus.

It is up to individual countries, but especially groups of countries, to be out in the lead. To do so, they should look to the advantages, which could outweigh the costs, certainly in the medium term. The EU has a fundamental role to play, and has already shown leadership in pushing to get the required number of countries to sign up to Kyoto to bring the agreements into being. Those that are in the vanguard in principle could be ahead of the game, in terms of economic benefits coming from technological innovation and social benefits, such as those accruing to public health. Since reducing emissions can be integrated with lessening energy dependency upon unstable parts of the world, there will be gains in energy security.

It is worth mentioning that, although the federal government in the US has kept its distance from climate change policies, some states have actually given a great deal of attention to it. The State of California has long been in the vanguard of environmental policies, even if the results have left something to be desired. In the 1980s California took the lead in introducing legislation that required car manufacturers to fit all their vehicles with catalytic converters. The state has recently produced a comprehensive and detailed study of how warming would affect California and has introduced new initiatives as a result. The governor of Wyoming has claimed that his state will be the first to shed completely its dependence upon oil, through the use of liquefied coal, purified of its CO_2. The mayor of New York, Michael Bloomberg, has initiated a greenhouse gas inventory that will be the basis for turning the city into an 'environmentally sustainable' one.

Climate Change and Citizenship

In terms of domestic politics, the normalization of climate change policy is crucial at this point. Environmental issues for the first time have to be brought within the framework of rights and obligations that constitute the citizenship contract between government and citizens, including both the fiscal and welfare systems. The guiding principle should be that the environment can no longer be treated as a free good.

I do not believe that self-denial should be the key basis of this shift. I'm not saying we can have it all, because we can't. Draconian measures will be needed in some areas, such as control of vehicle pollution, and these will be politically problematic. Yet tax incentives and tax credits, together with consciousness-raising, should, wherever possible, be the motivating factors of lifestyle change, for citizens, public organizations and business firms.

What should be the positive values associated with environmental policies? Here I think Labour should distance itself somewhat from the green movement. At first sight this seems a strange thing to say, now that environmental questions are so prominent. Isn't such an idea, to say the least, ungrateful, given the part that the greens have played in planting the issue in public consciousness? Shouldn't we all instead become Friends of the Earth?

Actually, it wasn't the green movement that alerted us to the dangers of climate change: it was scientists. Large sectors of the green movement have their origins in a quite different body of thinking. They are to be found in the writings of those hostile to modern industry, which was seen as destroying the integrity of nature – essentially a romantic, conservative reaction to industrialism. This fact explains why so many greens are either hostile to science and technology, or at least ambivalent about them.

Because the green movement grew out of a romantic critique of modernity, it has always been linked to the idea of setting limits, of cutting back, a sort of hair-shirt philosophy of everyday life. An article was written recently by one of the most prominent British environmentalists, entitled 'How sport is killing the planet'.[14] Motor racing, that author says, is simply incompatible with reducing climate change and hence, he implies, should be abandoned. The Olympic Games, involving as they do the building of stadia and a good deal of air travel, should be closed down in their current form. We should encourage spectators to stay at home and watch major sports events on the TV. The best and most involving sport – he seems to say this in all seriousness – is playing in the local park with a frisbee.

I'm not a fan of motor racing and hold no particular brief for it. Yet the technology developed in motor sport has in fact contributed perhaps more than any other single factor to the increased fuel efficiency (and safety) of everyday cars. The process of technological advance is oblique and complex.

The values underlying environmental policy should in some part be the same as those that inform other policy areas. One is solidarity – in this case with our children and future generations. Another is equality – as far as we can we should make sure that dealing with the effects of climate change do not concentrate disproportionately upon the poor. This theorem applies on a national and international level. The less developed countries are more vulnerable to the destructive effects of climate change than the more affluent ones. Improved public health should be another major goal, since there are win–win consequences. There is a positive gain in all respects if a person walks more often on local journeys, and comes to enjoy doing so, rather than using a car.

There are basically four strategies to follow in domestic efforts to reduce emissions. First, carbon-pricing is a necessary part of no longer treating the environment as a free good. The government must decide the most effective means of fixing prices for carbon use. Pricing carbon will have the consequence of forcing individuals, businesses and other agencies to accept the consequences of their actions. Different policies can be used to achieve this end. Taxation – such as congestion-charging – has the advantage of coupling behaviour change with a flow of revenue that can be put aside for environmental purposes.

Some have suggested that carbon could become a form of currency for individual consumers, just as it is in carbon-trading schemes on a larger scale. Credit cards could store carbon points in the way they do orthodox money. Users would use up carbon points whenever they made transactions such as buying fuel or energy, up to limits set by the government. Unused carbon points could be exchanged for money at the end of the year.

If we only have a ten- to twenty-year window in which to mitigate the most damaging effects of climate change, is it fanciful to suppose that such a scheme could actually be implemented by then? Not according to some researchers: no major technological development is needed; the main difficulties would be practical and political – would voters accept such an idea, and could it be made to work both efficiently and equitably? Studies carried out by the Tyndall Centre suggest that there is a clear possibility that the answer is 'yes' to both these questions.[15]

The EU Emissions Trading Scheme is a pioneering development, which has influenced other countries and areas around the world. California, for example, has announced it is adopting a similar scheme. Their version is only in its early stages, and does not at the moment apply to air traffic, although there are proposals to extend it in this way. The scheme will work so long as there are clear rules, such that risks to investors, especially in long-term projects, are clear and manageable.

There is a lot more to do at the European level. Several major countries still heavily subsidize the worst polluting industries.[16] For example, Germany pays large subsidies to its coalminers. Transport policy is not effectively coordinated. Thus some of the new member states of former East Europe are busy spending public money on building motorways while at the same time scaling back their railways. The Emissions Trading Scheme itself needs a thorough overhaul. It works through setting limits for carbon emissions for heavy industry and energy firms. They are allocated permits to pollute, which can be traded. However, at the moment member states set the limits, rather than the EU as a whole, and their average level is not high enough to be truly effective.

The second necessary element of a climate change strategy is to introduce policies that would facilitate rapid technological advances. The greater the pressure, the more likely are dramatic technological developments. UK spending on R&D is currently well below that of the leading countries in the world, no doubt adversely affecting the country's chances of being at the cutting-edge. Toyota has just become the biggest car-maker in the world. Their investment in environmentally friendly hybrid vehicles has helped give the company the edge over its rivals, especially the American firm General Motors. State-provided subventions or tax incentives will be needed to support start-up ventures in areas where the initial costs are high – as in the generation of electricity.

Some technologies involve long lead-up times, especially nuclear power. Should nuclear power be part of the energy mix, in the UK and elsewhere? Some countries, such as Germany, have decided to take the non-nuclear route (although the country currently gets about a third of its energy from nuclear power stations). The objections that can be levelled against extensive reliance upon nuclear power are considerable. If nuclear power is to be embraced, or renewed within the developed countries, it is difficult or impossible to argue that less developed ones should not have it. Yet although there are proposals on the table in the international agencies concerned, it will be hard to separate the widespread use of nuclear power from the possibility of further nuclear proliferation.

Nuclear power stations are vulnerable to terrorism, so there are costs involved in providing adequate levels of protection. Although the number of deaths as a result of accidents involving nuclear power stations, including Chernobyl, is very low – compared, for example, to coalmining – such accidents can potentially be dangerous. The problem of disposing of nuclear waste, which remains radioactive for thousands of years, has not yet been adequately solved.

So the decision is not an easy one. All these issues must be coped with. In addition, a country that invests in nuclear power for twenty years ahead might find itself outflanked by as yet unknown technological innovations. But on balance I think it would be sensible for the UK to invest in renewing its nuclear capacity, just as Finland, a highly environmentally conscious country, has done. Its neighbour, Sweden, is hesitating on the issue, having decided earlier to go non-nuclear. The Swedish government has announced proposals to become a wholly carbon-free economy by 2020, a date not that far in the future. The country is in a good position to do so, since it reacted more forcefully than most others to the oil crisis of the 1970s. Much of its electricity already comes from renewable sources.

Without nuclear power there might be a huge gap in the UK's non-carbon energy resources in some years' time. Energy security is likely to be a major problem for most nations over the next few years; indigenous sources of energy will be essential. It will be necessary, however, for successive governments to monitor the programme as it unfolds, in the light of developments that might occur on the energy front. Flexibility is by definition difficult to build into a nuclear power programme, given the high level of sunk costs involved, but the more adaptability there is, the greater the chance of finding the right energy mix.

Decisions made by households contribute to well over 40 per

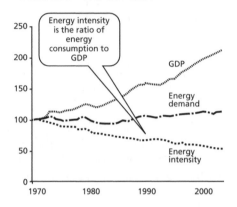

UK energy consumption continues to rise gradually despite efficiency gains
Index 1970 = 100, 1997–2004

Figure 6.1: Economic growth is causing rising demand for energy, posing severe threats to the sustainability of the planet

cent of total emissions in the UK. How can change in consumption patterns best be achieved? One way is to set up policies that are creative in terms of overlap. For instance, campaigns to improve public health, such as persuading people to walk and to combine walking with using public transport, can have significant environmental benefits. Since cars that consume large amounts of fuel per mile travelled tend to be owned by the more affluent, raising tax duty on them could also be redistributive. Some of the revenue raised from environmental taxes can be used to lower the tax burden on poorer groups.

Specific attention has to be given to businesses, to create the right sort of tax breaks, but also to ensure that the environmental responsibilities of firms are spelled out and consistent across different sectors. A very interesting initiative is being taken in California, one with wide potential ramifications. California has filed a lawsuit against the major car manufacturers, suing them for the environmental damage their products have caused. According to the state's case, the defendants have produced more than 289 million tonnes of carbon dioxide over the past five decades. This pollution, the state alleges, has, among other changes, reduced

California's snow-pack, thereby also reducing its available water supply, raised sea levels, increased ozone pollution in cities and heightened the risk of brush fires. The cost to the Californian economy runs into millions of dollars and the state is suing to get it back.

Finally, but just as important as the preceding points, as a matter of some urgency there should be a national assessment of vulnerability, since global warming will have an impact whatever happens, and if effective action is not forthcoming that impact will be correspondingly more radical. The situation in respect of adaptation is quite different from the endeavour to limit climate change as such. Local action can be taken that will have immediate benefits in terms of risk protection and reduction in the damage done by environmental changes. Markets, especially the private insurance market, can play an important role, by sending signals about shifts in risk to businesses and government.

However, the state will have an indispensable part to play too. It will have to provide much of the information upon which risk assessment can be built, and integrate this task with its other responsibilities. For instance, effects of climate change such as prolonged heat waves have obvious health implications: one might recall again how many died in Europe during the heat wave of 2003. Regulations have to be set for the building industry to take account of the implications of warming for infrastructure. Areas at risk of flooding will need extra protection.

Since there could be local catastrophes, there must be proper preparedness for emergencies – think of how ill-prepared the American authorities, local and federal, were for the flooding in New Orleans. As always, those with the least resources tend to suffer most. They are the least likely to have the personal resources to cope and many are not covered by any form of private insurance, whether personal or for the protection of property. As elsewhere, this fact implies the need to bring environmental measures directly within the framework of a reformed welfare system.

In the next chapter, I move on to consider yet another dilemma for the welfare system, that posed by the increasing diversity of Britain's population. Chapters 7 and 8, in fact, relate closely to one another: each is about our national identity being reshaped.

Tony Blair is greeted by Sayed Abdu Majid Al-Khoei, second right, who is the head of the Shia Muslims in the United Kingdom, Shaykh Dr. M. A. Zaki Badawi, right, and Shiekh Fadhel Sahlani, left, who are from the New York Al-Khoei Foundation, as he arrives at the Al-Khoei Foundation in northwest London, where he addressed an Islamic conference on Thursday, 25 October 2001.

7

No Giving Up
On Multiculturalism!

Former US Vice-President Dan Quayle is reputed to have said: I was recently on a tour of Latin America, and the only regret I have was that I didn't study Latin harder in school so I could converse with these people.

Reported in a British newspaper: The Home Office refused asylum to a Bosnian Croat who claimed he had received death threats in Sarajevo. He was told: 'The Secretary of State notes that the threats made against you were not carried out.'

Through the influence of modern communications, all of us come into daily contact with other cultures, should take the trouble to find out why others think and act as they do. Dialogue with others can help self-understanding as well as promote mutual tolerance. And for a country that values its tolerant attitudes, the Home Office is setting the bar rather high.

In the London bombings on 7 July 2005, fifty-two people died. Who were they? They included five Muslims, from widely removed parts of the world, such as Tunisia, Afghanistan and Bangladesh. One was a young woman described as 'a thoroughly modern Muslim, a girl who loved her Burberry plaid handbag and fashionable clothes while at the same time respecting her family's wishes that she sometimes wear traditional *salwar kameez* at home. She went shopping in the West End of London with friends but would always be seen at the mosque for Friday prayers.'[1]

Others who died included three Polish women. One was working as a cleaner; another was an assistant manager at a college hall of residence: both had been in London for three years. The third was a young woman who had come for four months to study English. Others had arrived in London from Romania, Italy, Nigeria, Israel, New Zealand, Vietnam, Mauritius, Australia, Sri Lanka, Grenada, India, Ireland and Jamaica.

London is one of the most diverse cities in the world, although other European cities are catching up fast. Since 1997 the flow of legal immigration into the EU countries has numbered well over one million a year. An estimated half as many again have come in illegally. This figure does not include the large population movement within the EU, where of course there is free mobility among citizens, with the partial exception of those from very recent new member states. Britain was one of only a few EU countries that allowed free entry from all new member states after the enlargement of the Union to twenty-five members in 2004. Large numbers of workers have come into Britain since then, especially from Poland, the Baltic states and the Czech Republic. There is immense diversity in all this movement in terms of who comes from where and in which countries they settle, or attempt to do so.

Not all who come to the UK are poor or jobless by any means. They include bankers, executives of multinational companies, doctors and other medical staff and many others. The tabloid press would have us believe that Britain is being overrun with asylum-seekers and migrants from poor countries. Yet asylum-seekers are a small minority of immigrants. The two largest groups coming to this country are from the US and Australia. Among all categories of immigrants, considerable numbers are temporary – they are planning to stay only for a while. There is a good deal of emigration from Britain too. About 5.5 million British people now live abroad. Over the past four decades, 67,000 more Britons have left the country each year than have returned. Forty-one countries in the world have British-born populations of 10,000 or more.

In the mid-1990s most new migration into Europe was concentrated in Germany, with some countries still having negative net migration – more people were leaving than entering. Net positive inflows now exist in all the more affluent EU states, and especially those, such as Spain or Italy, that border the Mediterranean. Most of the countries of North Africa and the Middle East, in notable contrast to Europe, have large numbers of young people who make up the bulk of the migrants.

The population of the EU15 states grew by about twelve million between 1995 and 2005. Migration accounted for two-thirds of this increase, given that the average birth rate in these countries is low. In some countries the influx of immigrants has started to reverse low birth rates. For instance, in Spain the birth rate has begun to climb again after years of decline. In spite of the prominence and heat of the controversies around immigration in Europe, North America and Australasia, migration flows around the world are lower today than they were in the early years of the twentieth century and in the 1950s. Migration has even been termed 'the missing link of the current era of globalization'.[2]

Immigration: Danger or Opportunity?

I have on my bookshelves a whole raft of books predicting disaster for the West if the current patterns of immigration continue. They belong to a right-wing tradition that goes back at least as far as Oswald Spengler, who many years ago wrote of the imminent collapse of the West.[3]

The American author Tony Blankley's book *The West's Last Chance* carries an endorsement from Henry Kissinger, no less. Blankley's book is dedicated to his parents, who were living in London at the time of the Blitz in the Second World War. 'They saw', he says, 'Europe threatened, redeemed to freedom, and now in the twilight of their years, again threatened.'[4] The source of Europe's vulnerability? It is 'the terrible danger posed by radical Islam'. 'It bears repeating', he continues. 'An Islamified Europe would be as great a threat to the United States today as a Nazified Europe would have been to the United States in the 1940s.'[5]

Bruce Bawer's work *While Europe Slept* has a similar theme. Its sub-title is: 'How Radical Islam is Destroying the West from Within'. Bawer is an American living in Europe. The political elites in the European countries, he says, are turning a blind eye to what is happening in the fast-growing Muslim enclaves, where 'women [are] oppressed and abused, homosexuals persecuted and killed, "infidels" threatened and vilified, Jews demonised, barbaric traditions (such as honour killing and forced marriage) widely practised, and freedom of speech and religion firmly repudiated'.[6] Europe is living through a 'Weimar moment', he concludes, in which most people seem unable to grasp the nature of the threat.

Then there is the grand old man of the American right, Patrick Buchanan, who has released his own version of this argument in *The Death of the West*. His book is more firmly about the US, and not so concentrated on Islam. In 1960, the vast majority of Americans could still trace their ancestors to Europe. Now they are in danger of becoming a minority. Well over a quarter of Americans today are from other parts of the world. As a consequence, '[m]illions have begun to feel like strangers in their own land'.[7]

The British do not seem to have been either so prolific or apocalyptic, but we have our own more sober and restrained versions of these diagnoses. The NGO Migration Watch UK denies having any political connections, but it does concentrate on a particular point of view. It dismisses most of the claimed benefits of immigration and focuses instead upon its threat. As the organization's website says, it 'is concerned about the present scale of immigration into the UK'. It declares that Britain will have to cope with a net inflow of two million immigrants every ten years for the foreseeable future, and that there must be serious doubts about the society's capacity to absorb numbers on that scale. Government figures were released in 2005 arguing that the benefits of immigration amounted to an extra £4 billion to the economy per annum. Migration Watch rejects those claims forcefully, saying that the economic benefits of migration are very close to zero – they amount to the 'equivalent of a Mars bar every month'.[8]

A completely opposing argument is made in a recent book by Phillipe Legrain, who argues for the opening of borders to let migrants come and go as they please. He quotes the celebrated economist J. K. Galbraith, who once wrote: 'Migration selects those who most want help. It is good for the country to which they go; it helps break the equilibrium of poverty in the country from which they come. What is the perversity in the human soul that causes people to resist so obvious a good?'[9] Legrain wants to make the 'missing link' with globalization. The case for free migration, he says, follows on logically from the case for free trade. Those who want to help the poor countries of the world could do so best by allowing freer international migration. Don't try to keep them out – on the contrary, let them in!

Free migration, according to Legrain, would benefit everybody, for the reason given by Galbraith, and for other reasons too. Virtually all forms of migration, he says, bring economic benefits to the host country. Immigrants work hard and pay their taxes. The diversity stimulates creativity and innovation. Unskilled immigrants do jobs that natives often wouldn't do, while skilled ones fill gaps where there are labour shortages. Contrary to popular prejudice, immigrants contribute more to welfare systems than they take from them. On average they tend to have more children than the host population, offsetting, to some degree, the dramatic drop in birth rates in some areas. Legrain gives short shrift to the idea that cultural minorities are a threat to the core values of the West.

Many Muslims in Europe, he points out, are not religious at all. Most are not socially conservative and do not hold antiquated views about women. Among those holding culturally conservative views, the majority want integration without assimilation: they wish to be active in the wider society, but without discarding their religious views and practices. There are not in fact many ultra-orthodox Muslims in Europe. And we should remember, Legrain concludes, that the Christian churches have their share of the ultra-orthodox, as do Jews; we do not judge these religions by their ideas, and we should not do so in the case of Muslims either.[10]

It is not remotely likely that the developed countries will open up their borders to all and sundry. Nor should they. The immigration of low-skilled workers is problematic, especially at a time when unskilled work is drying up. Such migrants come into poorer neighbourhoods, and it is clear that they might add to the pool of unemployed, or lower the wages of workers already in the area. Where their children do not speak English, there are significant costs incurred to provide the special needs training that might be required. If they are from a peasant background, where the rhythm of work is variable and seasonal, it may be difficult to adjust to a quite different work discipline. The anxieties that many feel about immigration might be stoked up by the tabloids, but it would be quite wrong simply to see the public as irrational and leave it at that. When large numbers of immigrants move into an area, the nature of the neighbourhood can change massively as far as local residents are concerned. Think of how different Bethnal Green is now from how it was half a century ago. One of the most famous works of social science, *Family and Kinship in East London*, written by Michael Young and Peter Wilmott, published at that time, described the nature of working-class life there.[11]

When Young and Wilmott carried out their research, in the 1950s, virtually all the inhabitants of the area were white, although there were certainly some immigrants among them. Geoff Dench and Kate Gavron spent twelve years studying the area much more recently. It has now become part of the London borough of Tower Hamlets. They carried out well over a thousand interviews with people of different ethnic groups living in the area, to try to trace the experience of the white families that had been studied by Young and Wilmott years before.[12]

Today, there is a large and youthful Bangladeshi community in the area, amounting to a third of those living in the borough, as well as other ethnic groups. These all coexist reasonably well, but there are also significant tensions, and a good deal of simmering resentment on the part of the indigenous whites. They complain about the habits and customs of the Bangladeshis. Their main resentments, however, concern the rights of the Bangladeshis to housing and other benefits provided by the welfare system. Some of these complaints, the authors accept, come from misunderstandings about how welfare entitlements operate. Others, they say, are based on a real sense of social injustice.

Since the 1980s there has been a struggle over housing, which is in short supply. The housing shortage in the area was exacerbated by a policy of selling council houses to their occupants, without any replacement building programme. The waiting list for social housing was once based on giving priority to applicants with established connections to the area, but now it is allocated according to whoever is deemed most needy – a policy that the white inhabitants feel unduly favours the Bangladeshi families. One of the consequences is that the networks of support and community among the whites that Young and Wilmott found are breaking up.

Of course, there are larger social processes involved in all this too, but the sense of social injustice comes from what the whites experience as a dismissal of the investment that they, their parents and grandparents had put into the area – often, as they see it, against the odds, since it was always a place where people struggled to make ends meet. Their attitudes don't seem to stem from racism. Few respondents saw the immigrants themselves as being at fault, and few denied that many Bangladeshi families live in greater poverty than themselves. Many who resented the system of housing allocation were friendly with their Bangladeshi neighbours.

The white working class might be in steady decline statistically, but it still comprises millions of people. There has always been a streak of authoritarianism in working-class communities, and xenophobia too. But Dench and Gavron's argument that there are well-grounded resentments among the 'forgotten white working class' is important. Such feelings fuel a disengagement from politics, and a turn towards far right populism among white groups. We will not be able to respond to these problems effectively if such feelings are not properly understood, or dismissed as rank prejudice.

Controlling immigration

British policy towards asylum-seekers and economic migrants has been far from consistent, and this is one of the reasons why concerns over immigration among the public have risen so steeply. As in other countries, the government was caught out by the changing nature of migration, which initially it tried to deal with in more traditional terms. The new system introduced in 2005 when Charles Clarke was the Home Secretary was the most sophisticated. When he set it up, Clarke argued that it was lack of confidence in the preceding approaches that had helped foster bigotry.

Under the system, high-skill workers, such as software engineers or doctors, can come to Britain without a job offer. Others at a rather lower skill level, such as nurses and teachers, will be able to come if there is a labour shortage in their area of work. Only skilled workers will be able to stay permanently, after passing English language tests. Migrants who work in sectors open to abuse have to post financial guarantees to ensure that they return home when the work finishes. The automatic right of immigrants' families to entry has been ended. To help limit illegal immigration, employers who use illegal workers face fines. Refugees will get permission to stay in the country for five years before a decision is taken about whether it is safe for them to return to their countries of origin. The system is designed to stay in place for some while and it would be wise to keep it that way unless major deficiencies appear. Endless changes simply erode public confidence, and demoralize the officials who have to apply the policies.

Persuading highly skilled migrants to come to Britain will not be an easy task, and more will have to be done if they are to be attracted to the UK. Australia has been by far the most successful country in these terms: it has attracted about ten times as many overseas graduates as it has lost of its own to emigration. The UK is faring poorly. The country has in fact a net outflow of high-skill workers – more leave to work abroad than come in. Among European states, only Sweden and Switzerland show a 'brain gain'. Between 1987 and 2002, 100,000 people with a basic university degree or higher qualification left Sweden; but 180,000 with those qualifications entered the country during that period.[13] Quite a few of these were Swedes returning to the country; others were highly qualified workers going in from trouble-spots, such as Bosnia.

Movement into the UK from the new entrant countries to the European Union is not immigration, but the free movement of citizens of the Union as a whole. However, with the enlargement in 2004 to twenty-five members, only the UK, Sweden and Ireland allowed open entry to workers from the ten new member states. Far more workers came into the UK than was originally anticipated, especially from Poland, which has high rates of unemployment. In all, around 420,000 workers from Eastern Europe have sought entry into the UK. Many were in fact already in the country, but were working illegally. Employers have mostly welcomed them, and the vast majority of them have quickly found jobs. Many are skilled artisans – plumbers, carpenters and people working in the building trade. The figures bandied about in the press are seriously misleading, since they do not include figures for those who have moved on. A high proportion of such workers say they intend to return to their home country after a few years. Others have already left. In 2004, net migration from Eastern Europe was only 48,000.[14]

The government has not followed its open door policy in the case of workers moving from the two states that became members of the EU on 1 January 2007, Romania and Bulgaria. Low-skill workers from these countries will be restricted to existing quota schemes to fill jobs in agriculture and food-processing. Skilled workers will be able to work in Britain under the Highly Skilled Migrant Programme. The scheme will be reviewed every twelve months. The European Commission expressed its disappointment at the decision, saying that member states should make a bigger effort to allow workers to move freely across the EU. The UK, after all, was one of the most forceful advocates of enlargement.

In Praise of Multiculturalism

Labour should defend multiculturalism, especially in the face of the more ignorant attacks to which the idea is subject. However we should distinguish between naive and sophisticated multiculturalism. Naive multiculturalism is the thesis that different ethnic or cultural groups should be left alone to get on with their lives as they see fit, no matter what the consequences for others; and the notion that their beliefs and practices should not be challenged. Naive multiculturalists see a society as simply an aggregate of different cultural communities, in which the majority or host population is just one ethnic community among others.

In a recent book, Amartya Sen makes a similar distinction, using different labels. He separates multiculturalism as such from what he calls 'plural multiculturalism'. The first refers to 'two styles or traditions coexisting side by side, without the twain meeting'. This version 'seems to get most of the vocal and loud defence from alleged multiculturalists'. Plural multiculturalism involves active interaction between cultural communities. For instance,

153

there was no chilli in India until it was brought there by the Portuguese, but now it is used very widely in Indian cooking. Hence, 'Indian food ... can genuinely claim to be multicultural.'[15]

Sophisticated multiculturalism has its origins principally in Canada. It emphasizes the overarching importance of national identity, with its symbols, laws and ceremonials. Rather than encouraging the development of separate cultural communities, there should be an insistence upon fostering connections between them, and with the overall national community. National law and international law override all specific cultural beliefs and practices. Political correctness is rejected in favour of policies that promote social solidarity across cultural divisions.

In the academic world, there has been a long-running debate about multiculturalism, one that is still continuing. However, no one of any intellectual standing argues that multiculturalism implies denying overall values, the need for a common identity in a society, or advocates the separation of society into distinct cultural segments. The leading advocate of multiculturalism is the Canadian philosopher Charles Taylor.[16] Taylor says that two concepts are involved when we discuss equal rights as applied to minority groups. One is that all people should have equal dignity, whatever culture they might belong to or lifestyle they might follow – this is a principle of universal citizenship within a society.

The second, just as important, is respect, or what Taylor, following Hegel, calls 'the politics of recognition'. Acceptance from others, Taylor argues, is crucial to a sense of self-worth. Our identities are defined in interaction with others. Multiculturalism is not about separate identities, but about mutual recognition, and therefore interaction. It is exactly when members of minority groups are treated as 'separate and alien' that problems arise. A democratic society cannot possibly be a patchwork of disconnected cultures. As Taylor puts it: '[T]he societies we are striving to create – free, democratic, willing to some degree to share equally – require strong identification on the part of their citizens.'[17]

Commitment to equal respect is therefore an elemental part of multiculturalism. Equality of status, however, does not in any sense imply uncritical acceptance of beliefs and practices of others. 'It is how we do things' is an acceptable defence of cultural principles where they don't impinge upon those of others, but not where they do. The clearest case is that of the law of the land, which has to be accepted by all. In Britain, for example, like other citizens, Muslims cannot by law practise polygamy, engage in honour killings, practice female circumcision or prevent freedom of speech.

Practices that are perfectly legal, but which impinge on public space, have to be open to critical discussion, whatever is eventually decided about them. Around the edges of such encounters, it will always be difficult to take decisions, since there are grey areas where the different principles can collide. For example, should a woman who works in public settings, where there is constant interaction with others – such as a teacher in a classroom – be able to wear the full veil, in which her face is almost completely covered? Personally, I would say no, because interaction with others is only open and free if one can see the face of the other, since facial expressions are so important to communication. The value of preserving public space should override other considerations.

All sorts of people have attacked multiculturalism over the past few years. Among the most surprising of such broadsides was that by Trevor Phillips, chairman of the Commission for Racial Equality. He has argued that multiculturalism is out of date and no longer useful.[18] Such a view seems simply to be out of touch with what the concept actually means. Discussing Phillips's speech, Tariq Modood quite properly pointed out that: 'Those who say multiculturalism means separatism clearly are not talking about the multiculturalism that is found in the main texts of academics or public policy practitioners.'[19]

How should we define multiculturalism? It must not be confused with cultural diversity as such. We cannot call a society 'multicultural' simply because it contains people of many different cultures. People talk loosely, for example, of 'multicultural London', but this usage is not helpful. (Sophisticated) multiculturalism refers to a set of ideals, backed by policies. These ideals are:

- valuing diversity, as a means of enriching the life of all members of a society;
- recognition, in Taylor's sense – respect for others whose way

of life is different from one's own, and getting similar respect back;
- interaction between diverse cultures, fostering mutual understanding;
- acceptance of a common overall identity as members of a national community, as a 'community of fate' – that is, being bound by laws and collective decisions that affect everyone.

Trevor Phillips claims that we should forget multiculturalism and concentrate upon being British. We need to 'assert a core of Britishness', he says. But there is no contradiction at all between the definition of multiculturalism that I have given and asserting the importance of building a common British identity.

Some say Britain is now too culturally variegated actually to be a 'community of fate'. Not only Scottish nationalists advance such an idea. It was put forward in quite a different form in a controversial essay written by the editor of *Prospect* magazine, David Goodhart.[20] Because of the diversity of British society today, he argued, we spend much of our time with strangers. Sharing and solidarity become correspondingly diluted. Will citizens go on supporting progressive taxation and a common welfare system when they feel they have little in common with other members of society? We are much more inclined to share with those with whom we have a shared history and who are similar to ourselves. Casual observation would seem to back up the idea. Thus, culturally homogeneous societies, like Scandinavian states up to twenty years ago, it could be argued, have lower rates of inequality than more diverse ones.

The essay drew furious responses from a variety of critics. Trevor Phillips felt as strongly about Goodhart's arguments as others did about his own condemnation of multiculturalism. 'Nice people', he commented, 'do racism too. ... Some very nice folk have decided that the nation's real problem is too many immigrants of too many kinds.'[21] His defence, somewhat perversely, leans exactly upon multiculturalism such as I have defined it above. When we look at Britain's welfare system, he points out, it shows the real value of diversity – and how it can support welfare institutions rather than undermine them. The NHS was launched by a Welshman, in hospitals and clinics built by Irish labourers, and works because of the skills of nurses and doctors it employs from many different parts of the world.

Goodhart did not deserve the abuse he received. He was not the first to make the arguments he did. However, his conclusions do seem to be wrong. For the past ten years scholars have been debating the issues. In 2003, more than a hundred academics from different disciplines got together in Brussels to discuss the same topic.[22] Looking at the evidence from different societies, their conclusions suggested that, in fact, cultural and ethnic diversity do not undermine welfare systems.

This finding has been reinforced by subsequent research. Will Kymlicka and Keith Banting carried out a detailed study of specific countries, including the United States, Britain, Canada, The Netherlands and Germany.[23] They distinguish two arguments that some make about diversity and welfare. First, it has been claimed that ethnic and racial diversity as such makes it more difficult to support redistribution through the welfare state; and second, that multicultural policies developed to recognize or accommodate immigrant groups tend to undermine national solidarity. On the basis of their study, they dispute both assertions. Their conclusion is that there is no inherent tendency for either ethnic diversity or multiculturalism policies to erode the welfare state.

Islam in the Context of British society

In spite of its problems, the UK can lay fair claim to being the most successful society in Europe in coping effectively with cultural and ethnic diversity. (Since 2000, Labour has adopted some of the Canadian policies, such as obligatory citizenship ceremonies for migrants gaining British nationality.) Studies, even in cities where there have been open ethnic battles, show a high level of assimilation. In his research into segregation, based on the 2001 Census, Ludi Simpson found that Britain is becoming increasingly mixed in racial and ethnic terms, not more segregated. In the areas he studied in Manchester and elsewhere, he found that black and Asian families, just like white families, move out of the inner city when they have the chance to do so. There are nearly 9,000 electoral wards in England and Wales. In only fourteen of them does a non-white ethnic group account for three-quarters of the population or more. In none does a single ethnic community account for over half of the population.[24]

Worries about multiculturalism used to centre mainly upon race, both in the US and in the UK. Blacks were consistently at the bottom in terms of earnings and social position. A book entitled *American Apartheid* claimed that the level of segregation between white and black was higher in the US than in South Africa, at that time – the late 1980s – still under the apartheid regime.[25] The UK had and has a lower proportion of blacks than the US, but people of African or West Indian descent were mostly firmly rooted at the bottom too.

These difficulties have not gone away, but they have been overshadowed by the new anxieties over Islamic groups referred to earlier. There are people from a diversity of Muslim countries living in the UK. Some do much better than others in terms of criteria of economic success. For instance, those from Malaysia on average do almost as well as indigenous whites in terms of educational success and average earnings.

There are real problems in improving the life-chances of some groups, but these are not where current anxieties are focused, which are concentrated on Islam as a form of religious practice and mode of life. Given the conflicts going on in the wider world, people of Pakistani background find themselves caught up in major clashes. It is awareness of the global struggles involving Islam that stands behind the radicalizing of some Pakistani groups in the UK.

For most migrants there is a sequence in terms of assimilation. First-generation immigrants (from any background) often feel themselves to be not truly part of the society to which they have come. They may not even master the local language. Second-generation immigrants take over English as their first language, but quite often feel torn between two cultures, especially if making progress in the host society is difficult. In many cases, third-generation immigrants manage to get beyond these difficulties, regardless of whether they hang on to pre-existing cultural beliefs and habits.

This sequence has now been broken, at least for some groups.

They might be to all intents and purposes well integrated. It is either the fervour of religious conviction that leads them to alter their world-view, or the conflicts affecting Islamic groups in different parts of the world, or both. After the London bombings, many were shocked that such an act could be carried out by individuals born in this country and apparently well integrated in it. But this pattern in fact fits most second-generation recruits to jihadist terrorism. The majority have actually become born-again Muslims in the West. As Olivier Roy puts it: '[W]e are not dealing with the reaction of a traditional Muslim community, but with a reformulation in religious terms ... of the more general revolt of a generation adrift between its culture of origin and Westernisation.'[26]

Most of the controversies surrounding Islam have a global tinge to them. The debate about the headscarf (hijab) and the full veil (niqab), for example, is going on in dozens of countries across the world, some where there are large Muslim majorities, others (like Japan) where there are hardly any Muslims at all, save for a few recent converts. In many countries, some younger women are wearing the headscarf or full veil where their mothers did not. They may give as their reason not religious tradition, but feminism: the full veil shields women from the sexual gaze of men.

The headscarf debate has serious geopolitical ramifications. In Turkey, for instance, it is the focus of a struggle between those who want to preserve the country's secular traditions (most of whom want Turkey to join the EU) and more traditionalist groups who want to bring Islam into the state sphere – and who oppose Turkey's potential membership. It is difficult to separate religion and culture here. Neither the partial nor the full veil has any direct legitimacy in the Qur'an. It is enjoined upon women only to dress modestly.

No question on religion was included in the census until 2001. The census taken in that year found that there were 1.6 million Muslims living in the UK. Over 70 per cent of the population registered as Christian, compared to 2.7 per cent Muslim, the second largest category. More than 40 per cent of British Muslims are of Pakistani origin; half the South Asian population as a whole were Muslim. The Muslim population has a quite different age distribution from the non-Muslim one: 34 per cent are under the age of

15, compared to 20 per cent for the rest of the population. It is this imbalance that fuels fears of apocalypse among authors such as those discussed earlier. The main outcome, however, is likely to be much more benign – a welcome marginal increase in the birth rate of the country, coupled to continuing integration of people of Muslim background.

To minimize clashes involving religious groups, we have to restrain fundamentalism, which exists in all religions, as well as in other areas of belief and practice. Freedom of speech and action are under threat from other groups besides extremist Muslims – such as radical Christians who attack abortion clinics, or animal rights activists who do the same to scientific establishments.

However, in these religions as in others, it is a truism to say that faith is normally a socially beneficial influence. All the 'world religions' incorporate principles of care for others, especially towards the most deprived. Their stress upon community is a force for cohesion as much as division; all have promoted community welfare. There are certainly more faith-based groups promoting religious tolerance than there are those which foster separation or antagonism, and the large majority of believers tacitly or otherwise support such groups, as well as wanting to be part of the wider society.

Some clear policy conclusions can be drawn.[27] It is in the public interest for the state to support faith groups that endorse the overall values of the society, and which further mutual understanding between faith groups and between faith-based communities and secular organizations. Faith groups that meet such criteria should receive public funding on exactly the same grounds as other third-sector organizations. Faith schools, public and private, should be carefully regulated to ensure that they operate on these principles. In practice, they are expected to teach the national curriculum and also offer places to children outside the faith in question. The evidence shows that faith-based schools more often help to promote social cohesion than undermine it – because they are obliged to relate religious belief to other world-views.

It follows that the state should make life difficult for religious groups that refuse to accommodate to the values of the liberal order, even when their position draws sustenance from the major faiths. Multiculturalism has to turn aggressive at this point. The government's legislation to ban preaching that incites hatred was extremely controversial – some saw it as an attack on free speech as such – but I believe it was correct and necessary. It is right also that religious leaders who are not from the UK should be carefully scrutinized if there is a good chance they will preach in this manner.

The main theorist of citizenship rights, the sociologist T. H. Marshall, thought of such rights in an evolutionary way. The legal rights of individuals were first established in the late eighteenth century, followed at a later point by their political rights, including the universal franchise, and then later still by their economic rights, as developed in the welfare state. Marshall tended to assume that, once they had come into being, all these rights were secure. In fact they remain contested and potentially subject to attack. This is manifestly true of freedom of speech. Protection of freedom of speech has to be asserted all over again in the face of the threat of violence, whether from religious groups or others. A distinction should be made, however, between the right to say or publish something, and whether or not in a particular context it is a responsible action. The Danish newspaper that published cartoons depicting the Prophet Mohammed in an unflattering way had a perfect right to do so. But I don't think it was a responsible action. Hostile feelings toward Muslims were running high in Denmark and the cartoons pandered to established prejudices.

Multiculturalism is an orientation. There will always be controversies around the edges and many of these have to be resolved in a pragmatic way, with solutions differing between countries and communities within them. Should Christmas cards be abolished in favour of greetings cards sent round at Christmas time? The answer is surely 'no', at least in terms of any intervention by the state. But in fact, conventional practice is already changing. Nativity scene cards are far less common than they were even ten years ago; and internet cards, many of which are non-denominational, are replacing orthodox cards, at least among the younger generation.

Gordon Brown lays a wreath as he pays respects at Rajghat, the memorial of Mahatma Gandhi, in New Delhi, India, Thursday, 18 January 2007. Brown was heading a 150-member British trade delegation to India.

8

Shedding the Island Mentality

Jay Leno: You know the world is going crazy when the best rapper is a white guy; the best golfer is a black guy; and Germany doesn't want to go to war.

Jay Leno again: CNN said that after the war, there is a plan to divide Iraq into three parts – regular, premium and unleaded.

No real comment necessary, except to say that the war in Iraq wasn't only about oil. But would it ever have happened if there were no oil in the Middle East?

Being British

How can we renew our national identity if there are divergent views of what it is? Gordon Brown's discussions of the subject are a beginning, but certainly need to be given more substance. The problem for most nations today is finding an identity where the war-like antagonisms that provided common cause in the past have disappeared or shifted their nature. That is precisely why the majority of countries are struggling with identity issues.

In her celebrated studies of the subject, the historian Linda Colley emphasizes that Britishness was forged through opposition to other nations, above all France. Britain went to war with France no fewer than seven times over the period from 1689 to 1815. Almost up to the outbreak of the Great War, many commentators continued to see France as the biggest threat to the UK.

France was an imperial rival, had a larger army than Britain and was a Catholic country. What enabled Britain to be invented as a persuasive identity, and be superimposed on more archaic ones, was unity produced either by war or a state of readiness to fight it, in Europe or in regions of the empire.

Not that people in the eighteenth or nineteenth century thought of things in those terms. It seems that the very term 'national identity' did not come into existence until as late as the 1950s, the time at which Britain had to come to terms with the loss of most of its imperial territories. National identity and nationalism, like religion, with which they have often been connected, are famously Janus-faced. We wouldn't have any of the achievements of the liberal state without them, since national identity is the basis of citizenship and the rights created around it. Yet national identity would seem to be by its very nature exclusionary and, moreover, can lend itself to authoritarianism. The left has mostly been suspicious of nationalism – as it has of religion – seeing it as a force that militates against social justice internally and against international collaboration externally.

If the left is to reappropriate nationalism, its shaping of national identity should meet a number of criteria, which have been well laid out by Bhikhu Parekh.[1] It has to be inclusive in the sense of respecting, up to the limits noted above, prevailing ethnic and cultural differences. It should be continuous with the nation's history but has to project into the future, above all in a period of rapid change such as today. As such, it should incorporate a set of ideals that will inspire loyalty but also motivate. These qualities are what create the community of belonging, not the other way around. A national community differs from others because of its identity; it is not actually founded upon difference. Hence it is entirely possible and normal for a national community to share many common traits with others.

The state always plays a part in moulding national identity. But forging a common identity also demands the involvement of the population as a whole. Where elites have attempted to impose identity, as in post-colonial regimes in Africa, the result has been state-nations rather than nation-states – with an overall sense of emotional commitment to the nation missing.

Because of the left's problems with nationalism and with sovereignty, the political right has long held a stranglehold over the issue. The rightist view of Britain's identity has been highly consequential, since it has helped shape the UK's fractious relations with the EU. Enoch Powell articulated the ideas that impressed Mrs Thatcher and, even more, the Tory far right. Powell's views drew upon the basic idea of Britain as an 'island nation', separated from its Continental neighbours. For centuries, Britain faced away from the Continent and towards its dominions overseas. British identity is bound up with the sovereignty of Parliament – its independence goes along with British independence. Britain is a society that has cherished the rights of the individual, but has a strong sense of 'we-ness' that comes from its island history.

Powell's idea of British identity led him to reject devolution of government to Scotland and Wales, since it would reduce the sovereignty of Parliament. The welfare state was corrupting, since it was not compatible with British individualism. Powell's notorious 'rivers of blood' speech argued that the British should never accept immigrants from poorer nations, who should be repatriated or have their rights reduced.[2] He did not believe there should be a close relationship with the US either; the two nations have different trajectories.

Most of these ideas reappear in the speeches of subsequent Tory leaders. Mrs Thatcher's views were certainly more restrained than those of Powell. She, of course, favoured the transatlantic relationship. Early on, she was more sympathetic to the EU and played a basic role in integrating the UK more firmly within it. However, she insisted that the national character of Britain is 'quite different from the characters of people on the Continent' and she asserted that the nation 'bears little resemblance to the rest of Europe'.[3]

In 1998 these themes were picked up by William Hague. His speech was a riposte to Labour's third way, and featured instead 'the British way'.[4] He spoke firmly in the Powellite tradition: British identity is bound up with its separation from other nations and with its parliamentary sovereignty; the ethic of individualism and enterprise that characterizes the country is many centuries old; in contrast to many of its Continental counterparts, but in common with the US, the UK has been free from invasion and external conquest; a closer involvement with the EU would threaten British identity because it would reduce our sovereignty; unlike some of the major Continental countries, Britain is not a federal nation and should not become one: it is a country of 'neighbourhoods', not regions, and one of local loyalties. Hague does differ from Powell and Thatcher, however, in stressing that Britain is an open and mobile society, which should find a place for people from many backgrounds.

For a couple of decades, up to somewhere in the mid-1990s, such views of national identity also commanded the support of large numbers of the electorate. They no longer do so, as surveys show. Cameron has not yet elaborated an idea of what should replace them from a Conservative point of view. Britain has become a more cosmopolitan country in terms of attitudes and composition, so this shift is hardly surprising. The rightist view meets few of the criteria mentioned earlier; it is historically highly questionable and society is changing so rapidly that some of the core ideas are obsolete. It is true that there is a long tradition of British individualism, possibly going back as far as the twelfth century.[5] It is indeed intertwined with some positive features of British life, including the protection of personal liberties and a robust tradition of civil law. Yet no nation could be built only on the basis of individualism, and there are just as many traditions of solidarity and care for others, having religious as well as secular roots.

Colley and others have stressed the closeness of Britain's European connections. The metaphor of the island nation is a misleading or false one. In the past, the quickest mode of communication and transportation was by sea. Rather than being a force for separation, the sea between us and the Continent was a means of close connection. For hundreds of years, the ruling class – the aristocracy – treated the Channel as no boundary at all, since their possessions were scattered widely.

Building a more relevant and well-grounded interpretation of British identity is relevant at this point for several reasons. The version just discussed has helped feed a defensive and isolationist view of the world, appropriated in its more extreme versions by the far right. The Union Jack should be a respected symbol of the national community, not one taken over by a small minority, and not a cover for a reactionary form of nationalism either. National identity is perhaps the one area where Labour's rethinking has not managed sufficiently to dent the preconceived ideas of the right, since the effort to promote Cool Britannia petered out. Our relationship to the rest of Europe is largely shaped by what we think of ourselves, and attitudes towards the EU are likely to shift if a new conception of national identity can be found. A forward-looking identity, widely accepted, is likely to prove crucial to generating the dynamic attitudes Britain needs for economic success and political influence in the global age. Finally, a new notion of identity will be central to making Britain's new-found diversity a force for the good.

Gordon Brown is quite right to be thinking in terms of symbols and ceremonies, since both have a unifying quality. It is also right to ground these in British traditions of freedom and tolerance, seeing these as values to defend in the here and now, and for the future. We should emphasize Britain's global heritage, so relevant to the world we live in now. Of course we should not forget its seamy side – for example, the fact that citizenship was denied to most of the subject peoples in the Empire. Yet Britain has long been open to the world, economically, politically and culturally. Some of the symbols of Britishness actually express our cosmopolitan past, such as our fondness for tea.

No country is sovereign in the way it might have been in the past. Many of the opportunities open to the UK, and the problems with which it must deal, cross-cut sovereign power: economic development, climate change, terrorism, migration – the list is almost endless. We have to give serious attention to what sovereignty can mean in such a world. Is it best preserved by clinging to the idea that we can somehow resolve most of these issues in national terms? Or would we be far better served by consistent collaboration with other nations, inside the EU and in other parts of the world? The answer is the second of these options. We should regard our membership of the European Union as adding to our sovereignty rather than detracting from it. I call this 'sovereignty plus': we get more influence over our own fate, and over the rest of the world, from being part of the EU than we would ever get if left to our own devices.

What about our relationship to the US? How important should it be in specifying our national identity? In my view it cannot be a defining feature, or if it is so, it is bound to be very largely a one-sided one. The conditions that underpinned the 'special relationship' are fast unravelling. When it was an imperial nation, Britain was a world power more or less on a par with the US. Today it is a large economy in world terms, but is a nation of sixty million people in a world of six billion. The US looks towards Asia, the Middle East and Latin America as much as it does Europe, much less specifically to Britain. There are clear linguistic and ideological affinities, but English is now in fact becoming the global language, spoken increasingly by the younger generation everywhere. The Anglo-Saxon emphasis of the US and its leadership is becoming more and more diluted, while the ethnic diversity of the US is growing. While we must seek to sustain a close connection with the US, this should depend in the future for Labour upon what type of government is in power there.

Britain is a country that cannot even decide what it is called. Is it 'Britain' or 'Great Britain'? Or is it 'the UK'? I have used 'Britain' and 'the UK' synonymously in this book, but a distinction is sometimes drawn between them – 'the UK' is said to include Northern Ireland, whereas 'Britain' does not. Surely, at least, the term 'Great Britain' should be forgotten, since it is a relic of the imperial past? Well, yes – but the term 'GB' is still widely in favour, and is used on number-plates when the British travel abroad. In addition, 'England' is often used interchangeably with 'Britain', though today only by those actually living in England.

Such an ambiguous and complicated way of referring to ourselves: is it a source of weakness, because we haven't seriously defined who we are? One could say, rather, potentially at least, that it is it more a source of strength. Flexibility is the name of the game today, as is multiple identity. An identity that is narrowly and dogmatically defined would prove a handicap. To be British is an inclusive identity. More than 80 per cent of members of ethnic minorities in the country as a whole are happy to be 'British'; fewer than 40 per cent regard themselves as 'English'.

Is Britain really a country of neighbourhoods and localities, apart from its controlling centre in London? It is not. The country includes three nations. It boasts a range of major cities, all of which have direct relations with the global economy. It is true that the regions in England do not have strong identities, with one or two partial exceptions. Yet the experience of other countries – such as Spain – shows that regional identities can be created and that they have important contributions to make. Regional identity can be crucial in attracting inward investment, in tackling problems that cross-cut localities and in providing the dynamism needed to succeed in the global economy.

The year 2007 marks the 300th anniversary of the union of Scotland with England and Wales, followed later by Ireland. The English are by far the dominant group demographically, at 50 million people. Scotland has a population of just over 5 million, Wales 2.9 million and Northern Ireland 1.7 million. The anniversary of the union coincides with a time in which the forces of separatism seem to be on the march, not only in Scotland and to a lesser degree in Wales, but also in England. Polls show the Scottish nationalist party ahead of the other two main parties as the elections in May approach. Some Tories have mooted the idea of a separate English parliament, although this is not official party policy. The Campaign for an English Parliament is running a cogent and well thought-through website to help secure its goal. Scotland and Wales have parliamentary assemblies, and one has been offered to Northern Ireland. The Campaign seeks the creation of a parliament in England based on the Scottish model, with power devolved to the body from the UK Parliament.

A BBC poll taken just before the anniversary of the union, on 16 January 2007, found that 61 per cent of people in England, 51 per cent in Scotland and 48 per cent in Wales supported the creation of an English parliament.[6] Blair has spoken out against the idea as strongly as Brown has against Scottish separatism, dismissing it as 'completely unworkable and unnecessary'.[7] In attacking the Scottish nationalists, they have both tended to concentrate upon why separatism is a bad idea, rather than upon why the union is a good thing. It would mean, they have suggested, that millions of Scots would be threatened with alien status, immigration controls, accompanied by a collapse in business confidence.

They haven't been so clear about why it is important for the UK to stay together as a unitary state. I believe it is indeed important. The UK is a cosmopolitan nation, with high levels of tolerance. A split into the separate nations would cut across this principle, since there would almost certainly be a surge of nationalist sentiment in each of them. Three smaller countries would undoubtedly not have the influence that Britain has.

Britain needs to change its image in the world, Brown says. The rightist view defines Britain mainly in terms of its past; and this is the idea many people overseas have of the country. It is not seen as a place of innovation and of new ideas, but rather as a fusty mix of royalty, beefeaters and ancient traditions. Tony Blair tried to correct these prejudices in speaking of Britain as a 'young country', but rebranding will not work on its own. To change the image of Britain we have to change the country itself.

The Question of Europe

The EU remains a difficult issue for the Tories, and will be so whatever standpoint Cameron ultimately adopts. In fact, the party risks being split over it in a way that Labour – at this point in its history at any rate – does not. Could the EU for the first time become a real source of strength for Labour? I was on a panel recently discussing the issue with a prominent journalist. She pooh-poohed the notion, saying simply that the EU is a 'toxic issue' for the British – with the implication: all parties, keep away! I didn't agree then and I don't agree now. Only in conjunction with the rest of the Union does the UK have a chance of making a serious impact on climate change, energy security and control of international crime and immigration.

The 2006 Labour Party Conference was a very important one, and coincided with a time at which there seemed to be a coup forming against Blair and in favour of Brown. Many issues were discussed, but the EU got little mention. Giving his last conference speech as party leader, Tony Blair affirmed his commitment to Europe, but almost in passing. Gordon Brown made no reference to Europe at all in what was at that point the most important speech of his career so far. Both main parties seem content at the moment to downplay Britain's EU involvement. Yet EU membership is one of the core features of this country.

For the past year and a half I have been taking part in a project on the future of the EU, concentrating especially on the 'social model' – Europe's systems of social protection and welfare. Together with colleagues from Policy Network, I have met with many different EU leaders and those around them. A substantial group of academic colleagues from around Europe were also involved.[8] The experience has brought home to me forcefully how different Britain is from most – well, actually, all – other EU countries that I visited during the course of it. If you are working on 'Europe' in Britain, you are outside the mainstream of policy-making.

During his ten years of power, Blair has not managed to change this very much. There are two main areas where he has made a strong and practical impact on the European scene. The British played a significant role in creating the Lisbon Agenda, initiated in 2000, concerned with improving Europe's competitiveness in the global marketplace. It has proved hard to implement, but has provided goals that have commanded general agreement. Blair also took the lead in arguing for improved EU military capability, especially in the creation of a force capable of rapid deployment in trouble-spots. Blair signed up to the constitution. But it was clear that he felt relieved when French and Dutch voters said 'no'. He called for a referendum in Britain not for democratic reasons, but to defuse the issue during the last general election. In other European capitals he was seen as sacrificing principle for expediency.

Blair has given his best speeches about the EU late on in his premiership. The most effective was one delivered in the European Parliament in June 2005, concerned with how the EU should react to the demise of the constitution. It is Blair's only speech on the EU that really struck a chord in other EU countries. He declared himself firmly pro-European, but argued that greater innovation and change are necessary if the European social model is to survive and prosper. The reasons for the rejection of the constitution were not primarily to do with the document itself. Rather, the referenda in France and The Netherlands provided a vehicle for the expression of much wider discontents about unemployment, job security, living standards and migration. Without social and economic reform, much of which has to be at the national level, there isn't much chance of further European integration.

Yet in this speech, as in his others, Blair avoided spelling out what, in his eyes, the future of the EU should be and Britain's place in it. So too has every other top Labour figure. We all know what the Labour leadership thinks the EU should *not* be: an integrated system with too much power taken away from member states. But is the EU in Blair's eyes a political project at all – and if so, what kind?

Gordon Brown has done something Blair has not – he has published a pamphlet on the EU, entitled *Global Europe*.[9] The Treasury has also produced a longer document on the problems of, and possibilities for, the EU upon which Brown's pamphlet drew. The focus of the EU, Brown says, has been inward- rather than outward-looking. The EU must 'reach out to the rest of the world', upgrade skills, technology and education and achieve greater flexibility in labour, capital and product markets. One of the odd things about the work is that it is written almost as if no one had thought of these points before. Most of the ideas suggested by Brown are actually in the Lisbon Agenda. In his 2005 European Parliament speech, Blair put things more succinctly. What we must do, he said, is simple: implement that agenda.

Brown's pamphlet met with a critical reception in other EU countries. In France, for instance, Zaki Laïdi, a prominent political commentator, wrote that 'according to Gordon Brown there is no point in the existence of the EU'.[10] Brown's economic formulae, he pointed out, could be applied by nations regardless of whether the EU existed or not. Brown is widely thought to be more sceptical about the EU than Blair. If and when he becomes leader, should those of us who believe that the EU is essential to Britain's future abandon all hope? I don't think so. Being outside the euro is not the barrier to a British voice in Europe it once was. Europe's elites have had to accept that the euro is only a partial success. It has not helped to generate the return to growth that its proponents hoped for.

Even more important, given the range of the EU's problems, it isn't possible to be naively pro-European any longer. A 'critical pro-Europeanism' can resonate more closely with British euro-scepticism, at least of the more reasoned kind. We need a new account of the benefits the EU can bring to Britain, but one that connects with the changed agenda emerging in domestic politics.[11]

If it is to deliver sovereignty plus, the EU has to be a political project, not just an economic one. But what kind of political project? There is a major opportunity for Britain here. 'Federalism', in the peculiar sense that term has acquired when Europe is discussed, is dead. There is no chance that the EU will become a super-state. However it is, and has to be, more than a sort of regional UN, a loose collection of formally independent nations. The nature of the EU will be defined by certain basic decisions taken by member states over the next few years, including the ticklish question of its limits. Where are the EU borders to be? My own answer would be that Turkey and the Balkan states should be given the opportunity to join, as the EU has in principle already agreed, assuming that they have made the necessary changes (quite a big 'if' as things stand at the moment), but after that, 'full stop': no further full members to the East, whatever special privileges might be offered to countries such as Ukraine, Georgia, Moldova or the states of North Africa.

In spite of the German Chancellor, Mrs Merkel's, attempts to revive it, the constitution will probably have to be abandoned for the immediate future, but some of its prescriptions will have to be enacted if the EU is going to deliver on sovereignty plus. There should be a single EU foreign minister instead of a job divided in two, as is the case at the moment. The proposal in the constitution to have an elected president of the European council, serving for a term of at least two years, should be endorsed. The current six-month rotating presidency is a recipe for lack of continuity in decision-making and the rule of inertia. Difficult though the issue is in the context of British politics, there has to be more majority voting on the council, and more effective rules for reaching decisions than those inherited from the Nice agreements of a few years ago. If Gordon Brown does not agree with these points, he will have to say why, since other European leaders will press for them.

173

Foreign Policy

Foreign policy will be crucial for the fate of the next Labour leader, but it is far too large an area for me to discuss in great detail here. Tony Blair built much of his foreign relations strategy upon the idea that Britain could be a bridge between the US and Europe. During the Clinton days it stood him in good stead – and was manifest in the close personal ties established during the progressive governance meetings. I had the chance to see it all at close hand.

At the turn of the century, thirteen out of the fifteen EU countries were governed by centre-left parties or coalitions, in addition to the US and Canada. When Bill Clinton and the Canadian Prime Minister Jean Chrétien came to the gatherings in Florence, Berlin and Stockholm, for instance, they could meet virtually all of Europe's leaders. The very meetings, as it were, were a bridge between North America and Europe.

I remember vividly how different the French leader Mr Jospin was from the others. He was ambivalent about going in the first place, since he saw himself as much truer to the traditions of the left than the rest of the participants. On the one or two occasions he attended, he would stand in a corner of the room by himself, talking to his aides. And he was distinctly underwhelmed by Clinton. The American Democrats have in fact never been part of the Socialist International, to which most social democratic parties in the world belong, since they are not regarded by the more doctrinaire parties as qualified to be in the club.

What worked well when the centre-left was dominant in North America and Europe later came under strain. There was a Republican president in the White House and the right took over in a number of European countries. According to the British ambassador to Washington, Christopher Meyer, he had instructions from Tony Blair's Chief of Staff, Jonathan Powell, after the election of George W. Bush to 'get up the arse of the Americans and stay there'.[12] If that was in fact said, it was a crude metaphor for a policy that – if I can put it that way – backfired badly.

I have been a consistent supporter of Tony Blair and still regard him as an outstanding leader. But I don't understand why, to change the metaphor, he put all his eggs in the Bush basket. Blair has consistently supported multilateralism in world affairs, and made this perfectly clear in his speeches. Yet the Bush Administration announced from the beginning that it was not going to hold to some of the main international agreements. The new US National Security Doctrine explicitly argued that America's interests should be put ahead of all other considerations. Condoleezza Rice, Bush's National Security Advisor (later Secretary of State), spoke derisorily of 'the illusory international community'. The Bushites rarely missed an opportunity to run down the UN. All of this happened well before 9:11.

By redefining international relations as a house of power, with the US at the head, the Bush government undermined the work of several decades in the international system. The Americans previously had usually been in the lead in declaring the need for international cooperation and following it up with institution-building. In 2002, the distinguished expert on international relations, John Ikenberry, wrote that Bush's doctrines form a vision 'in which the United states arrogates to itself the global role of setting standards, determining threats, and using force. These radical ideas could transform today's world order in a way that the end of the Cold War did not. The administration's approach is fraught with peril and likely to fail. If history is any guide, it will trigger resistance that will leave America in a more hostile and divided world.'[13] As they say in religious texts, and so it came to pass.

Britain couldn't be a bridge between the US and Europe when Europe was so divided about Iraq; consequently, it was at most a conduit between those countries that supported the war and the Americans. I don't think it was in fact ever the right approach, even when the Democrats held the presidency in the US.[14] It implies yet again that Britain isn't really part of Europe. You can't be a bridge to somewhere you already are. Tony Blair continues to speak in the same vein even today. In a speech on defence given in January 2007, he said that British foreign policy 'has as its foundation, two alliances, with America on the one hand and Europe on the other'.[15] To me, it is an extraordinary way to put it, making clear how distant 'Europe' is. Are we

Europeans or not? While the special relationship isn't wholly a myth, no single member state can or should be the main channel of EU–US relations.

The time when people used to think the US could build a new world empire is over. After nearly two terms of George W. Bush's government, the influence of the US has actively shrunk. It may be easily the world's pre-eminent military power, but the adventures in Afghanistan and Iraq have made it plain how limited the practical use of such power really is. The jihadists claimed victory over the Russians in Afghanistan, and they will do the same when the US pulls out of Iraq. The world's mightiest army has proved quite unable to deal with local armed insurrection. In the meantime, just as Ikenberry predicted, American prestige around the world is the lowest it has been for decades.

The war has also been enormously expensive for the US. The direct cost to the American tax-payer, as of spring 2006, stood at $400 billion, and there is much more to be paid out, whatever happens.[16] Even given the size of the US economy, this represents big money. Combined with tax cuts, it has helped produce the record budget deficit that America now has. (Before Clinton left office, the budget was in surplus. He wanted to spend most of this on improved welfare measures, but was blocked by the Republican Congress.)

The decline of American power and influence could have far-reaching implications for the foreign policy arena. Those who wanted a more multi-polar world may be getting their wish, or something close to it. The outcome for the world, however, could be uncomfortable and dangerous, especially since it coincides with a marked loss of the authority of the UN. It means the UK should work hard to promote a return to multilateralism, hopefully in the near future together with an America recommitted to the same ideal.

What should Gordon Brown do? Concretely, he must make plain his intention to take the British troops out of Iraq, and in the relatively short term. However, it has to be done with due sensitivity to the troops there and to the local situation when they leave. The British troops in the south have done a good job in very difficult circumstances, even if no one any longer boasts how much better we handle being an occupying power than the Americans. Brown has to find ways of proposing how the Iraq situation should be handled internationally. Neighbouring Middle Eastern countries will have to be involved, as the Baker Report in the US suggested.[17] Brown must distance himself from the current American administration, even though he will have to work with it for a while. He can do so without sacrificing a wider Atlanticism. The Democrats, after all, control the Congress. He should substitute a different approach on terror, emphasizing far more the need to win over hearts and minds. This approach is entirely consistent with recognizing the dangers that international terrorism continues to pose.

What should we put in place of the War on Terror? This seems a simple question, but demands a complex answer.

1 International terrorism, as I have emphasized earlier, is a real threat. It is not purveying a politics of fear to say so. Those who declare that it is all overblown are wrong. Everyone has their favourite risk, as it were, that they like to say is exaggerated. For some – usually on the political left – it is jihadist terrorism. For others, mostly on the right, it is global warming. For yet others, it might be avian flu. The truth is that they are all real, and in each case it isn't easy to calculate what the actual level of risk is. These situations aren't like the ones that insurance companies deal with, where risk can be calculated on the basis of a long series. An insurance actuary could tell you what the risk is that you will die in an accident in your own home. He or she couldn't tell you what the risk is that you will die in a terrorist incident. International terrorism is an example of what in the risk trade they call low-probability high-consequence risks. They are very difficult to manage. There will always be people who say they are not risks at all. Yet since the consequences can be catastrophic, such risks must be managed and defended against.

2 International terrorism involves widespread networks of activists, usually deploying modern high-tech communications to organize themselves. Yet such groups still normally need a base, inside one state or another. That is why military

options can still be relevant in countering them. It was the right decision to intervene in Afghanistan, although there was a failure to marshal the resources needed to stand a chance of pacifying the country. However, in the vast majority of cases diplomatic pressure has to be used, as in the case of Pakistan.

3 Development projects that help lower unemployment, especially of young men, and which improve conditions of life more generally in poorer countries are important in reducing the threat of terrorism. Yet we must recognize that terrorism is not just the outcome of poverty. Jihadist movements are driven by religious conviction and/or may have geopolitical objectives.

4 The risk of a serious terrorist incident in the UK is not just the result of foreign policy in Iraq, or closeness to the Americans. It will not go away if either or both of these change. It is not even true that religious fundamentalism is the only source of terrorist threats. Timothy McVeigh, who planted a bomb in Oklahoma City that killed nearly two hundred people, was a member of a far right group. Partly as a result of the internet, both the materials and the know-how needed to make destructive weapons are now readily available.

5 The worst-case possibility as far as terrorism is concerned is that a group may acquire a nuclear weapon. A large amount of nuclear material has gone missing in recent years, especially from the ex-Soviet Union. No one knows where it is. A state with nuclear capability might decide to give help to a terrorist organization. The struggle to prevent nuclear proliferation, trace missing nuclear materials and hold the line on chemical and biological weapons is therefore directly relevant to containing risk.

6 Britain should upgrade its capacity to deal with potentially cataclysmic risks in general. They come from different sources, but the results, should things go wrong, can overlap quite a bit. All might cause mass panic; city centres might need to be speedily evacuated; the capability of rescue services might become overloaded; hospitals might be swamped; communications might be disrupted. Some forms of preparation can cover many or most potential disaster situations.

7 International collaboration in passing on information, surveillance and so forth will be essential. As discussed earlier,
there must be a compromise between liberty and security in
the case of international terrorism. To some degree this theorem applies to other risk situations too.

Simple nostrums must be avoided. One of the most damaging
was the Manchian idea of the Axis of Evil. Yet George W. Bush still
seems to believe in it, and in its dog days the Bush Administration
might decide to bomb the nuclear installations in Iran. The Israeli
leadership could opt to do so before a new American President
comes on the scene. Such an action would provide Brown with his
first major foreign policy decision. Should he condemn such an
attack if it comes? In my view he certainly should.

The broader issue of containing nuclear proliferation will
remain, as will the difficult question of the obvious hypocrisy of
the existing nuclear states. After all, Brown has stated his support
for renewing Trident. If possession of nuclear weapons makes us
safer, why shouldn't this apply to other nations too? Britain at present is not even committed to a 'no first use' policy. In practice, the
decision to renew Trident has mixed motives: Labour's desire not
to appear weak on defence or be outflanked by the Tories; the
wish to avoid a situation where France would be the only nuclear
power in Europe; and the belief that being a nuclear state carries
extra clout in world affairs.

We have now come well beyond the debate that the American
author Robert Kagan unleashed in 2002, with his discussion of
'power' and 'weakness'.[18] Kagan ruffled more than a few feathers
in Europe with his thesis that the Europeans are from Venus, the
Americans from Mars. The US possesses the use of force and can
get its way for this reason; the Europeans have to use the feminine
arts of persuasion and negotiation. How outdated this view seems
already!

The Iraq war and its aftermath has actually been a humbling
experience for both sides in Kagan's equation. The next few years
could be difficult ones for the world community. The chaos in Iraq
and Afghanistan has quietened those who believed that military
intervention could be used to reshape world danger spots. But

negotiation and multilateralism are not always effective against nations firmly bent upon a given course of action, as has been seen in the case of Iran. There is a lot of rethinking to do.

The idea of multilateralism could do with closer scrutiny, given the casual way in which it is often used. So also could its nominal opposite, unilateralism. Not much is done unilaterally in a pure sense of that term. The US in Iraq, for example, did not act on its own, but with the active support of a range of governments, whether they contributed troops or not. 'Coalitions of the willing' will be needed to tackle quite a few of the world's problems in the future, since there will be many situations where there will not be a sufficient consensus among the generality of nations for action. The military intervention in Kosovo, which won widespread support, was one such coalition.

A disposition towards negotiation, collaboration and respect for international law are not, as Kagan said in his Nietzschean way, signs of weakness. On the contrary, they are forms of power, and more influential in the longer run than the use of force. Yet he was right in his assessment that multilateral approaches without military backing may be ignored by those at whom they are aimed. We should adopt a stance of what I would call assertive multilateralism – recognizing the key importance of international collaboration, but accepting also that the use of force may be needed to back it up. Britain should continue to press for greater military capability for the European Union. Progress has been made. As of 2003–4, about 70,000 EU troops, excluding those involved with NATO, were capable of being deployed as a rapid reaction force.

The UK should continue to support reform of the UN Security Council and G8, difficult though each has been to make progress with. The Security Council still reflects the world of 1945, more than sixty years later. India, Japan and Brazil all have claims to permanent seats, but no consensus has been reached. Neither China nor India is part of G8, which should become G10.

There are two areas where Gordon Brown has a respected presence on the world scene – one is in relationship to poverty in Africa, the other his influence in world economic councils, as one of the longest-serving finance ministers. The second is one main area where he could assert an immediate impact as Prime Minister, since he has already played a part in the debate about reform of global economic governance.

Like the UN, the two main world economic institutions, the World Bank and IMF, have seen their influence decline. Capital is widely available in financial markets without the same conditionality as the Bank and the IMF apply. Because of perceived failures of the IMF regime of lending, countries in Latin America and Asia have turned away from it. Although the World Bank and IMF have changed their roles over the years, the only major institutional reform over the past century has been the creation of the WTO – and even that grew out of GATT. There have been many ambitious proposals – for example the establishing of an Economic Security Council, or Global Competition Authority, but none has come to fruition. In this situation, clear dangers are a return to economic nationalism and/or the separation of the globe into different regions, the economic version of a multi-polar world.[19]

Energy security is one of the main factors driving nationalism, both among countries that are energy-rich and among those scrabbling for supply. Russia is a prime example of the first of these, reasserting itself in world affairs on the launch-pad of high energy prices. Mr Putin's idea of 'sovereign democracy' in Russia is far more about sovereignty than it is about democracy. Russia is selling nuclear materials to Iran, an assertion of its independence from the larger world community; and has pressurized the Shell Oil Company into forfeiting its control of the oil and gas development at Sakhalin, in Eastern Siberia. China is a state very much in the second category, searching for supplies to fuel its rapidly growing economy. The geopolitical ramifications are considerable. For example, China is very unlikely to agree to support international sanctions against Iran to block that country's pursuit of nuclear capability, since Iran is a major supplier of its oil.

Regionalism is also emerging as an important force in world society. In the field of trade, more regional agreements have been made since 1995 than in the previous half century. The case of the EU is the most striking and developed, but analogues exist in Latin America, Africa and, above all, Asia. The Asian crisis of 1997–8 was the stimulus to regional monetary and financial agreements negotiated by the East Asian countries with one another. At the same time, four Asian countries – India, Pakistan, China and, most latterly, North Korea – have become nuclear states. They could be followed by Japan if Iran acquires nuclear weaponry, and perhaps also South Korea. Economic cooperation might help to reduce the enormous dangers such a situation would bring, but major tensions are also possible, not only between India and Pakistan, or North and South Korea, but also between China and Japan.

Central Asia is becoming an area of great strategic significance, after spending centuries in relative obscurity in global terms. In 1994 Russia and China got together with three central Asian republics, Kazakhstan, Kyrgyzstan and Tajikistan, to form the Shanghai Five.[20] They demilitarized their thousands of miles of common borders and signed trade agreements. Uzbekistan joined in 2001 and the group became the Shanghai Cooperation Organization. It now has a permanent administration in Moscow, and has developed further mutual agreements, and could in the future be either a worthwhile partner for, or, more ominously, a rival to, NATO. India, Iran, Mongolia and Pakistan have joined as observers. Should they at some point be full members, the group would include four nuclear states, massive natural resources and a combined population of some two and a half billion people. No wonder the EU, the US and Japan are deeply worried.

Regionalism can undermine global governance, but it doesn't have to be that way. Appropriately cultivated, it could contribute to producing more effective global institutions. The EU is the leading champion of binding rules of multilateral governance, which have clear advantages in principle for nations as well as for regions.[21] Since global interdependence cross-cuts all nations and regions, it is generally to the advantage of everyone if there are clear rules and means of settling disputes, in trade as in other areas. Global institutions offer all countries, large and small, the possibility of influencing the shape of world development. They are themselves a form of capital, because they cut costs by allowing actors to follow established rules, rather than having to negotiate solutions each time an interchange is made.

It is clear enough that G8 is not able to provide the economic governance that it might have done in a simpler global trading and power system than the one we have today. Brown has spoken extensively about the economic challenges created by the rise of China and India, but the strategic implications are at least as large. On all of these issues it is hard to see Britain getting far without the EU, and the same is true of other pressing international questions, such as making headway with the deteriorating situation in Gaza and the Occupied Territories. It is even more obviously true with problem areas within Europe itself, such as the Balkans, where there is no hope of stability without the continuing direct involvement of the EU and the eventual possibility of EU membership.

Tony Blair speaks at a news conference on the last day of campaigning before the General Election, London, Wednesday, 4 May 2005. Blair was joined on stage by members of his cabinet, at front from left, Jack Straw, John Prescott, Gordon Brown and Margaret Beckett.

9

How to Build a
Progressive Consensus

A platoon of British soldiers is wending its way through the jungle, when suddenly they come to a large river full of man-eating crocodiles. The platoon commander asks for a volunteer to swim across with a rope so everyone else could get safely to the other side. For a while everyone is silent. Then a skinny Scot pipes up and says he'll do it. He gets into the water and reaches the other side completely unharmed. The commander calls across to him, 'That's amazing, how did you manage it?' In response, the Scot strips off his shirt. Across his chest there is a large tattoo, proclaiming: 'Glasgie – the fairest city in the whole wide world.' And he says: 'Nae crocodile would ever swallow that!'

Good slogans can have a lot of persuasive power, but it is the reality behind them that counts. Politicians please listen!

We live today in a world of instantaneous communication, in which the internet and other communications media have revolutionized many aspects of our lives. They form a crucial part of what globalization actually means, as well as being deeply involved in its expansion. There is no doubt that the internet will in fact have a big role in elections from hereon in. The internet, blogging and YouTube shaped much of the recent mid-term American elections. They have not, of course replaced the ortho-dox media: they intertwine with television, radio and the press.
The internet reflects, as the same time as it furthers, major

changes in social life and the very nature of politics. It is quite often said that our society is becoming less and less democratic, and that this process is expressed in political apathy and disengagement. I would turn this argument on its head. Democracy for the first time has been reaching deep into the heart of our lives, because information control has passed out of the hands of elites. I call this process 'everyday democratization', and it is expressed also in day-to-day freedom of choice, the capacity to travel and open access to a diversity of media.

Everyday democratization produces voter dealignment – parties can count less and less on automatic voting support from their followers. More important, the act of voting itself becomes conditional, no longer the core component of citizenship it used to be, and I do not see any chance of this situation reversing itself. It follows that a low election turnout, especially in a first-past-the-post system, does not necessarily signal dissatisfaction with a government. In the last national election, voters basically got the outcome they wished. They didn't want the conservatives back in government, and they weren't about to turn to the Liberal Democrats. Perhaps *faute de mieux*, voters (and non-voters) wanted Labour to stay in power, but with a reduced majority – and that's what they got.

Voters may be more dismissive of politicians than they were a generation ago, although the evidence about this is far from conclusive. I would say that citizens are on average more rational and calculative than once they were, as both cause and consequence of the retreat of tribal political affiliations. It won't in fact be until the next national election that we will be able to speak of a trend towards a pronounced decline in levels of voting in the UK. Such a decline might continue, but nobody really knows. The turnout could very well climb again next time, given that the parties all have new leaders and will have new programmes – and everyone will be aware that the outcome could be very close.

Recent work has shown that the expressed level of interest of the public in politics has not changed over the past thirty years. About one-third of people say they have 'a great deal' or 'quite a lot' of interest in politics; some two-thirds say they have at least some political interest. These figures tend to rise during an election year. The figure of 71 per cent interest for 2005 was in fact the highest since 1974.[1] It is not easy to say what accounts for the discrepancy between people's continuing interest in politics and falling voting levels. One can say with confidence that it is not just a British phenomenon, and that therefore any explanation or suggested remedies that depend too much upon factors specific to this country will not be convincing. The 'vanishing voter' is doing the same disappearing trick in many of the developed countries, although with considerable variations.

That non-voting is not always an expression of political disinterest is shown by intensive research done after the 2000 US presidential election. The outcome of that election hung on a few hundred votes in Florida. There was widespread regret among those who had not voted. A poll taken by CNN showed that over 50 per cent of them wished in retrospect that they had.[2]

There is an obvious paradox here. Participation appears to be falling in the countries with established democracies. Yet democracy is one of the world's success stories over the last several decades. Most military dictatorships have disappeared. There are something like four times as many democracies today as there were four decades ago, even using strict criteria of what counts as a democracy.

What explains such a paradox? I would say that the same factor that accounts for the spread of democracy also explains its travails in its heartlands – the global role of the media and information technology. We live today in a world information society, from which few, rich or poor, are excluded. Dictatorships thrive upon secrecy and information-control, which are much harder to achieve than in the past. At the same time as authoritarian regimes diminish, or have to adjust the basis of their rule, democratic institutions come under strain where they are well established.

The communications media have a dual role in relation to democracy. On the one hand, the easy availability of information opens up new possibilities for effective discussion of public issues. On the other, the media tend to close down the very space they have opened up by relentless focus on personalities, negative reporting and trivialization of difficult issues. It is not a question of blaming individuals in the media industries. The problem is more structural. We know that people have not lost faith in democracy as such. Well over 90 per cent of respondents in surveys in all the advanced countries see democracy as the only system they want to live under.

Democracy, it has been said, is like sex. When it's good it's very good; and when it's bad it's still pretty good. Yet the nature of democracy and people's expectations of it have clearly changed. We live for better or for worse in a media democracy. The media are no longer just the messengers; they set much of the tone in which public debate is carried on and political consciousness formed. A politician may feel obliged to respond to a request from the *Today* programme as a matter of greater urgency than whatever he or she might say in Parliament. The presenters sound affronted when a political leader declines to appear on the show, as if it is a failure of the democratic process.

However, it is highly important to recognize that the media themselves, printed and electronic, are changing, and possibly changing quite radically, in line with the process of everyday democratization. Via emails, quite often discussed on the programme as it goes along, the *Today* presenters and their guests interact in a regular way with the listeners. And this practice is being echoed in media programming throughout the world.

It is worth remembering how extremely recent all of this is. In 1998, shortly after Tony Blair had come to power, I gave the BBC Reith Lectures. To find a new format for them, I gave three of the five in different cities abroad. One was in Delhi, one in Hong Kong, another in Washington, with the remaining two in London. In each place there was a discussion with an invited studio audience, which was broadcast along with the programme. It was only the second occasion in their history that the lectures had had a studio debate, and the first time that an international audience had been involved.

We also organized a global internet debate around the lectures. The subject was globalization and I wanted the internet audience to be an example of what the lectures were about. Questions and comments from the internet audience were fed into the debates going on in the studio after each of the lectures. What was remarkable – in terms of how things have progressed since – is that the BBC website had only just been set up by then, and was still regarded by many in the organization as an esoteric experiment. Change since then has been amazingly rapid, with 70 per cent of the British population now using the internet at least once a month or more.

We live in a much more reflexive world than previous generations, where in one way or another we are, as it were, forced to interrogate our own lives, almost on a day-to-day basis. The media are changing in line with these transitions, and not only by engaging over the internet. Reality shows are a perfect example of the active engagement of the media with its audience. The process appears at first sight to be one where the quest for celebrity trumps all else, underlining the power of the media over their audiences. I would interpret what is happening as the opposite: the audience is getting hold of the media and reshaping them in a much more interactive way.

Passive versus Active Trust

I am suspicious of the idea that people trust politicians less than they used to . A more compelling interpretation is that, in a reflexive society, trust is less of a passive, taken-for-granted phenomenon than it once was. Consider those groups which, according to surveys, are most trusted. They are not people who are elected. In fact they conspicuously belong to groups who have little connection with the electoral process – doctors, the military and (although not for all members of the population) the police. Do people really trust them more than others, or is it rather the case that they are in areas of life least penetrated – so far – by the trend to reflexivity?

I would say it is the second of these. Traditional trust mechanisms we could call passive trust – it is where confidence in a given type of person or institution comes from accepting their authority. It isn't necessarily unquestioning, but it does mean accepting that the other has access to privileged sources of knowledge over which he or she is the arbiter.

Today, passive trust is on the retreat everywhere, even in the area of the professions. 'Doctor knows best' is an attitude that still exists – among both doctors and their patients – but it is coming under assault, and quite rightly too. The monopoly of information that once fed professional authority is a monopoly no longer. Studies show that on some occasions a patient actually knows more about his illness and how it should be treated than a doctor, especially a GP, who is, by definition, a generalist. People therefore might have less faith in any individual doctor than before, but it doesn't follow that they have lost trust in the medical profession as a whole, or in medical knowledge. On the contrary, as the basis of trust starts to shift, they make use of these resources to form judgements about individual doctors.

Active trust is an ongoing process. Trust in these circumstances is contingent and is a transaction – the basis for it has to be demonstrated. I don't think it means that social bonds are weakened, but rather that they are expressed in a different form. Communication (on both sides) becomes more central to trust relations than in the case of passive trust. This has happened in the sphere of personal life as well as in more formal settings. Several decades ago, marriage was a 'state' – either one was married or one was not. It was based upon a division of labour between the sexes, at the risk of over-simplification, the housewife and the bread-winner. Of course, ideally there was close communication between husband and wife, but the two by and large occupied different spheres. Nowadays marriage depends upon 'intimacy' – it is a 'relationship', in which trust is gained through the mutual communication of feelings and desires.

How does all this translate into the domain of politics? It means that what philosophers call discursive or deliberative democracy becomes more important than it has been in the past. It won't and can't replace representative democracy, but hopefully can be used to strengthen it. Discursive democracy means providing spaces in which issues of public concern can be openly debated in an informed way.

Not only do citizens today know, and expect to know – or be able to find out – what their leaders are up to; it is a necessity for a successful leader to do the same for the citizenry. Government by focus groups has been widely criticized, and rightly so. A leader who simply did what focus groups wanted would not be a leader at all. Moreover, those in the focus groups simply supply views that the government then 'listens to'. They don't have any interchange of ideas or attitudes with those who take political decisions. Focus groups thus represent a halfway house towards discursive democracy: but they do at least mean that the politician who uses them is trying to find out what citizens think. It is a communication process of sorts, but mainly one-way.

Two-way communication needs to be established. The demand is there. Research conducted for the 2006 Power Inquiry into the state of democratic participation in Britain found that almost all non-voters in the last election were prepared to specify issues that 'really mattered to them'. Over 70 per cent said they would be interested in getting involved in a debate about how local council money should be spent.[3]

A variety of forms of deliberative process have been suggested and tried out in recent years. They are likely to become more and more central to how modern democracies work, although they raise plenty of problematic issues too. Current experiments mostly take a similar overall form. They aim to elevate the level of public debate and citizen involvement by ensuring that certain conditions are met. The participants have to be in possession of relevant facts and perspectives on a given issue or range of issues, and have the opportunity to think about and discuss them in a critical way. The information made available to those taking part should be clear and comprehensive. It can take the form of written information or interviews with experts.

The numbers involved can vary widely, from a small group of a dozen to quite large assemblies of people. They can happen at a national level, with many such groups being involved. The time allocated can vary from a few hours or several days through to considerably longer periods of time. Those who take part should be chosen to represent the different groups or interests in a given community. Treating each person's contributions in an equal way is just as important. Finally, there should be a clear indication from the beginning of what impact the debating process is likely to have, especially since the point of such processes is to move towards a future in which they will be the basis of regular two-way dialogue with decision-makers.[4]

The types of deliberative process pioneered in different countries across the world are numerous. In their survey of the subject, Viki Cooke and Deborah Mattinson list about thirty. These include citizens' juries, citizens' deliberative councils, e-dialogues, learning circles and 'decision days'.[5] Citizens' juries are the oldest version, and consequently the most thoroughly researched. They were initiated in the US as early as the 1970s. They allow small groups of people, one or two dozen at the most, to meet and hear evidence – much like in an ordinary courtroom – from different witnesses about a given topic. Their conclusions are then given to the convening authority to feed into decision-making. In Germany, 'planning cells' have been in existence for some while, involving simultaneous juries all debating the same issues with the same information.

Research shows that citizens' juries can make quite an impact on government when they have a fairly permanent existence. There is time to learn and absorb information, as well as test out ideas on others, such as family and friends. An example is workshops set up in the UK to explore public opinion on the use of embryos for tissue donation. Discussion groups for members of the public were set up that were later reconvened. Initially most participants had little or no knowledge of what was involved in this area of regulation. After six extended group discussions, most felt at home with the debate and the available options. The conclusions they submitted led the regulatory agency, the Human Fertilisation and Embryology Authority, to change the policies they had initially proposed.

Deliberative workshops can involve hundreds or even thousands of people. They allow more chance of getting the involvement of all significant groups in a community. An example is the deliberative polling initiated by the American political scientist James Fishkin. It has been used in a range of countries, including in the UK, the US, Denmark and China. Several hundred people are normally involved. They are given balanced material on a given issue to be discussed, which are debated in small groups. They then meet with experts and political leaders who put their opinions to them. The attitudes of those taken part are measured before and after the deliberative process to see how far they have changed.

In these various methods there is rarely a systematic involvement with government. However in the 'consensus conferences' held in Denmark, findings are incorporated into parliamentary discussion as a matter of routine. So far these discussion circles have mainly concerned questions of science and technology, such as whether or not GM crops should be banned. But they have directly influenced parliamentary decisions in such areas. There are plans to extend them more widely.

Obviously the internet has added a whole new dimension to deliberative processes. There is a host of initiatives going on, using it in different countries – including some of the poorest, where wireless technology can now be introduced at relatively low cost. What was claimed as the world's first e-democracy project was set up in the Swedish city of Kalix in 2000.[6] It was designed to give the inhabitants of the city the opportunity to influence the renovation of the city centre. The project ran over a two-week period. Detailed information was offered on rival possibilities. Those taking part could participate by letter, telephone or fax, as well as on-line; 86 per cent chose the on-line option. Only people entitled to vote could take part, which was ensured by setting up a password system. The outcome was the creation of a design that won popularity among the large majority of the community as a whole.

There are objections that can be made against most or all of these projects. Some are expensive to mount. They consume time and energy, for the citizens involved as well as others. The object is usually to reach consensus, but in some areas divisions of opinion are embedded and consensus might be impossible. Most thus far are consultative without real influence flowing from them. There is also the factor of what social researchers call the 'halo effect'. Schemes that work when a few people take part, and when they are new, might not work at all if they become commonplace. Some are only feasible at local level. They could lend themselves to populism, in the way referenda do. If not properly regulated, they could be used by those in power to legitimate what they have already decided to do. Finally, they have not for the most part given voice to the most disenfranchised groups in society.

These are all good reasons to reaffirm the point made earlier, that the expansion of discursive democracy is not a replacement for representational democracy, but the two ideally should advance together. Part of the reason for having fixed terms of government is that it allows for leadership. A good leader should be in touch with the wishes of the citizenry, but also be prepared sometimes to take decisions that go against what the majority thinks or feels at a particular point in time.

What position should Labour take on all these questions at this point? It is impossible to ignore the yearning for greater consultation that a more reflexive citizenry naturally brings into being, and the fact that it is a process already under way. Labour should seek to incorporate extended discursive democracy into its new constitutional settlement, and base that settlement in some part on such processes. First of all, real decentralization naturally opens up greater possibilities of using some of the mechanisms described above. Local authorities should be encouraged to try some of the diversity of versions on offer, and integrate the results into their own deliberative procedures.

Second, efforts should be made to introduce deliberative procedures to the more marginalized groups in society, even though the social context for doing so might initially look completely unpromising. If they are perceived as providing voice for those who are normally not listened to, they might actually have more impact than among more privileged groups. The same applies to the up-and-coming generation. Only 37 per cent of people aged 18–24 in Britain voted in the 2005 election. Survey evidence among non-voters in this age group shows their average level of interest in politics is almost the same as that of the rest of the population. The issue is therefore once again one of engagement.

Third, the government should continue to experiment with deliberative methods and keep a close eye on new developments in other countries. Labour's on-line consultations have not so far been conspicuously successful. The Big Conversation was supposed to feed opinions and ideas into Labour's manifesto for the 2005 election, but it is not clear how much value the exercise had. More regulated exercises with specific targeted outcomes would be an advance.

Fourth, if British identity is to be a theme of Gordon Brown's premiership, then it would make sense to build some deliberative exercises into any new national celebrations that are planned. Thus in the US it has been suggested that there should be a new national holiday in the year in which there is a presidential election, called 'Deliberation Day'. On that day, there would be debates organized across the whole country to give citizens the chance to debate questions likely to be crucial in settling the election outcome. Perhaps it would be worth trying something like that here in Britain.

Trust and New Labour

Having said this, Labour's problems with trust are all too plainly not just structural. They are to do with the track record of the government and its leader. The sources of disillusionment with Labour are several. One is the version of political campaigning that New Labour cultivated, again borrowing quite heavily from the Democrats in the US. Another concerns promises not kept, or seen as not being kept. A third is the personal style of leadership that has been cultivated at the top. A fourth is the allegation of cash for peerages and other intimations of sleaze. A fifth, and perhaps the most important, is the unfolding debacle in Iraq. As a Labour supporter myself, I have to admit that it is quite a list.

Joe Klein, the American political commentator, has just published an interesting book on American politics, called *Politics Lost*.[7] It carries the subtitle: 'How American Democracy Was Trivialized by People Who Think You're Stupid'. Who were the trivializers? They were the pollsters and political consultants, geared to branding and image-making. Their history in American politics stretches back a long way, but they became more and more prominent in the 1980s and early 1990s. Bill Clinton's campaign in 1992 to become President started poorly: there was the Gennifer Flowers issue, draft-evasion and smoking marijuana at Oxford. To counter the bad publicity, Clinton's consultants initiated what they labelled, tongue in cheek, the 'Manhattan Project' to repair the damage.

Rather than the Rhodes Scholar from Oxford, he was reintroduced to the American public as the folksy Man from Hope (Hope was where Clinton was born, in Arkansas). He played the saxophone on a TV show, did a whole round of non-political talk shows; a film was produced showing him, as a young delegate to Boys' Nation, shaking hands with John F. Kennedy in the Rose Garden at the White House.

James Carville was the forerunner of Alastair Campbell. He was there wherever Clinton was, a 'walking sound-bite', as Klein puts it, and a favourite of the press. A new language was invented via testing slogans out on focus groups, much as filmmakers do before they release a film. In the 1980s the Democrats used to talk about the needs of 'working families'; instead, Clinton spoke of the 'forgotten middle class'. It didn't always work with Clinton himself, whose political sense, Klein says, 'was better than any poll' – he frequently disregarded what his consultants advised.

Focus groups were actually invented by a sociologist – a very famous one within the profession – Robert K. Merton of Columbia University.[8] He designed what he called the 'focused group interview' as a tool of social research. It was intended to get behind the answers people give in opinion polls and explore their attitudes in greater depth. In the hands of PR consultants it became almost the opposite of what was intended.

Rather than focus groups as such, however, it was the whole PR paraphernalia that eventually rebounded on New Labour. Before 1997, few people in Britain spoke of spin, spin doctors, sound-bites or control freaks – all American terms that entered the language at that point. The origins of the words 'spin' and 'spin doctor' are uncertain, but the terms probably came from baseball. A spin doctor is someone who coaches a pitcher in the art of deceiving the player on strike with the degree of rotation put on the ball.

Spin is not new if it simply means trying to put a good face on things. All organizations try to do that, as do all governments – as well as individuals in everyday life. It is different if this goes along with a whole technology of manipulation, staging and deliberate image-building, as well as control of information. Without putting too fine a point on it, New Labour was deeply into such a technology. It wasn't a good start for a government whose leader wanted to be 'whiter than white' – although this phrase itself was actually taken from an advertising jingle for a well-known washing-powder.

I don't mean to be too critical of all this, as so many have been in a facile way. There were very good reasons why those involved with New Labour wanted to have their say about stories appearing in the press. The *Sun* newspaper, rightly or wrongly, claimed to have a determining effect on the 1992 election, after running an extremely critical – and highly personalized – series of articles about the then Labour leader Neil Kinnock. 'Rapid rebuttal' was introduced as a way of countering false stories about Labour in the media in the run-up to the election. Newspapers like to excoriate spin, but much of what appears in them is exactly that, in the sense that considerable resources might be spent to promote a particular line on events. The media, printed and electronic, may deploy these resources to run campaigns in relation to individuals or issues. It was and is a thoroughly twisted circle indeed.

As far as the media are concerned, it has long been the case, as the saying has it, that bad news is good news. The reverse applies just as strongly – it is very difficult to get any positive achievements reported upon. However, studies show a large rise in negative reporting over the past two or three decades, as well as in personalized journalism, in which the journalist or presenter gets far more air time that the politician whose speech is being reported upon. Parliamentary debates are rarely described at any length, and then quite often simply to satirize them. There was a further factor after Labour won such a big majority in 1997. Some sections of the media took it upon themselves to represent the opposition, the Tories being too weak to do so effectively, or so they proclaimed.

Yet there is no doubt that some New Labour zealots took it all too far, and that the concentration on news management subverted itself. Jenny Kleeman, an investigative journalist, got a job in Labour's London press office that dealt with regional and local affairs. She was part of an effort made to influence the content of the letters pages in local newspapers. Party members were asked to put their name to pre-scripted letters defending Labour's policies. The sample of published letters the reporter traced all contained the same phrases.[9]

Early on New Labour also tended to produce statistics which, under scrutiny, didn't show what was claimed for them. Thus 'new' money would be announced for projects of various kinds which included funds that had already been publicized earlier, as if the total sum were fresh investment. Whatever effect that might or might not have had, surveys show that official statistics are widely mistrusted. A survey by the Office of National Statistics showed that 68 per cent of a national sample of respondents believe that official figures are constructed to support the government's policies.[10]

Labour has responded to the moral climate which, at least in some part, it helped create by re-jigging its approach. The monitoring of statistics by independent agencies, setting up league tables and audited targets, were designed to provide more reliable benchmarks. Yet these also have led to problems, since targets themselves can lead to games-playing and even downright deception in the way that public bodies present themselves. As Chancellor, Gordon Brown has introduced legislation to implement the conclusions of the Statistics Commission in a report published in 2004. The Commission was charged with advising on the integrity and quality of UK official statistics. A Statistics Board will be set up, replacing the Office for National Statistics; it will operate at arm's length from government.

'Call me Tony' – was that a sensible approach to leadership? The media might have decided to call Blair by his first name regardless of what he did. After all, Mrs Thatcher, who was a quite forbidding figure as Prime Minister, was widely referred to as Maggie, even by those who protested vociferously against her policies. However, Blair, with his ready smile and charm, decided to develop a much more personalized style than she had. It worked very well in the beginning, helping Labour reach beyond their traditional supporters. One Italian study of Blair describes him as 'the boy', and indeed he was only 43 when he became PM.[11] His boyishness hid a strong will and great determination – he was no 'Bambi' in spite of media attempts to apply the tag. But it certainly added to his personal appeal. Perhaps sofa-style government came naturally with it.

Personal appeal works when things are going well, but it can prove a handicap when they begin to sour. The emotional tie upon which it is based can go into reverse, in a milder version of what happens in relationships when love turns to hate. Blair's support for the Iraq invasion was the catalyst for many, especially when the premise upon which the war was based, that Saddam possessed weapons of mass destruction, turned out to be wrong.

The key question, of course, is where to go from here. If a Brown-led government cannot overcome at least some of the feelings of distaste that many people feel about Labour at the current time, all will be lost. What remedies, then?

It is tempting to say simply: be more straight-speaking, speak your mind – it's what the public likes. This quality is why people take to politicians such as Mo Mowlam, Clare Short, Tony Benn or Ken Livingstone. Well, yes, but if you are a front-line politician you simply cannot speak your mind at will. Mo Mowlam had to observe this principle when she was Secretary of State for Northern Ireland, and when she didn't it caused all sorts of trouble. Clare Short has always been forthright, but it is much easier for her now that she has stepped down from office.

This is not a new issue, but intrinsic to politics as such. Remember Samuel Johnson's definition of a politician, published in the first edition of his dictionary in 1755: 'A man of artifice; one of deep contrivance.' Ken Livingstone had to modify his rhetoric significantly when he became the first elected mayor of London – he couldn't go off into the diatribes against the business community that he was once so fond of. Tony Benn: he said that he left Parliament in order to devote himself to politics, and it was an apt observation. Actually, one of the disappointments of my youthful life was hearing him speak in Cambridge many years ago. He was in the Cabinet at that time. I expected bold talk, but all we got was a 'typical' politician's performance. Since he left 'politics' he has of course expounded on all sorts of subjects.

Why can't politicians speak their minds more often? The reasons are obvious enough: the press says 'government wholly divided' if discussions are always held openly; in any government, ministers have to support policies they may not agree with; at any one point, a policy programme might still be in the process of construction, such that public statements of commitment cannot yet be made; and a host of similar situations.

So one shouldn't be unrealistic about all this. But it doesn't follow that there is nothing that can be done by a Brown-led govern-

Box 4 Democracy and Trust

1 Everyday democratization is having a profound effect upon political attitudes. Voters are more discriminating and calculative than in the past; non-voting is not necessarily an expression of lack of interest in politics, and is a complex act.

2 Active trust is replacing passive trust in most areas of life, including politics. One consequence is that discursive or deliberative democracy comes, or should come, to play a more important role alongside representative democracy.

3 It is a mistake to suppose that discursive democracy could ever replace representative democracy, even at a local level, but it can be a means of strengthening it.

4 (East European joke): A democracy is a system in which, when someone knocks on your door at 6 o'clock in the morning, you think it's the milkman. One should never forget the basic point that a democracy consists of far more than just parties, parliaments and political leaders. The rule of law, an independent judiciary and freedom of speech are its underpinning.

5 Trust cannot be manipulated or manufactured, at least not for too long. This theorem applies with even more force when secrecy has more or less been obliterated. Active trust has to be earned.

6 A clear move away from sofa-style government, coupled to constitutional reform, could allow Labour to wipe some of the slate clean.

7 A progressive consensus now exists in this country, since otherwise Tory policy would not have had to change so much. 'Progressive' here, however, means able to deal with change, innovation, reform. Not Labour but New Labour; not New Labour, but New, New Labour ... and so on.

ment to rebuild public support. Action can be taken in each of the five areas that have affected people's views of, and feelings about, New Labour.

- Any government these days is going to consult PR and media consultants. It's one thing to use them, and quite another to be patently dominated by them. Labour should cut back on the image-making, and use images that correspond to realities. The era when it was thought that anything could be achieved just by branding is long over. Advertising only works if there is substance behind the message.

- In the area of promises, be very careful – especially be careful about the inflation of expectations. Labour's massive new investments in health and education have not got the recognition they deserve, partly because a spiral of increasing expectations was generated in each case. As I mentioned earlier, Tony Blair's promise to raise health care spending to average EU levels probably accentuated this effect.

- Gordon Brown has already spoken, quite rightly, of his intention to move away from sofa-style government. In terms of personal style he cannot match the direct appeal Blair has, but he can compensate with gravitas.

- Reform of the Lords should help with the cash for peerages issue, even if such reform turns out to be quite minimal. For instance, appointments to peerages could be taken completely out of the hands of the Prime Minister. A clear distinction could be made between working peers, who would be expected to attend, speak and vote on a regular basis; and the award of honours. Currently, a peerage mixes these together. The question of party funding needs to be resolved, although it won't be easy. In the interests of transparency, Labour obliged donors giving substantial sums to political parties to declare the fact. It was this change that underlay the troubles that the party found itself in. It was a foolish move to accept undeclared loans. The whole thing has affected the party in a serious way even if no charges are pressed in the police investigation. The donors want their loans back – quite rightly, because that's what a loan is. In the meantime Labour finds itself with major funding problems.

- Brown will have to consider the state of the party itself, a tiny part of the public but obviously vital for Labour's future. Party membership is now below 200,000, the lowest it has been since the 1930s. This phenomenon should not be interpreted in too parochial a way. It is structural, since it is found in all the developed countries. All sorts of remedies have been proposed, including the idea that an inner party of full-time members should be complemented by a network of supporters working on a more sporadic or issue-driven basis.

• Decisive action in relation to Iraq will be necessary, as discussed elsewhere in the text.

A Progressive Consensus

These considerations suggest that how Brown performs over the first year will be crucial. He won't have too long to make count the fact that he is a fresh face as Prime minister. My feeling is that, as soon as he becomes leader Gordon Brown should get on the road and embark on an exercise to get in touch with the public on a personal level. He should talk to as extended a range of people as possible, and also use the full range of media to do so. He also has to talk widely to party members. There has been much talk of surprise policy announcements, but this tactic should be avoided. He should have a clear outline programme, and the policies on hand to back it up; but in the beginning these should be offered provisionally.

The two main parties are contesting the centre-ground, and the Tories have abandoned some of their most cherished beliefs to do so. How can Brown put clear water between Labour and the 'New Tories'? His not so secret weapon is still the economy. Surveys show that under half of the electorate believe that the economic success of the past decade has much to do with the government. Yet it is actually the result of good management and bold decision-making (the decision to transfer control of interest rates to the Bank of England). When the election approaches, will voters risk their prosperity by electing a party with no recent experience in government?

No real substance (either to Cameron or to his party); no sound economic theory; no underpinning analysis of the Tories' new ideological stance; the weakness of the idea of social responsibility;

no full consensus in the party; major inconsistencies of approach to different policy areas – these should all be the focus of Labour's critique.

David Cameron's decision to avoid policy commitments provides a major opportunity for a Brown-led Labour government to return to the driving-seat in British politics. Assuming he does not call a snap election, which he is highly unlikely to do, Brown will be in power for two, perhaps three, years before he has to face the electorate in a national vote. Unlike Cameron, he has the ability to actually enact policy changes during that period, and therefore to lead from the front.

Today, except to a dwindling number of Tory supporters, to most electors Thatcherism is a dim memory. Labour has defined a new terrain of its own, for better or for worse (much of it is for better, as I have argued). A new storyline is needed for the country. Is the one Gordon Brown has devised so far good enough? If fleshed out properly, I think it is. It involves a stress upon the core importance of British national identity and citizenship, not as dissolving in the face of globalization, but as vital to responding effectively to it. Adapting to change is the motif, but in such a way as to reinforce the cohesion of the society as far as possible. Thus getting a high proportion of people into work, investing in public services, concentrating upon education, radically cutting back on child poverty, dealing with the skills gap, all help to reinforce the integration of the country. It is right, as I have said, to stress the national identity of the UK as a cosmopolitan country within which different ethnic and cultural groups can coexist.

Should the name New Labour be dispensed with? I don't think it can be. One consideration is tactical: if Brown stopped using the term, the Tories would have a clear avenue of attack. Brown would immediately be accused of turning back the clock and reverting to the stance that kept the party out of power for so many years in the 1980s and early 1990s. The main grounds, however, are those of substance. Labour must continue be reformist, prepared to adapt or discard old policies in the face of change, and indeed to step up further the pace of reform.

What about Gordon Brown's personality? What about his Scottishness – will it be a handicap? It has been said that 'For

Tories, the day that Brown becomes prime minister cannot dawn too soon. Champagne corks will pop in Tory Central Office.'[12] Part of the reason is that some Tories think it will be easy to proclaim Brown as a Labour traditionalist (it will not), but part is also because he lacks 'Blair flair'. He will be seen as a dour Scot with little empathy for the country as a whole. Brown did very well (to shift the partnership metaphor) when he was Scottie to Blair's Captain Kirk, but who could imagine Scottie actually commanding the Starship Enterprise?

Scottish origins or involvements have never been much of a problem for British prime ministers before. Several twentieth-century prime ministers have sat for Scottish seats. Churchill once represented Dundee, while Blair was born in Edinburgh and educated at Fettes.[13] Of course, it could be that the situation is different now there is a separate Scottish parliament, since it is impossible to imagine an Englishman or woman being First Minister in Scotland. Brown has to worry these days about Scots who think he has deserted his own roots, not just about what voters in the rest of the UK might think.

He can assuage English voters' reservations about his Scottishness in several ways. It may not prove a big difficulty in and of itself. He can make sure his cabinet is not only fresh, but ecumenical. Given that he endorses further devolution, he will be redressing the imbalance between Scotland and the English regions. In turn, he can try to get the Scots to listen to the economic lessons that have been successful for the country as a whole, since the governing coalition there is building up commitments for public spending that are simply not sustainable.

Professionalism, party discipline – these are definitely attributes of New Labour that have to be sustained. Since the pace of revisionism must be kept up, Brown will face dissenters in the party just as Blair did. It remains to be seen how well he will cope with them, but a great deal will hang on this, since the electorate strongly dislikes fractious parties and governments. A firmer emphasis upon Labour's public purpose, and a more sustained commitment to egalitarianism, such I have suggested earlier, should help provide a clear base for overall party unity.

However, the Tories are likely to have even bigger problems of internal division, and it will be up to Labour tacticians to exploit them. The current situation of David Cameron in the Tory party is not the same as Blair's in the early days of New Labour. Cameron has sought to break with party traditions – particularly those associated with Thatcherism – in a much more radical way. How far will he be able to control the right when push comes to shove? How many votes will the Tories lose to the United Kingdom Independence Party?

Gordon Brown has spoken of building a progressive consensus for future Labour electoral success, but has not fleshed out what that actually means. Is it a viable idea? In my view: yes. Like all left-of-centre parties today, Labour has problems with its erstwhile base in industrial areas, because the class structure has changed so much. There have always been 'working-class Tories', but in the declining strongholds of traditional industry disaffected voters are more likely not to vote at all, and some are turning towards the populist right. Levels of voting in general are higher among the more affluent and among older people than among the young.

A progressive consensus has to be cross-class, but it is a mistake to speak of Labour as having to appeal to 'middle England' or the 'middle class'. With the emergence of a post-industrial society, the middle class has changed just as much as the working class. In effect, there is no middle class any more. Instead, one can distinguish three overlapping groups.

About 10 per cent of the working population are in professional and managerial jobs, but the nature of many of these jobs has changed significantly. They have become penetrated by information technology, while professional expertise is now subject to much greater public scrutiny than in the past.[14] A further 20 per cent work in high-tech or knowledge-based jobs – work demanding advanced qualifications and expertise. 'Apple Mac' jobs of this sort include work in the communications industries, the media, publishing and other areas. Another 18 per cent are 'wired workers' as defined earlier (chapter 1) – people who work with computers most of the day, but in fairly routinized settings – in banks, insurance companies, travel agents and so forth. Lower down the scale, the industrial working class is now smaller than that of workers in low-level service jobs, so-called 'Big Mac' jobs, who make up about 22 per cent of the labour force.

The fact that there are as many women in the labour force as men marks one of the biggest changes from earlier generations. Women are prominent among wired workers and in 'Big Mac' jobs, but the division between women and men, including the pay differential, is quite a lot smaller than it was, even ten years ago. Women's share of household income is increasing, currently standing at 37 per cent (in some countries, such as Denmark, at 42 per cent it is approaching parity with men).

A progressive consensus will demand substantial backing from industrial workers and 'Big Mac' workers, but Labour's potential support stretches across the other class groups too, as well as across the gender divide. In terms of class, the essential difficulty is reconciling a post-industrial agenda with achieving support from those in more traditional occupations. 'Apple Mac' workers tend to be progressive in terms of liberal causes, such as women's rights, gay rights and human rights more generally, and sympathetic towards environmentalism. They accept the importance of public services, but have reservations about a large role for the state.

Industrial and 'Big Mac' workers are generally happier about extensive state involvement in social and economic life. However, what has been called 'working-class authoritarianism' is a common-place aspect of their outlook – indifference or hostility towards liberal causes, and a traditionalist outlook towards the family. Finding a programme that cross-cuts these different class groups is one of the most difficult tasks in left-of-centre politics. Labour will need solid working-class support in the next election, but how to mobilize it (without conceding anything to authoritarianism and protectionism) is a serious and problematic issue.

A Populus poll taken in November 2006 indicated the Tories had gained a seven-point lead over Labour among women, a lead that rose to 12 per cent if Brown were leader. The significance of these figures can be disputed, since the sample size was small. However, they appear to be confirmed by YouGov measures, in which the Tories were ahead among women voters in every poll save one since September 2005.[15] It is possible that Cameron's strong stance on green issues accounts for much of this difference, since women are on average more sympathetic to environmental policies than men. The gap seems to have closed somewhat early in 2007, but it remains an issue to which Brown must give close attention.

One doesn't have to be a PR fanatic to see that in the next election Labour must have a core message, and one that voters can identify with. That message can't be just a message, as I have argued throughout the book – it must be backed with developed ideas and with policy substance. But elections are not won without such a main theme. What should it be? My best bet would be 'Safer With Labour'. It is a message that encapsulates what I have called a Contract with the Future. Safer with Labour (and with Gordon Brown) because we live in a turbulent world where a safe hand on the tiller is essential; safer because Labour is now the established party of government, with a wealth of experience to draw on; safer because Labour will defend and advance those institutions that really count, such as the NHS; safer because Labour is thinking ahead, to the disturbing problems waiting down the line if we do not act now.

Brown will be a 'newer' figure than Cameron as party leader and Prime Minister. Hence it is possible that existing poll figures don't mean very much, since much will depend upon how he establishes himself in office. Forging a progressive consensus will depend a great deal upon finding policies that will persuade 'traditional' labour voters actually to turn out and vote, while at the same time appealing to the core support that Labour has built up among the new class groups, wired workers and those in high-tech occupations.

How likely is it that the next election, whenever it happens, will produce a hung parliament? It is certainly a possibility. Hung parliaments are rare in British politics. The last one was in the general election of February 1974, and lasted until a further election in October of that year. Some say that a hung parliament is simply a situation of coalition, as would happen anyway under proportional representation. Yet in the UK under the current system it tends to lead to a situation of uncertainty and lack of leadership. I am a believer in the wisdom of crowds. I don't believe voters will want a hung parliament, and therefore they are likely to prevent it happening.

Clare Short, who has now left the Labour Party, says she will actively campaign for a hung parliament in the next election, although it is not clear exactly how. If such an outcome were to occur, the Liberal Democrats would hold the balance of power, and would have to decide with which of the other two main parties they would form a government. The fact that no one could be clear which one they would choose is indicative of the difficulties the party has in locating itself ideologically.

It is all to play for in British politics at the moment. Should the economy go wrong, it would almost certainly destroy Labour's chances. Events in the wider world could count for a lot, for or against. The fact that Bill Clinton was in power in the US in 1997 was certainly a positive influence for Blair. The same could be true for Brown if a Democrat is elected as President next time in America.

I hope both things will happen. There won't be any more trips to Washington to the White house on Concorde for me, or anyone else. But I'd be just as happy to be going in an Airbus A380 should I ever get invited again – let's say, should there be a second Clinton administration.

10

Labour's Contract with the Future

Groucho Marx: The future isn't what it used to be.

George Burns: Too bad all the people who really know how to run the country are too busy driving cabs and cutting hair.

Variously attributed to Tony Blair, Glenn Hoddle and Madonna: I never make predictions and I never will.

Actually the future isn't what it used to be given the scale of the tasks that face a globalizing world. Climate change wasn't an issue when Groucho was around. Running the country is like being manager of the England football team – everyone thinks he or she can do better than the current incumbent. Both are in their different ways thankless jobs. Successes are taken for granted and failures excoriated (sometimes successes are too). Glenn Hoddle was once England manager. I don't know if the observation about predicting the future was indeed one of his bons mots, but it does make a point. Prediction is a difficult business, but we have to do it or we could not plan for anything.

The following is really a summary of the book, but it might help to restate it all in brief. Labour's aims, I have argued, are to create a society in Britain that is prosperous, fair and open, and ensure that these qualities can be sustained – for this generation, but also for generations to come. It asks citizens to contribute to securing these aims.

When I was originally writing this concluding précis, I thought I would order it in terms of areas where policies didn't need to be changed versus those that do. But I have come to the conclusion that there is hardly any area where policy innovation is not necessary, although in some it is needed much more than in others.

The integrating theme of the Contract with the Future is globalization – our capability as a society to cope with and to profit from it. Most of the challenges we face we simply cannot deal with alone. The worst move we could make at the moment would be to look for security by turning away from the international arena. We can become more secure, but only by engaging with the forces of change that are all around us.

Domestically, my argument is that at this point we must move well beyond the original New Labour agenda. New Labour developed many successful policies in 1997, but a different approach is now required to move to a further stage.

New Labour wanted to break away both from the Old Left and from Thatcherism, without sacrificing their insights – to establish a third way. However, it was unable fully to create a new synthesis. It remained too caught up in the old divisions: should a given service be provided by the state, markets or the third sector, or a combination of all three? The state remained largely unreformed, being seen mainly as a delivery vehicle, while the nature of markets was not properly interrogated, let alone the wider structure of capitalism.

Today we have to try to make both the state and markets the servants of the people. 'Servants of the people' sounds much too trite to be interesting, but what it signals is important. The two 'p's – people and participation – provide the guiding thread. The public services need to be opened up in such a way that citizens are able to exercise choice where possible, and voice wherever necessary. Decentralization and independent management are what matter, rather then whether they are provided by the state or other agencies, including commercial ones.

Capitalism has to be made to work in the interests of consumers, and in the long-term interests of society. Corporate responsibility should be as high up the list of Labour's concerns as the reform of public services, and we should be opening a wide debate upon how to make it more than just words. There are many investment demands that will entail collaboration between public agencies and private companies, especially in the now pressing area of the environment. Energy projects, for example, normally need long-term investment, as well as technological capacity, that will have to be provided mainly by the private sector. Yet unless government gets the conditions right, there may be no incentive to invest over such lengthy periods.

Gordon Brown talks of the need for a new constitutional settlement in Britain. A better way to put it might be that we should be looking to democratize our democracy. Two tasks are involved. One is to complete the constitutional revisions that were begun in 1997. These include: helping to resolve the 'English problem' through effective devolution; reform of parliament, especially of the Lords; further reform of the criminal justice system; and other changes. The second task, however, is getting to grips with the complexities of what I have called everyday democratization. In this area we have to be prepared to be experimental. There are deep transformations going on that no one fully understands.

Identity politics are likely to have a key part to play over the next few years. Two overlapping political arenas are involved. One is containing the centripetal forces of nationalism, which threaten British identity itself. There are many perversities here. Consider the UK Independence Party. It might as well retitle itself, because if Britain left the European Union, the Scots would want to rejoin it as a separate nation, and quite probably Wales too. There would no longer be a United Kingdom but a Disunited Kingdom. The other task is to make our cultural and ethnic diversity add to Britain's strength rather than corrode it. There is only one means – to make a success of multiculturalism.

The following list of 'clauses' in the contract is brief and schematic – it doesn't substitute for reading the volume itself!

1 Economic success is the basis of so much else that it makes sense to give it prime place. The goal of Labour is to maintain, but also further amplify, the successes that have been achieved thus far. Macroeconomic policy should aim at stable growth, coupled to continuing low inflation. There should be no return to protectionism. Flexibility is an objective in all areas of the economy, above the floor of a steadily

increasing minimum wage and the furtherance of active labour market policy (the New Deal). More effective investment in skills will be needed to increase productivity, and also improve the life-chances of those at the bottom. Labour should continue to encourage the development of a business-friendly environment, but not shy away from regulation where needed. 'Regulation' should be based as far as possible upon incentives, not restrictions. That this aim is consistent with improving levels of social justice is shown by the success in both areas achieved by the Scandinavian countries.

2 The state is needed in many domains of our lives, although there are few in which it should be in exclusive or even dominant control. It has to work in collaboration with many other agencies, in the market sector and in civil society, and with citizens directly. Citizens must have voice and choice in state-based services, in all areas where either or both are possible. The state is an ensuring state – it aims to provide resources that will empower citizens, but also to work with them to ensure that desired outcomes are achieved. There can be no going back to the era of the top-down state. It is crucial not to equate the state with the public sphere – the mistake of the traditional left. Conversely it is wrong to argue that turning to commercial providers must mean betraying the public purpose.

3 Devolution should be a major part of the reform package, in the fields of government itself, education and health. It has to be a real devolution of power, not just token concessions from a central government that can't let go. The government should recognize how fundamentally political life is changing and be prepared to experiment with discursive democracy.

4 Controlling and adapting to climate change must be made integral to the rights and obligations of citizens. Efforts should be redoubled in the international arena to secure real advance, especially in conjunction with the rest of the EU, by far our best chance of having a serious impact. Technological innovation will be highly important, and should be stimulated by tax breaks and other means. A variety of levers need to be used to ensure responsible behaviour from state agen-

cies themselves, companies and citizens. A national assessment of vulnerabilities should be instituted immediately.

5 The pattern of taxation has to be shifted to give more prominence to environmental taxes and tax incentives. Hypothecated taxes may play an important role. Tax incentives should have as large a part as possible, as should taxes that have other desirable social effects – such as stimulating healthier lifestyle habits. Increases in green taxes should not be used to raise extra revenue without corresponding tax cuts elsewhere. Care has to be taken that environmental taxes have a progressive dimension to them. Since the poorest are always the most at risk, the consequences of climate for social insurance will have to be thought through.

6 Labour should come out more explicitly as an egalitarian party, making the case that continuing high levels of inequality, and of poverty, have harmful consequences for everyone. Labour's egalitarian thinking has to be different from that of the traditional left, because the economic implications of social policy (and vice versa) always have to be spelled out. Policies that simultaneously further economic dynamism or job creation at the same time as reducing poverty have to be kept in the forefront.

7 A guiding principle should be: children first! The nation's future by definition lies with its children. We must not only aim to give all children a good start in life, but guarantee that we will not usurp the resources that belong to them and subsequent generations. The principle 'children first' also applies to combating poverty. The commitment to reduce child poverty by half, in relative terms, by 2010 is one of the most radical the government has made, and policies should be put in place that can ensure it happens. The aim to eliminate child poverty by 2020 should be kept firmly in view. Utopian it may be, but it is a goal that could have great motivational force to generate future policy developments. After all, some countries – the Scandinavian ones – already have very low rates of child poverty.

8 No systematic change in the lives of children can be made without giving policy priority to improving the position of

women, in the workforce and in the home. Work–life balance is, on the face of things, an odd term. Work is part of life and for many people a very important one. What it means is reconciling work, the family, and other concerns and obligations. Many women still have a domestic job on top of their paid work. A range of strategies can be deployed to help women, such as policies that allow those in low-level service jobs to have the chance of promotion into management.

9 Education and health must continue as major priorities. Education is the lynch-pin of our continuing prosperity, but is just as important for its contribution to tolerance and a cosmopolitan outlook. Life-long education must cease to be a somewhat empty mantra and become a reality. Reform of the NHS must continue, whatever the roadblocks. Serious attention should be given to freeing it from direct government control, a process that is in fact happening but should be further radicalized. The health care agenda, however, ranges far beyond the NHS.

10 Labour should be committed to sustaining the integrity of Britain, as a cosmopolitan nation. The identity of the country should be based upon an outward-looking perspective, drawing sustenance from the global role the country has had in the past, and should assume a different guise today. Sovereignty now depends upon international collaboration and the pooling of resources by member states in the EU. We must break away from the narrow, explicitly insular conception of national identity fostered by the political right. We should seek to celebrate national achievements and tie them to the endeavour to up-date the image of the country in the rest of the world.

11 Immigration must be policed in a rigorous way. Britain should continue to provide a haven for genuine refugees, but the mechanisms for doing so have to be improved radically, to the satisfaction of the public. The key task is to reduce illegal immigration; collaboration on a European level, and more widely too, is the prime way of doing so. The economy cannot absorb large numbers of unskilled immigrants, but positive efforts should be made to persuade skilled migrants to come.

12 The identity and values of the society are the backdrop to what should be a continuing endorsement of multiculturalism. Multiculturalism, at least in its sophisticated version, means that minority groups should accept the principles of the liberal state and abide by its laws. The state should pursue policies that develop ties between different groups, and between those groups and society as a whole. Multiculturalism means taking a critical approach to the values of others, not one in which cultural practices trump all other considerations. No cultural community is above criticism. The preservation of freedom of speech and action must be pursued with fresh vigour.

13 The theorem 'tough on crime, tough on the causes of crime' should stand, but has to be unpacked more carefully than Labour's policies to date imply. Major policy revision is called for. Labour has relied too heavily on the criminal justice system. The distance between the criminal justice system and the causes of crime is considerable, since so few crimes are actually punished. Moreover, there are limits to how many people should be in prison. Being 'tough on the causes of crime' *is* 'being tough on crime', not a wholly separate task.

14 International terrorism is different in nature from, and potentially far more lethal than, the local terrorism we have been familiar with in earlier periods. Appropriate measures must continue to be taken against it, nationally and internationally. The legislation that allows the police to hold suspects without charge for an extended period, subject to judicial approval, should be maintained. The rhetoric of a 'war against terror', however, and some of the implications drawn from it, should be abandoned.

15 Our membership of the European Union is crucial to Britain's future. We must use our influence as a key member state to promote effective policies on climate change, energy security, control of international crime and human trafficking plus, as noted above, migration. The EU cannot run effectively with the decision-making arrangements it has now, and these must be sharpened. Britain should continue to press for the completion of the Single Market, and for economic and social reform within the low-performing EU states.

16 Labour should remain committed to an activist foreign policy, recognizing the interdependencies of globalization. Britain should work to strengthen world governance and restore the standing of international law. The country may have a large economy as measured in terms of GDP. Yet in world terms it is a small country. If the Euro-sceptics get their way, Britain could be a minor island stuck in no man's land between the US and the rest of Europe with little influence on either.

Taken together, these points show what kind of Britain Labour should want to bring into being. It is a country confident in the face of change; with a newly developing cosmopolitan identity, outward and forward-looking, not an island mentality; which believes in open markets, but just as fervently in a strong public sphere; where environmental issues are right at the forefront; where power is devolved to regions, cities and localities in a meaningful way; where public service reform continues, giving primacy to voice and choice; in which poverty, and especially child poverty, are in steep decline; where standards of education rival the best in the world, and where education is a continuing process; where crime continues to drop; in which the family is strong, but diversity in family forms is not stigmatized; which is secure in the face of new global threats; which recognizes the crucial advantages the European Union offers in the global age; which remains a leader on the international stage; and where the present generation does not exploit generations to come.

Notes

Preface

1 Anthony Giddens, *The Third Way* (Cambridge: Polity, 1998).

Introduction

1 See Akbar Ahmed, *Journey Into Islam. The Crisis of Globalization* (Washington, DC: Brookings, 2007).
2 Olivier Roy, *Globalised Islam* (New York: Hurst/Columbia, 2005). See also the interesting recent essay by Francis Fukuyama, 'Identity and Migration', *Prospect*, February 2007.
3 Brown has defended the record on inflation, pointing out that, since 1997, in countries such as the US, Germany, Australia and Sweden, inflation has deviated more often from stated targets than in the case of the UK. 'So UK inflation has not only been lower on average than in other major economies – but also more stable.' Economic Brief From the Office of Gordon Brown, 18 January 2007, p. 2.

Chapter 1 After Ten Years: Labour's Successes and Failures

1 David Osborne and Ted Gaebler, *Reinventing Government* (Reading: Addison-Wesley, 1992).
2 Ibid., p. 263.
3 See, for example, Ed Kilgore, 'Safer streets and neighbourhoods', in Will Marshall and Martin Schram, eds, *Mandate for Change* (New York: Berkley, 1992). This book as a whole is the best exposition of New Democrat philosophy.
4 Will Marshall, 'US global leadership for democracy', in Marshall and Schram, eds, *Mandate for Change*.
5 See, for example, Richard Layard, *Welfare To Work and the New Deal*, Centre for Economic Performance, LSE, January 2001.

6 1997 *Labour Party Manifesto: New Labour: Because Britain Deserves Better.* London, Labour Party, 1997, p10.
7 Tony Blair, 'Environment: next steps'. Speech given on 6 March 2001, p. 3. Available on the Downing Street website.
8 Peter Dunn, 'Blair, plausible psychopath, "set to implode"', *New Statesman*, 1 July 2003.

Chapter 2 The Contenders: Brown versus Cameron

1 Ipsos MORI, 'Political monitor: satisfaction ratings 1979–present'.
2 Populus Poll, 9 January 2007. Available on the *Times Online* website.
3 Ipsos MORI, 'Political monitor'.
4 Gordon Brown, *Moving Britain Forward* (London: Bloomsbury, 2006), p. 158.
5 Ibid., p. 161.
6 HM Treasury, *Investing in Britain's Potential* (London: HMSO, 2006); *Prosperity for All in the Global Economy* (The Leitch Report, 2006).
7 Brown, *Moving Britain Forward*, pp. 43 and 13.
8 Tom Nairn, *The Break-Up of Britain* (New York: NLB, 1977). See also Nairn, *After Britain* (London: Granta, 2000).
9 Gordon Brown, 'We need a United Kingdom', *Daily Telegraph*, 13 January 2007.
10 Brown, *Moving Britain Forward*, p. 262
11 Ibid., p. 264.
12 Cameron, speech to the King's Fund, 9 November 2006.
13 Cameron, speech to the Foreign Policy Centre, 24 August 2006
14 Cameron, speech at the Conservative Conference, 4 October 2006, p. 14.
15 Cameron, speech on general well-being, 20 July 2006.
16 Cameron, speech to the Centre for Social Justice, 10 July 2006.
17 Cameron, 'Bringing down the barriers to cohesion'. Speech given in Birmingham, 29 January 2007
18 Menzies Campbell, 'The Liberal Democrats – a party on the up'. Speech given in East Fife, 24 February 2006, p. 2.
19 *The Liberal Democrats: Fairer, Simpler, Greener.* Policy Paper no. 75, 2006.
20 Campbell, Speech to launch his campaign to be leader of the Liberal Democrats, 19 January 2006, pp. 1–2.
21 *The Orange Book: Reclaiming Liberalism* (London: Profile, 2004).
22 For the original inspiration, see Marvin Olasky, *Compassionate Conservatism* (New York and London: Free Press, 2000; Introduction by George Bush).

Chapter 3 The World in Flux: How to Respond?

1 Martin Wolf, *Why Globalization Works* (New Haven: Yale University Press, 2004), p. 14.
2 Gene Grossman and Elhanan Helpman, 'Out-sourcing in a global economy', *Review of Economic Studies*, 72 (January 2005); Alan Blinder, 'Off-shoring: the next industrial revolution?', *Foreign Affairs* (March/April 2006).
3 Robert Winder, *Bloody Foreigners. The Story of Immigration to Britain* (London: Little, Brown, 2004), p. 8; Defoe, quoted in ibid., p. 9.
4 The Young Foundation, *Britain's Unmet Needs* (London, 2006).
5 Richard Layard, 'Mental health: Britain's biggest social problem?' Paper prepared for the 10 Downing Street Strategy Unit, December 2004. Available on the London School of Economics website.
6 See David Held, *Global Covenant?* (Cambridge: Polity, 2005).
7 See Montserrat Guibernau, *Nations Without States* (Cambridge: Polity, 1999).
8 See Nicholas Veron, 'Farewell national champions', *Breugel Policy Brief* (Brussels, June 2006).
9 Gordon Brown, *Pre-Budget Report statement*, 6 December 2006 (London: Treasury).
10 For the best discussion of these issues, see Lutz Leisering and Stephan Leibfried, *Time and Poverty in Western Welfare States* (Cambridge: Cambridge University Press, 2001).
11 Quoted in Robert Cheshire, 'A soaring number of inmates', *Observer*, 28 January 1997.
12 See David Downes and Kirstine Hansen, 'Welfare and punishment in comparative perspective', in S. Armstrong and L. McAra, eds, *Perspectives on Punishment* (Oxford: Oxford University Press, 2006).

Chapter 4 The Public Services: Putting People First

1 See Folke Schuppert, 'The enabling state', in Anthony Giddens, ed., *The Progressive Manifesto* (Cambridge: Polity, 2003).
2 Ibid., pp. 55–7.
3 Referred to in the OECD study *Integrating Transport in the City* (Paris: OECD, 2000), p. 43.
4 Reform (a think-tank), *Investment in the NHS – Facing up to the Reform Agenda* (London, 2006), p. 20.
5 Martin Summers, 'Only connect: toward a new democratic settlement', in Mark Perryman, ed., *The Blair Agenda* (London: Lawrence and Wishart, 1996), p. 87.
6 Dawn Primarolo, reported in Ashley Seager and Ian Cobain, 'Ten held after VAT fraud raids in Britain and Europe', *Guardian*, 7 February 2007.

7 *Releasing Resources to the Front Line* (London: Treasury, 2004). Group chaired by Peter Gershon.
8 Martyn Hart, 'The Gershon Report and the value of outsourcing', *eGov Monitor* (22 March 2005), p. 1.
9 Julian Le Grand, 'The Blair legacy? Choice and competition in public services', Public Lecture, London School of Economics, 21 February 2006 (available on the LSE website). See also Le Grand, *Motivation, Agency and Public Policy* (Oxford: Oxford University Press, 2004).
10 Robert Hill, 'Bag of clubs', in Geoffrey Filkin and Patrick Diamond, eds, *Public Matters* (London: Methuen/Politico's, 2007).
11 Ibid..
12 Peter Robinson, *How Do We Pay?* (London: IPPR, 2006).
13 Ibid., pp. 21–2.
14 Julie Foley and Malcolm Ferguson, *Putting the Brakes on Climate Change* (London: IPPR, 2006).
15 For one of the best discussions of the state of the NHS, see Nick Bosanquet et al., *NHS Reform: The Empire Strikes Back* (London: Reform, 2007).
16 Michael Porter and Elizabeth Teisberg, *Redefining Health Care* (Boston, MA: Harvard Business School Press, 2006).
17 Ibid., p. 8.
18 Bosenquet et al., *NHS Reform*, pp. 43--4.

Chapter 5 We Can Have a More Equal Society

1 See Alena Ledeneva, *Russia's Economy of Favours* (Cambridge, Cambridge University Press, 1998).
2 Stewart Lewis, *Corporate Brand and Corporate Responsibility* (MORI: MORI House, 2003).
3 Julia Finch and John Vidal, 'You've checked the price and calorie count, now here's the carbon cost', *Guardian*, 19 January 2007.
4 Sebastian Mallaby, 'Hands off hedge funds', *Foreign Affairs*, January/February 2007.
5 CISDM Research Department, 'The benefits of hedge funds: 2006 update', Isenberg School of Management, May 2006.
6 Fabian Society, *Paying for Progress* (London, 2004).
7 Institute for fiscal Studies, *The UK Tax System and the Environment* (London, 2006).
8 See Wolfgang Merkel, 'How the welfare state can tackle new inequalities', in Patrick Diamond and Matt Browne, eds, *Rethinking Social Democracy* (London: Policy Network, 2004).
9 Institute for Fiscal Studies, *Poverty and Inequality in Britain, 2006* (London, 2006).
10 Mike Brewer et al., *Micro-Simulating Child Poverty in 2010 and 2020* (York: Rowntree Foundation, 2006).

11 D. Hirsch, *What Will It Take to End Child Poverty?* (York: Rowntree Foundation, 2006).

12 Lisa Harker, *Delivering on Child Poverty* (London: Department of Work and Pensions, 2006).

13 Brewer et al., *Micro-Simulating Child Poverty*, pp. 27–35.

14 See Günther Schmid, 'Towards a new employment contract', in Günther Schmid and Bernard Gazier, eds, *The Dynamics of Full Employment* (Cheltenham: Edward Elgar, 2002).

15 See Gene Sperling, *The Pro-Growth Progressive* (New York: Simon and Schuster, 2005).

16 Lori Kletzer and Robert Litan, 'A prescription to relieve worker anxiety', *Institute for International Economics Policy Brief*. Available at <http://iie.com/publications/pb/pb01-2.htm>.

17 See Julian Le Grand, 'Assets for the people', *Prospect* (December 2001) and other publications.

18 HM Treasury, *Investing in Britain's Potential* (London: HMSO, 2006), pp. 93–4.

19 See Schmid and Gazier, eds, *The Dynamics of Full Employment*.

20 Ibid.

21 *Women and Work Commission: Shaping a Fairer Future* (Report, London, 2006).

22 'Diet and exercise "transformed our children"', *Daily Telegraph*, 10 January 2007. Research initiated by Food For the Brain.

23 See Alan Smithers and Pamela Robinson, *Five Years On. Open Access to Independent Education* (Sutton Trust, 2006).

24 Edward Wolff and Ajit Zacharias, *Wealth and Economic Inequality* (Bard College: Levy Economics Institute, 2006).

25 Dominic Maxwell, *Fair Dues* (London: IPPR, 2004).

26 *The Economist*, 'Rich man, poor man', 18 January 2007.

Chapter 6 Changing Lifestyles: A New Agenda

1 See Richard Layard, *Happiness: Lessons from a New Science* (London: Allen Lane, 2005).

2 The phrase actually come from one of Bennett's characters in his play *The History Boys*, which at the time of writing is showing in both London and New York, and has been made into a film.

3 It is a term I introduced some years ago, but it never really caught on at that point – so I'll try again. See Anthony Giddens, *Beyond Left and Right* (Cambridge: Polity, 1994).

4 Bertrand Russell, *In Praise of Idleness and Other Essays* (London: Macmillan, 1932).

5 I first introduced this idea in *The Third Way* (Cambridge: Polity, 1998).

6 HMG Strategy Unit, *Improving the Life Chances of Disabled People* (London: HMG Stationery Office, 2005).

7   Dennis Selkoe, 'The ageing mind: deciphering Alzheimer's disease and its antecedents', *Daedelus*, Winter 2006.

8   Howard Stoate and Bryan Jones, *Challenging the Citadel* (London: Fabian Society, 2006).

9   David Boyle et al., *Life Begins at 60: What Kind of NHS After 2008?* (London: Young Foundation, 2006). (I have modified his list slightly.)

10 Ibid., p. 9

11 The Stern Report, *The Economics of Climate Change* (London: Treasury, 2006).

12 Quoted in David Adam, 'UN's vast report will end the scientific argument', *Guardian*, 27 January 2007.

13 Stern, *The Economics of Climate Change*, p. xi.

14 George Monbiot, 'How sport is killing the planet', *Observer Sport Magazine*, 29 October 2006.

15 Tyndall Centre, *Constructing Energy Futures*, 2006. Research reported at <www.tyndall.ac.uk/publications/publications.shtml>.

16 Stephen Tindale, 'The EU must do more on climate change', *Centre For European Reform Bulletin*, 46 (2006).

Chapter 7 No Giving Up On Multiculturalism!

1   Quoted in Philippe Legrain, *Immigrants: Your Country Needs Them* (London: Little, Brown, 2006), p.4.

2   Nicola Rossi, 'Managed diversity', in Anthony Giddens, ed., *The Progressive Manifesto* (Cambridge: Polity, 2003), p. 123.

3   Oswald Spengler, *The Decline of the West* (Oxford: Oxford University Press, 1926; originally published 1918).

4   Tony Blankley, *The West's Last Chance* (Washington, DC: Regnery, 2005), Frontispiece.

5   Ibid., p. 185.

6   Bruce Bawer, *While Europe Slept* (New York: Doubleday, 2006).

7   Patrick Buchanan, *The Death of the West* (New York: St Martin's, 2002), p. 5. For a much more sophisticated example of similar arguments, see Samuel Huntington, *Who Are We?* (Free Press, 2005), which concentrates upon the possibility of a divided America, separated into Anglo-Protestant and Hispanic cultures.

8   See <www.migrationwatchuk.org>.

9   Legrain, *Immigrants: Your Country Needs Them*, p. 1.

10 Ibid., pp. 298–305.

11 Michael Young and Peter Wilmott, *Family and Kinship in East London* (London; Routledge, 1959).

12 Geoff Dench and Kate Gavron, *The New East End* (London: Profile, 2006).

13 Ingela Bjorck, 'Sweden's brain gain', *Science Careers* (Stockholm, January 2004).

14 Le Grain, *Immigrants: Your Country Needs Them*, p. 328.

15 Amartya Sen, *Identity and Violence* (New York: Norton, 2006), pp. 156–69.

16 See Charles Taylor, *Multiculturalism: Examining the Politics of Recognition* (Princeton: Princeton University Press, 1994) and many subsequent publications.

17 Charles Taylor, 'Why democracy needs patriotism', *Boston Review*, 19 (1994), p. 72.

18 Reported in Tom Baldwin and Gabriel Rozenberg, 'Britain "Must Scrap Multiculturalism"', *The Times*, 4 February 2007.

19 Tariq Modood, 'Multiculturalism or Britishness: a false debate', *Connections* (Winter 2004/5), p. 2.

20 David Goodhart, 'Too diverse?', *Prospect* (February 2004).

21 Trevor Phillips, 'Genteel xenophobia is as bad as any other kind', *Guardian*, 16 February 2004.

22 See the proceedings of the meetings in Philippe Van Parijs, *Cultural Diversity Versus Economic Solidarity* (Brussels: De Boeck, 2004).

23 Keith Banting and Will Kymlicka, eds, *Multiculturalism and the Welfare State* (Oxford: Oxford University Press, 2006).

24 Ludi Simpson, 'Statistics of racial segregation', *Urban Studies*, 41 (2004).

25 Douglas Massey and Nancy Denton, *American Apartheid* (Boston: Harvard University Press, 1993).

26 Olivier Roy, 'Britain: home-grown terror', *Le Monde Diplomatique*, 5 August 2005, p. 1.

27 Charles Clarke, speech at Royal Commonwealth Society, 15 November 2006.

Chapter 8 Shedding the Island Mentality

1 Bhikhu Parekh: 'Defining British national identity', *Political Quarterly*, 71 (2000).

2 Enoch Powell, speech given in Birmingham, 22 April 1968.

3 Quoted in Parekh: 'Defining British national identity', p. 10.

4 'The Tory way is the British way'. Speech given at Conservative Party Conference, 9 October 1998.

5 See Alan Macfarlane, *The Origins of British Individualism* (Oxford: Blackwell, 1978).

6 '"Most" support English Parliament', BBC News, 16 January 2007. Available at <http://news.bbc.co.uk/1/hi/uk-politics6264823.stin>.

7 Helene Mulholland, 'Blair rejects calls for English Parliament', *Guardian*, 16 January 2007.

8   Two main publications came out of this project: Anthony Giddens, *Europe in the Global Age*, and a companion volume edited by Anthony Giddens, Roger Liddle and Patrick Diamond, called *Global Europe, Social Europe* (both Cambridge: Polity, 2006).

9   Gordon Brown, *Global Europe: Full-Employment Europe* (London: Treasury, 2005).

10 Zaki Laidi, 'According to Gordon Brown, there is no point in the existence of the EU', *Telos*, 2005. Available at Telos-EU.com.

11 For an excellent analysis of this issue, see Roger Liddle, *The New Case for Europe* (London: Fabian Society, 2005).

12 Christopher Meyer, *DC Confidential* (London: Weidenfeld and Nicolson, 2005).

13 John Ikenberry, 'America's imperial ambition', *Foreign Affairs* (September/October 2002), p. 1. See also the parallel work of David Held, *American Power in the Twenty-first Century* (Cambridge: Polity, 2004).

14 For an interesting and comprehensive view of the issue, see Peter Riddell, *Hug Them Close* (London: Politico's, 2004).

15 Tony Blair, speech on defence, Plymouth, January 2007.

16 Anatol Lieven and John Hulsman, *Ethical Realism* (New York: Pantheon Books, 2006), p. 97.

17 *Iraq Study Group Report*, chaired by James A Baker and Lee Hamilton (Washington, 2006; no publisher given).

18 Robert Kagan, 'Power and Weakness', *Policy Review*, 113 (2002). See also Kagan's *Of Paradise and Power* (New York: Knopf, 2003).

19 See Alan Aherne et al., 'The EU and the governance of globalization'. Paper produced for the Finnish EU Presidency, September 2006.

20 Mark Leonard, *Divided World* (London: Centre for European Reform, 2007).

21 Aherne et al., 'The EU and the governance of globalization', pp. 18–31.

Chapter 9 How to Build a Progressive Consensus

1   David Sanders et al., *The 2005 General Election in Great Britain* (Report for the Electoral Commission, August 2005).

2   Thomas E. Patterson, *The Vanishing Voter* (New York: Knopf, 2003), p. 3.

3   *The Power Report: Power to the People* (York: Rowntree Foundation, 2006).

4   See Opinion Leader Research, *Britain Speaks. Effective Public Engagement and Better Decision-Making* (London, 2006).

5   Ibid., pp. 26–9.

6   Ibid., p. 18.

7   Joe Klein, *Politics Lost* (New York: Doubleday, 2006).

8   Robert K Merton, *Social Theory and Social Structure* (New York: Free Press, 1949). Quite apart from focused group interviews, this is one of the great works of sociology in the twentieth century, on which, as young sociologists, we all cut our teeth.

9   William Dinan, 'Undercover in New Labour', *Spinwatch*, 24 May 2005.

10 Quoted in Polly Toynbee, 'It is New Labour, as much as the public, that lacks trust', *Guardian*, 22 November 2005.

11 Andrea Romano, *The Boy* (Milano: Mondadori, 2005; in Italian).

12 Andrew Roberts, 'The Tory dream ... Brown as PM', *Observer*, 8 June 2003.

13 Ibid., p. 3.

14 See Anthony Giddens, *Europe in the Global Age* (Cambridge: Polity, 2006), pp. 60–4.

15 'The voting intention gap'. Available at
    <http://www.ukpollingreport.co.uk/blog/archives/903>.

Index

Index

Index

Goodhart, David 156-7
Gore, Al ix
Green Party (Germany) 24
Greenpeace 99
Greenspan, Alan 48
Grossman, Gene 55

Hague, William 165-6
Harker Report 106
Hayek, Friedrich von 16
health care 214
  charges for 84
  choice and 81
  corporate responsibility 99-101
  jokes about 67
  lifestyle factors and 128-33
  market competition 36
  nuclear power and 141
  obesity 9
  older people 127-8
  private care 89-90
  self-esteem and 123
  smoking 129, 130
  two-tier 8
  see also National Health Service
Hegel, George W. F. 154
Hewitt, Patricia x
Hill, Robert 82
Hirsch, Donald 105-6
Hoddle, Glenn 209
homosexuality 21
House of Lords reform 43
housing
  immigration and 150-1
  poverty and 110-11
Howard, Michael 39, 46
Human Fertilisation and Embryology
  Authority 192
Hutton Report 30-1

ID cards 40
ideas, battle of 2
identity politics 59-60, 211
Ikenberry, John 175
immigration 10, 214
  control of 151-3

danger/opportunity of 147-51
economic 64-5
employment and 151-3
globalization and 57
New Tories 42
responding to the right 22
voter concerns and 34-5
see also multiculturalism
India 54, 182
individualism 5
information technology 6
Institute for Fiscal Studies 79, 103-4
Institute of Policy Research x
International Monetary Fund (IMF)
  181
internet technology
  deliberative democracy and 193
  democracy of 185-6
  health care and 88
  misunderstandings about 49
  rapid development of 53-4
  Reith lecture debates 188-9
Iran 182
Iraq war
  Blair and 30, 175, 198-9
  European allies in war 30
  future action in 176-7
  humbling experience 179
  justification for war 30-1
  Liberal Democrats and 43
  withdrawal of troops 11
Ireland 152
Islam
  in British context 157-61
  Danish cartoons and 161
  equal respect and 154-5
  perceived threat of 147-8
  radicalism in global context 10-11
  women's dress and 159
Israel 179, 183
Italy 25

Japan 182
jobs
  see employment
John, Elton ix